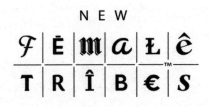

NEW

FĒMALÊ™ TRÎB€S

Shattering Female Stereotypes and Redefining Women Today

Foreword by Madeline Di Nonno
CEO of Geena Davis Institute on Gender in Media

RACHEL PASHLEY

1 3 5 7 9 10 8 6 4 2

Published in 2018 by Virgin Books an imprint of Ebury Publishing,
20 Vauxhall Bridge Road,
London SW1V 2SA

Virgin Books is part of the Penguin Random House group of companies
whose addresses can be found at global.penguinrandomhouse.com

Penguin
Random House
UK

First published by Virgin Books in 2018

www.penguin.co.uk

A CIP catalogue record for this book is available from the British Library

ISBN 9780753553008

Typeset in 11.5/18 pt Garamond MT Std
by Integra Software Services Pvt. Ltd, Pondicherry

Printed and bound in Great Britain by Clays Ltd, Elcograf S.p.A

For Lily

CONTENTS

FOREWORD

Madeline Di Nonno
CEO, Geena Davis Institute on Gender in Media

What Rachel Pashley has captured with this book is a significant narrative that corrects the story of women's contributions to society and our world history, as well as introducing the important concept of Female Capital – the value women bring to bear every day across every field.

Given the Geena Davis Institute on Gender in Media's long-standing mission to achieve gender equity onscreen in media, we are experiencing a pivotal time as we all strive for gender equity in business and in our lives. Our work addressing female portrayals onscreen along with movements such as #TimesUp and #MeToo contribute to our collective efforts to strive for systemic change. This change is manifesting itself around the world and across many industries.

That said, women's achievements are still vastly overshadowed and regularly airbrushed from our history and culture, depriving women and girls of powerful female role models. The reality is that women are leaders, we are multifaceted and we are intelligent!

The book makes a compelling argument as to how the commercial world can be a force for good: how we can dramatically influence the perceptions of women's value through our storytellers and marketing. We know from Rachel's research that women want to see themselves reflected in media as they are in real life. It challenges the unconscious gender bias so ingrained in all of us as adults. Our motto at the Institute is 'If she can see it, she can be it.' I believe we all can play a critical role in shaping the future – the future we want to *see*.

PROLOGUE

....

New Female Tribes: How this Book Began

This book is based on a survey we at J. Walter Thompson came to call 'Female Tribes'. To my knowledge, it is the largest female insight study of its kind conducted within the advertising industry. It was fuelled by over five years of desk research and it grew from the commissioning of our own global research study, the J. Walter Thompson Women's Index. The study reveals the dreams, ambitions and goals of over 8,000 women aged 17 to 70 years, across 19 different countries, and from different ethnicities and income levels, with the objective of understanding female progress.

We initially commissioned the study with what I now call the 'original global nine markets', a deliberately diverse global spread of countries to investigate women's progress beyond the realms of rich, white Western women. Those countries were the UK, USA, China, Brazil, South Africa, Russia, India, Australia and Saudi Arabia. As the project gained momentum, additional offices in the agency network participated in the study, so we expanded our research across the Middle East (Lebanon, Egypt) and Asia Pacific (Hong Kong, Singapore, Japan, Philippines, Thailand, Taiwan, Vietnam), and in Europe Italy came on board. By the end of commissioning for the Women's Index research, we had a truly global study and, frankly, a lot of analysis to do.

The results present a fascinating and diverse study of contemporary femininity from a wide spread of ages, ethnicities and geographies, and the degree to which women's role in society is advancing. Equally the results point to the fact that women's status in the real world is significantly out of step with the way in which women are portrayed on screen in popular culture, through advertising or in entertainment, i.e. the 'reel' world, and that is something I wanted to address in this book.

FEMALE CAPITAL: WOMEN AS VALUE CREATORS (NOT JUST CONSUMERS)

The aim was to explore the idea of 'Female Capital', the value that women bring to the world *as women*, to demonstrate that our equity in the world extends beyond bearing children or just as a lucrative consumer sales target in our role as 'main household shopper'. I wanted to reflect that the lives women are leading today do not follow the traditional pattern or 'life script' of dating, brief career, marriage, children, retirement; that, in fact, women are pursuing incredibly diverse 'life scripts', which may or may not include motherhood. By highlighting the findings of the Women's Index, my intention is to reveal the diversity of women's lives and 'Female Capital'.

NEW TRIBES: NEW LANGUAGE

Through our analysis of the Women's Index data, and scrutiny of values, motivations and aspirations, we have identified a rich variety of cohorts or, as I prefer to call them, 'tribes', many of them challenging female stereotypes and countering the received wisdom of what ambitions or life goals look like for women. While we saw that there were home- or family-focused 'Traditionalists' – arguably pursuing familiar roles for women – we also observed the high prevalence of achievement-focused 'alpha' characteristics present across geographies and, perhaps surprisingly, independent of age or marital and maternal status: busting the myth that motherhood dulls ambition. At the same time, though, we also identified what we term the 'anti-alphas', those women who are struggling to find their way in the world, perhaps still living at home with parents and grappling with emotional or financial insecurity. The prevalence of 'anti-alphas' tended to correlate to age – millennials being a key demographic – but also to those countries with troubled economies (Italy) or a 'hostile' work culture as regards women (Japan is a case in point). The prevalence was perhaps reflective of the fact that in economically turbulent times women are often the first to suffer, given that they are likely to be in lower paid or part-time work, or simply viewed as an expendable resource.

On a more optimistic note, we also identified what I refer to as the 'Altruists', women committed to philanthropy or activism and driven by a sense of social responsibility, and lastly the 'Hedonists', women for whom self-satisfaction, exploration and taking risks were driving forces; some would say these are more traditionally 'male' values, or at least values frequently associated with men.

The intention of the 'tribes' concept was not to find a new set of stereotypes in which to force-fit women (one can embody many different 'tribes'), but to stop using such simplistic or binary terms as 'Busy working mum' to define *all* women. The new tribes concept would help us to refer to women beyond their parental and caring responsibilities, and create a language that credits women with ambition, aspiration and attitude.

My hope is that we can begin describing women in a much more meaningful, inspiring and profound way that will serve to influence not just advertising but product design and service creation; this will start to change the way the world works for women. Advertising is a central part of our culture and, in my view, we have a responsibility to change the one-dimensional way women are portrayed throughout the world.

CHAPTER 1

Women and the New Rules of Engagement

'It's never too late. Never too late to start over, never too late to be happy.' **Jane Fonda**

There has never been a better time to be a woman, or so say 83 per cent of women around the world in our J. Walter Thompson Women's Index study.[1] Admittedly you might have a different opinion depending on where you live in the world, but this is reflective of a bigger trend, a sense that something is happening for women: and it is a movement to be excited about. What startled us in the results of our study was the universality of optimism. We fielded research in deliberately diverse corners of the world, from Saudi Arabia to Singapore, Brazil and the US, India, Russia and South Africa, and the sentiment was shared. It's clearly too simplistic to suggest the push for equality has in any way been won and that we can now sit back and soak up the rewards of our new-found freedom. Women's lives are evolving, however, things are changing: let me put forward the evidence.

THE ERA OF THE FEMALE HERO

If like me you grew up in the 1980s, you may have wondered why Ferris Bueller got to have the day off driving the Porsche while Molly Ringwald's sole preoccupation was to be pretty in pink. Aside from Princess Leia, Purdey in *The New Avengers* or *The Bionic Woman*, there were precious few kick-ass female role models when I was growing up. As part of the cultural surround sound of social conditioning for young girls, films and television served to reinforce our normative role in society: to be the mother, supportive wife or girlfriend hovering in the background and to leave the fighting, leading and achieving to the menfolk.

Fast forward to the new, empowered Disney heroines, or the *Star Wars* reboot, *The Force Awakens* and *Rogue One*, each with a female lead and smashing the box office. In 2016, *Rogue One* was the number-one box office hit in the US[2] by a long way, earning half-a-billion dollars and cementing the significance of the female lead.

A 2018 study by the BBC revealed that female-led movies were significantly more profitable,[3]and in the past decade the top 25 movies about women earned $45 million more than the equivalent for men.[4] Recently *Wonder Woman* became the largest grossing live-action film directed by a woman (Patty Jenkins), but even that feels like faint praise because, in fact, the film is set to earn a spot in the top ten highest grossing superhero films of our time: not bad for a woman. *Atomic Blonde*, featuring Charlize Theron, further demonstrates our appetite for female action heroes, or rather anti-heroes, and surpassed *John Wick* in earnings, with an ultimate revenue of $90 million worldwide.

In fact, in a dismal box office in summer 2017 in the US, the only movies to earn significant revenues were female-led movies: alongside *Wonder Woman*, the all-female road movie *Girls Trip* has earned more than $100 million, with an all African-American cast and screenwriting duo demonstrating that there is a place in Hollywood for diverse talent.

Hollywood writers' guilds are now actively seeking female-centred screenplays as studios wake up to the earnings potential of female-led content, and within the TV world female show runners such as Shonda Rhimes are behind some of the biggest successes on the small screen. The more enlightened broadcasters like Netflix even enable subscribers to search for shows featuring 'a strong female lead'. So, it could be that female box-office capital will initiate a wake-up call among studio bosses: women are ready for their close-up after all. The advent of Hollywood's burgeoning promotion of the 'Alpha Female' with *The Hunger Games*'s Katniss Everdeen, female Marvel superheroes, Wonder Woman, *Star Wars*'s Rey *et al.* is a sort of cultural barometer that points to women's changing roles in society: the sense that we're at a cultural tipping point moving from 'best supporting actress' to 'leading lady'.

THE END OF THE 'LIFE SCRIPT' AND THE RETIREMENT BABY

It used to be that you could look at a woman's age and predict with some accuracy her 'life stage'. It would go something like this: twenties – single and working; thirties – married working mum; forties – stay-at-home mum; fifties – retired grandmother. For many women today, things have changed: it's now no longer the case that we can confidently predict we'll know everything about a woman based on her age. In fact, certainly in the developed world, I might go as far as saying that we can predict very little these days about a woman based on age alone. Never has there been more truth in the assertion that age is 'just a number'. We have witnessed recently UK Marks & Spencer senior executive Laura Wade-Gery, a high-achieving Alpha Female at the top of her game, taking time out from her career to have her first child in her fifties. Predictably the press baulked at her age, yet the fact that her husband will be a first-time father at age 67 passed almost without comment. Nevertheless, Wade-Gery is not alone in postponing motherhood. In January 2017 Dame Julia Peyton-Jones, former boss of the Serpentine Gallery in London, announced at the age of 64 the birth of her first child, leading to the suggestion that the 'retirement baby' is now a thing.

A woman's average age for the birth of her first child in the UK is now 30, compared to 22 back in 1950, and for the first time more women in Britain are having children over the age of 35 than under 25.[5] Increasingly we're also witnessing women postpone motherhood indefinitely in order to focus on their own lives, with a subtle shift in attitudes redefining 'childless' to 'childfree', and embracing life without children not as eternal 'spinsterhood' with the implied pejorative associations, but as a positive and powerful choice. In fact, the percentage of childless American women in their forties has doubled in the last 40 years and, according to the latest census data, some 43 per cent of American women aged 15–50 are childfree, with many women in this cohort actively seeking to redefine and challenge what it is to be a woman and willingly childless.[6] The Not Mom Summit is an event and organisation working towards 'redefining female legacy' and breaking the cultural trope of 'Mom with kids' as the only woman of significance or value.[7]

At the same time, women in their fifties are also more likely to get a divorce, and this is not confined to the UK and US; in Singapore, for example, women in their fifties and sixties are six times more likely to get a divorce compared to the same cohort 20 years previously.[8] What's driving this trend is partly that life expectancy, both in terms of age and anticipation of quality of life, is increasing. In Singapore, for example, women's increasing empowerment means they are less likely to stay in an unhappy marriage or suffer their husband's infidelities out of a sense of duty; and if you can expect to live another 30 years or more, why would you? From our own Women's Index study, we saw that Singapore was home to some of the lowest incidences of what I call the 'Spouse Focused' tribe, the traditional marriage model where the husband comes first, with only 9 per cent of women falling into this group.[9] Across Asia, we witnessed a pragmatic attitude towards marriage, with significantly more women 'not expecting to be in a

4

relationship forever', and accepting of the idea that 'love isn't the be all and end all'.

In the US, the divorce rate among the over fifties has doubled since 1990, and research indicates that divorce among this cohort is most frequently initiated by women; in fact, some two-thirds of divorces are initiated by wives.[10] This dynamic has meant that women we typically assumed were settled at home doting on grandchildren are now single and dating – another profound shift in life stage. Again, we saw this reflected in our Women's Index data, with the US, UK and Australia home to some of the biggest populations of what pop culture would call 'The Cougar' tribe, namely older unmarried women, actively dating and seeking to date younger men. Perhaps the most iconic example is Brigitte Trogneux, or Madame Macron as she is better known, the French President's wife who is 24 years his senior. An additional frisson of intrigue was added to her public reception on the revelation that she was once Emmanuel Macron's drama teacher.

THE FEMALE ENTREPRENEURS

At the other end of the spectrum we now have young women who should be at university racking up tuition-fee debt, but who are instead dropping out, starting their own businesses and achieving millionaire status before their twentieth birthday, making those of us who went to university feel a bit like gullible losers. Juliette Brindak started MissOandFriends.com at only 16 years of age; it's a community created by a teenager for teenage girls, selling products but also supporting self-esteem at a critical age. The company was valued at over $15 million three years after its launch. Meanwhile, Diane Keng invented MyWEBoo, enabling users to manage their online reputations (yet another pressure millennials have to wrestle with), at the age of 18; it was her third business and earned her projected millions in the process. These examples illustrate the new entrepreneurial spirit among teens to millennials – according to Deloitte, up to 70 per cent of millennials around the world want to start their own business.[11]

The idea of a teenage millionaire entrepreneur is not something you would have often encountered 20 years ago. What supports female entrepreneurship in this generation is access to a level of education previously denied or discouraged among their forebears, but also the empowerment that technology provides. Technology, in facilitating access to information, networking and design resources, in one sense democratises entrepreneurship – it's no respecter of age, gender or background. Arguably, internet access is all you need. According to the Women's Index,[12] 80 per cent of women globally felt that technology had empowered them. This sentiment was strongly felt across China, India, South Africa and Saudi Arabia, but most profoundly in India with 90 per cent saying technology had given them a voice. What proved perhaps most striking was the fact that, in India, women were saying technology trumped religion in serving to bring friends and family closer together.

It would be disingenuous, however, not to point out that it remains much more difficult for female entrepreneurs to gain access to venture capital: 85 per cent of all venture-capital funded businesses have no women in the management team, and while in the US the number of venture-capital funded female-led start-ups has increased threefold in the last 15 years, it still only stands at a relatively modest 15 per cent.[13] It's hypothesised that part of the problem is the unconscious bias within the venture capital community as to what represents a 'sound investment', and from analysing the figures superficially, the data would suggest that women are not seen as a sound investment. A 2017 study, analysing six years' worth of Q&A panels between investors and start-ups, added more evidence to the unconscious bias theory.[14] The results revealed that panels ask male entrepreneurs about potential gains, and female entrepreneurs about potential losses: so we expect women to fail, perceiving them as high risk, which by implication restricts funding.

What's most interesting is that when we remove the mostly male venture capital panels from the funding equation and look at, for example, crowdfunding. Although women use crowdfunding less than men, when they do crowdsource they are much more likely to achieve their investment targets than male entrepreneurs.[15] Women were 32 per cent more likely to achieve their funding target and this applied across all geographies studied, but perhaps more significantly across all business sectors.

THE RISE AND RISE OF ACTIVISM

In considering female activity and the exertion of power, and perhaps influenced by the connectivity and power of social networking, we cannot overlook the increased political and social *activism* among women of all ages and backgrounds. The women's marches around the 2017 US presidential inauguration were the largest global demonstration of their kind, with an estimated 100,000 people marching in London. Meanwhile, over in Hollywood, the Harvey Weinstein scandal has proved a watershed moment in highlighting the predatory sexual harassment and discrimination prevalent not just in the film industry but across many industries. The #MeToo movement has served not just to throw a spotlight on but to challenge toxic masculinity, with the resulting Time's Up organisation launched to support victims of sexual harassment: women are no longer going to suffer in silence.

As depressing as Hillary Clinton's loss was in terms of a desire to see the first female US President, there is no doubt that the increased alt-right conservatism sweeping the USA is in turn reawakening feminism the world over. There is, perhaps, a new wave of feminism intent on resisting a rolling back of female empowerment, and putting women's rights and their significance firmly back in the public consciousness. A poll conducted by the *Washington Post* revealed that 40 per cent of US female Democrats intended to become more politically active versus 27 per cent of their male peers,[16] and record numbers of women are applying to run for office. In 2017, over 19,000 women contacted Emily's List, a US advocacy group, about running for office compared to 920 in the previous year.

If we had been in danger of slipping back into sleepy complacency in the West, something has been awoken. You could say that social media is both a friend and a foe to the cause: it propagates fake news and 'alternative facts' that no doubt warped our sense of reality and subsequent election results, but at the same time the public scrutiny it supports means we have access to information as never before.

In our research, 84 per cent of women globally felt that technology or social media had made them much more aware as a global citizen, and this was particularly prevalent among millennials in our survey.[17] The relatively youthful face of political and social activism is perhaps best illustrated by Malala Yousafzai: a Nobel Prizewinner, activist and impressive orator, yet until very recently still a teenager. Global research highlights the significant phenomenon of activism among teenage girls, often stimulated by education, and posing an articulate and energised voice in what we must accept is increasingly a hostile world.[18] Jessica Taft's research discovered that girl activists often perceived themselves as better activists due to their more empathic nature and emotional intelligence, and the nature of their activism was not isolated to 'women's issues' but to broader societal and environmental issues around them, shattering the preconception that teenage girls' preoccupations centred only on Barbie and boys. To quote Michelle Obama: 'Adolescent girls are the future of their countries and their voices can move mountains if we let them speak.'

What we are witnessing is that the rules governing women's predictable life script and the resultant cultural stereotypes appear increasingly redundant as a means of characterising contemporary womanhood. Women we thought had settled down are kicking up their heels, dating again, becoming first-time mothers in their forties and even fifties; university students are dropping out of the rat race to pursue a life of self-employment and entrepreneurship; and political and social activism is being taken up by girls not yet out of school. This is nothing short of a cultural revolution and illustrates the diversity of Female Capital. For all the difficulties and inequalities in the world, it is an exciting time to be a woman.

THE J. WALTER THOMPSON WOMEN'S INDEX: THE MAGIC NUMBERS

While our desk research at J. Walter Thompson undoubtedly pointed out a 'quiet revolution' for women, in order to try and put a sense of scale to this phenomenon we commissioned our own proprietary research and were able to secure funding through the agency. We wanted to provide real, tangible insight into prevailing attitudes and ambitions: to explore contemporary femininity. We deliberately set out to speak to women across very diverse countries, cultures and ethnicities because we didn't want to imply that progress was purely the province of rich white Western women – from my time travelling around the world and witnessing boardrooms from Shanghai to São Paulo filled almost exclusively with women, I knew this wasn't the case. In Russia, for example, I observed what seemed to be something of a curious role reversal. On arriving at my client's offices, it was an exclusively male reception desk and men who delivered the coffee, but the boardroom was female. The most powerful person in the room was a very formidable woman who had the respect (if not hero worship) of everyone in the organisation, male or female. My experiences told me there were real shifts in the workplace, and we had to attempt to record and report it.

We launched the study at the end of 2015 initially with 4,300 women across 9 countries, and then started to roll the study out across the world, facilitated through our agency network, getting us to a final total of 19 countries and more than 8,000 women. The more we publicised the research through the agency, the more offices jumped on board to commission the study. We had more research than we knew what to do with, and making sense of what the numbers were telling us was one of the most challenging but ultimately rewarding experiences of this endeavour. It probably helped that I love numbers.

As any agency planner or researcher will tell you, numbers tell a story. Initially, certain figures leapt out from the page: the overriding sentiment that 'femininity was a strength not a weakness', not a burden to be overcome, no matter which country we looked at, gave us a clue to the global scale of female empowerment. Other data, seemingly innocuous numbers on a page, reminded us just how far we had to go. The fact that more than 40 per cent of women anywhere in the world felt that their gender was holding them back in their career was a consistent if depressing theme. To see that in black and white in this century still enrages me, and the gentle hum of that anger is what gets me out of bed most days, that and the will to do something about it.

The first nine countries in the study – the UK, USA, Brazil, China, Russia, South Africa, Saudi Arabia, India and Australia – are the core countries that constitute our 'global' all-market averages quoted across the book. As mentioned, we tried to achieve a representative balance of income, race and demography, and equally we spoke to women from 17 to 70 years old in order to understand how attitudes evolved with age.

The study comprised an online survey, consisting mostly of 'closed' or tick-box questions to facilitate ease of administration and analysis. We did include a number of open-ended responses, however, allowing for individual feedback. All countries participated in the same questionnaire, although we edited some of the questions on, for example, sexuality for some countries to respect cultural sensitivities. We decided that in order to really get a personal feel for what was going on for women around the world, we would ask the same sort of questions we would ask at a job interview or perhaps, given the more personal probing, a first date! We asked questions around earnings, ambition, education and aspiration, but also love and sexuality. For example, 'Do you expect a relationship to last forever?' and 'Are you comfortable dating a younger man?' We also probed their ideas of feminism and femininity: 'What does being a woman mean to you?' and 'What should women represent in the world?'

The results were fascinating. It took us months to extrapolate the findings, but immediately responses jumped out, making us take stock of what we were witnessing. We all had a moment of reflection when we zeroed in on the fact that one in four women in Brazil told us they had been inspired to leave an abusive relationship purely through seeing a strong on-screen female role model. When you consider that one in three women in Brazil is affected by domestic violence, then you start to understand the huge influence popular culture can play in people's lives – the fact that the moving image can be persuasive not just in selling products through advertising, it can truly change fortunes.[19] It seemed so absurdly simple, yet so powerful: the idea that having on-screen female role models could unleash what could be an incredible cultural ripple effect was and still is hugely compelling. It's a message that I will never tire of telling: role models could change the way the world works for women.

Within this book, I will attempt to unpack the rich insight of the Women's Index in order to highlight the value that women have in the world now, and the future of Female Capital. In constructing and analysing the results of the Women's Index, I have Mark Truss and Diana Orrico from our New York team to thank for their tireless work, not to say brilliance and patience in designing what initially was a 'quick survey' and very rapidly turned into a major initiative.

A NEW FEMININITY?

I remember once describing a woman to her face as 'feminine' and watching her nose wrinkle. Firstly, I realised that I ought to be more careful with what came out of my mouth (no filter), and, secondly, I wondered whether 'feminine' is such a great compliment anyway.

If you read through the various dictionary definitions of femininity, while some of the finer points may change a little, there are key themes that emerge, namely passivity, gentleness and being pretty or attractive. As a culture, we associate the word 'feminine' with sugar and spice: the soft, girly values of being a woman – great, for example, for hanging curtains or adding decorative appeal to a room. The word itself is derived from the Latin word, *femina*, simply meaning 'woman', so literally feminine means 'of a woman', but over the years it's acquired a more nuanced meaning, encompassing those qualities culturally associated with women, particularly 'delicacy' and 'prettiness'. One of the most interesting findings from our Women's Index research was the universal belief that femininity is not soft or passive: 86 per cent of women globally felt that 'femininity' was a strength not a weakness, so delicacy was not resonating. In China, when we asked women what values they aspired to have as a woman, 50 per cent chose 'aggressive' as a key attribute, another 50 per cent chose 'maternal', so we can see how the phrase 'Tiger Mother' was born.[20]

If you start digging into just what feminine strength entails, a very surprising picture is revealed, which starts to dissipate the 'sugar and spice' image of femininity and replace it with more steel. As we started to assess the data, what emerged was a much more empowered vision of femininity because what women aspire to embody today, as recorded in our Women's Index Study, is confidence and independence; 60 per cent pinpointed confidence and 57 per cent chose independence as key values, while 'caring' features at 49 per cent, and strong and determined are the next most important values.

Confidence, independence, strong and determined are not words associated with passive delicacy but with courage, heroism and leadership. A study we had conducted in 2014 revealed that 80 per cent of women would rather be described as 'strong' versus 'sweet', which tells you a lot about modern femininity.[21] Equally there are signs that societal attitudes towards gender and femininity may be starting to change or embraced more fluidity. For example, John Lewis recently announced that it will no longer separate children's clothes by gender, embracing a unisex approach, something that adult retailers (such as H&M, Rick Owens and J.W. Anderson) have embraced for some time. Whilst in Canada and Nepal citizens will be able to select a third gender, as distinct from a binary male or female definition, and although this marks progress, there is still a long way to go before we can assume true equality.

IS FEMININITY COMPATIBLE WITH LEADERSHIP?

So often it is assumed that women do not make good leaders, and are rather better as supporters because of our 'femininity'. When children were asked whether women would make good presidents, being 'girly' was given one of the chief impediments (notice here that in this context, femininity is used implicitly as a pejorative).[22] The truth, though, tells a different story. In the Zenger Folkman global study of over 16,000 male and female leaders, it was women who were the more effective leaders, and not just in relation to the traditional 'feminine' qualities of nurturing and team building.[23] They excelled in the typically 'masculine' qualities of drive for results, taking the initiative and championing change.

Equally the most surprising new research from the University of Cambridge reveals that, despite what we may verbalise about the incompatibility of femininity with leadership, we instinctively perceive women with the more 'feminine' facial features as the better leaders and, in an important twist to the findings, it's the presence of oestrogen – literally the hormone 'of a woman' – that is believed to not only physically manifest as 'feminine' features in the face but inspire competitive behaviour correlating to leadership characteristics.[24] So to return to the definition of femininity, if this is true, then we need to reconsider the meaning of 'feminine' because as a measure of those characteristics innate to womanhood, it is not delicacy and fragility but competitiveness and leadership that may ultimately define us.

THE LANGUAGE OF FEMALE ACHIEVEMENT

While we are redefining the idea of 'femininity', just examining the word itself throws up an important issue of language because, without wishing to state the obvious, it is language that is used to record, characterise and narrate or frame the story of female achievement. How that language is used will decide whether women's achievements are celebrated or diminished. Sport is a good place to start. If you were watching the Rio Olympics coverage, you could have been forgiven for thinking that there were two entirely different games going on: a serious men's athletic competition, and for women … well, the gymnasts in their fancy leotards 'might as well be standing around at the mall' (someone at NBC actually said that). The patronising language and reporting narrative means that women are not portrayed as serious athletes and, instead, the focus is on our 'lady' pursuits (mall shopping).

The significance of language or the issue of gendered language prompted Cambridge University Press to monitor the reporting narrative of sports coverage during Rio 2016.[25] The research, led by Sarah Grieves, revealed that not only were female athletes much more likely to be discussed either in the context of their appearance or relationship status (married, mother, engaged), when it came to the discussion of their performance women were subject to much more neutral language (compete, participate), whereas men's performance was characterised in much more heroic terms (dominate, battle, mastermind).[26]

In June 2017, John McEnroe suggested that Serena Williams would rank 'like 700 in the world' if she played on the men's tennis circuit, suggesting that women's tennis is of a lesser standard. Yet the Williams sisters' tennis achievements are phenomenal; one cannot help but think that, had they been born male and white, they would be held in far greater esteem, and they would not have had to overcome such intense scrutiny as to their body image and love lives, or racial discrimination and the belittling of their combined achievements. It's significant that despite winning more grand slams in her career than Roger Federer, and arguably being a more consistent performer, Serena attracts a fraction of the sponsorship deals that Federer has racked up. This tells you everything about how we perceive women's achievements.

The fact is that besides the obvious physical differences, female sporting performance is 'catching up' with men. Women's tennis serve speeds are in many cases equal or even faster than men's. For example, German player Sabine Lisicki has recorded a serve speed of 131mph, faster than Roger Federer can usually manage. In belittling women's tennis McEnroe is perhaps forgetting the 1973 'Battle of the Sexes', the iconic tennis match between Billie Jean King and former Wimbledon champion Bobby Riggs, once dubbed 'the best tennis player in the world'. The 55-year-old Riggs was arrogant enough to assume that he would thrash King, who was in her prime. She flattened him in three straight sets, despite Riggs's assertion that women 'lacked the emotional stability' to win! That particular battle has now been turned into a film featuring Emma Stone and Steve Carrell, and may prove a useful reminder to Mr McEnroe of women's capabilities.

A classic example of gender-focused tennis commentary came from BBC broadcaster John Inverdale about Wimbledon singles champion Marion Bartoli: 'Do you think Bartoli's dad told her when she was little "You're never going to be a looker. You'll never be a Sharapova, so you have to be scrappy and fight"?'[27] The BBC duly apologised, but once again a woman's sporting performance was overlooked and undermined.

The point is that by conflating a woman's achievements with attractiveness or home responsibilities, we serve to undermine her; we imply that her energies and concentration are focused not on the job at hand, but at home. In the case of a sportswoman, it implies she can't be a serious athlete. A case in point: according to a *Chicago Tribune* tweet, 'The wife of a Bears linesman' won a bronze medal at the Rio Olympics.[28] She didn't even get to have a name – it was Corey Cogdell. Perhaps by some fluke, in-between running errands and dropping off dry cleaning, 'the wife' had gone and won herself a medal.

It's not hard to understand how, in the workplace, this undermining emphasis on home responsibilities and relationships could rob a woman of opportunities for advancement – because she 'might have to leave early to take care of the kids'. This is how unconscious bias works. Another facet of unconscious bias that befalls women in the office is the lack of credit we get for ideas: that moment when you suggest an idea that everyone ignores only for the man next to you to repeat it, and suddenly it's brilliant. And his idea. Something not too dissimilar happens outside the office, too.

THE GUY WHO GOT HER THERE: GIVING WOMEN RECOGNITION

I call this phenomenon 'The guy who got her there', the man behind the scenes who is ultimately responsible for a woman's stellar performance – because she couldn't have done it herself. In Rio, this supposition was in evidence in epic proportions: for example, Hungarian swimmer and medallist Katinka Hosszú's sporting performance was almost incidental to that of her coach husband, 'the man responsible' for her victory. She beat a world record, by the way. Or gold-medal winning swimmer Katie Ledecky, who is the 'latest innovation' of coach Bruce Gemmell. If you read a *New York Times* article, you could have easily mistaken Katie for a Stepford-like swimming fembot designed by Gemmell, a former engineer, because 'he's never stopped innovating.'[29]

If you thought this was just confined to the sporting world, you would be wrong, because 'the guy who got her there' pops up just about everywhere, and he must be exhausted supporting women everywhere, because it's portrayed as a full-time job. There's Hillary Clinton, who has Bill to thank for her political career, and so newspaper editors felt justified in giving over their front pages to the husband, rather than to the first ever female US presidential nominee.

Or spare a thought for poor multi-millionaire Grammy-winning musical failure, Taylor Swift. The real meaning and credibility of her songs only seemed to become apparent when Ryan Adams sang them. I could bore you by listing all the female scientists whose achievement was credited to their husbands or male colleagues, or the female screenwriters whose storytelling genius is attributed to the male directors of their films ... Have you ever heard of Melissa Mathison, the writer of Steven Spielberg's *E.T. the Extra Terrestrial?*

The portrayal of 'the guy who got her there' robs many women of the real, hard-won credit they deserve. Plus, it implies that women lack the ambition and courage to strive and compete on their own terms, and that they need a man to be successful. It's the 'mansplaining of female success'. This I find curious, given the fact that more women than men are attending university in the US, women are attaining higher grades and we're increasingly the primary breadwinners. Perhaps most importantly, this phenomenon robs us of female role models and the opportunity to really acknowledge and celebrate female achievement.

WOMEN'S ACHIEVEMENT: THE TREE THAT FALLS IN THE WOODS

When it comes to female achievement, despite most women in our Women's Index Study telling us it had 'never been a better time to be a woman', there was observable and universal frustration with both the lack of female role models when growing up; 74 per cent of women wished they had more female role models as inspiration.[30] This sentiment was most strongly felt in China (89 per cent), Saudi Arabia (89 per cent) and India (86 per cent), which given the cultural context is unsurprising. Equally an almost universal 93 per cent of women felt that we need to understand the value that women bring to the world: as women.

The degree to which women's accomplishments had been airbrushed from the history books was a frustration shared by nearly six in ten women worldwide, with 82 per cent of women wanting to see more inclusion of women's achievement in relevant narratives. If over 8,000 women across 19 different countries support this idea, we're not all imagining it, so although this is a great time to be a woman and, yes, we're ushering in a new era of female empowerment and influence on culture at large, but like the tree that falls in the woods, if nobody hears about it, will it even matter?

Taking the philosophy of the Geena Davis Institute on Gender in Media, 'If she can see it, she can be it', the reverse is also true: without visible role models it's difficult to visualise a different life path to those other than the ones we are surrounded by. If a girl sees female astronauts or scientists the precedent is set, she believes she can also aspire – it becomes possible for her to imagine this in her future. Thanks to Katniss Everdeen, record numbers of young girls have taken up archery as the fastest growing American sport, with 70 per cent of girls citing Katniss as their inspiration.[31] Meanwhile *Hidden Figures*, the 2016 movie about the African-American 'human computers' of NASA, has already inspired hundreds of girls to consider a career in STEM (Science, Technology, Engineering, Maths), according to Techbridge, a Seattle-based organisation that seeks to inspire the next generations of innovators. For this reason, it's important to continually challenge the lack of representation, inclusion and celebration of women's achievements but also the language and narrative used to describe them – so that we can reap the rewards of the cultural ripple effects and make it even easier for future generations to follow in their footsteps. Role models can change the way the world works for women, but only if we can see them.

WHAT THIS MEANS:
KEY TAKEAWAYS FOR BRANDS

The end of the life script represents a fundamental shift for women – our lives are no longer dictated to or geared solely around our responsibility to others, and the fluidity and diversity of our lives today reflects women with the power to determine their own futures, who embrace the possibilities of being a woman and who are increasingly following a self-determined path: this is what makes it an exciting time to be a woman. We are less adherent to the expectations of others, we are less prepared to follow social norms and conventions based on when we *should* get married, when we *should* have children and how we should behave if and when we have children. What's more encouraging is that this phenomenon is not confined to women in the West; certainly, the data we have suggests this is a global phenomenon reaching into the lives of women of all ages. Women also display increased financial independence and determination, and there we saw enormous pride among women: 72 per cent of women globally were proud to be a good provider.[32] There was no sense that women were stepping up reluctantly to become the major breadwinner, it was very much an empowered independent choice, and one based on recognising the freedom that financial independence affords.

We do not fit into one box

If you take away one thing from this book, my hope is that I will have impressed upon you the fact that marketing to women is not as simplistic as may have been previously thought: we simply don't fit in to one or two boxes anymore, i.e. Busy Working Mom or Sassy Singleton. We are complex and diverse as an audience, and whether or not we have children or want to have children does not define us, a sentiment shared by 93 per cent of women in our survey.[33] So I can say with some confidence that many segmentation studies will fall very wide of the mark in accurately defining their target audience, certainly if that audience is female. When you consider that audience targeting and segmentation drives pretty much the entire direction of a business, and what it does, that's a big issue. I feel qualified to say this, because as a planner and strategist, I have seen very many segmentation studies over the years, and very few of them didn't make me want to scream inside, which is precisely why I started Female Tribes: the silver lining. The ramifications of our findings should be far-reaching – this is not just communication we're talking about here. They affect products, services, internal culture, business purpose and vision. In short, these findings should fundamentally rewire an organisation's DNA, which may sound terrifying but the potential rewards, when you consider women's consumer spending power and earnings, are huge.

The life script is dead: so are many segmentation studies

Part of the problem with audience segmentations, particularly or almost exclusively when it comes to women, is the idea that we know everything about a woman based on her age, because we assume that women's lives follow very particular and consistent patterns. Again, as I've pointed out, the life script as we know it is dead; it's much harder to define the 'typical age' for motherhood; it's also true that women in their fifties are not as likely to be settled, doting grandmothers. Consider, for example, that in the UK one in five festival-goers are over 45, and the Baby Boomers represent a key demographic at the Glastonbury festival.[34] So stop thinking so much about age and maternal status as key determinants of behaviour and start thinking about attitude and aspiration as a predictor of behaviour, just as you would for a segmentation of a male audience.

In reality, the Female Tribes study is a form of attitudinal segmentation, not that I want to put women into boxes or create more lazy stereotypes. Yet the simple act of discovering and exploring the 'tribes' is a way to demonstrate women's diversity to reveal new insights and to challenge everything we *think* we know about women, proving that women have as many different goals, dreams and aspirations as men, and that there is more opportunity in exploring the possibilities of being a woman versus focusing only on the parental responsibilities of being a woman.

No life script: new opportunities

One example of innovating in relation to the demise of the life script is some of our work within the jewellery and specifically diamond jewellery category. Previously diamond jewellery had been long associated with 'love gifting' in the form of diamond engagement and anniversary rings, but the problem with that narrative is that women are settling down later, if at all; equally implicit to this narrative is the idea that a woman has to wait for a man to buy her a diamond, she cannot reward herself. So much love-gifting advertising has relied on the old story of 'be a good girl, get a diamond', and it felt like time to disrupt the Cinderella story for once, recognising that women can and do gift themselves, and why shouldn't the ultimate self-reward be a diamond? Working with the De Beers Group on a campaign for 'A Diamond Is Forever' in the US, J. Walter Thompson developed the 'Right Hand Ring' concept, the idea being that while your left hand may reflect your engagement, your right hand is for your own self-expression. As an extension of this idea, working with Forevermark, the consumer brand that the De Beers Group launched in the US in 2011, our Female Tribes insight helped lead to the creation of the Forevermark Tribute™ collection, which celebrates women for the individuals they are, recognising their control over their own lives, and heralding all their unique characteristics and not merely their roles and responsibilities, and so represents a subtle nod to women's empowerment. The collection, launched in the US, has been enthusiastically embraced by the retail jewellery community, attracted much press and PR coverage, and opens up new opportunities for purchase.

Give her recognition: show her that you see her

I think a very simple way of summing up the 'new' rules of engagement for women, and the cynic in me would question how 'new' they really are, is that women are not the passive **objects** of their life story, they are the active **subjects** of their own story, as the diamond case study illustrates. We are no longer appendages to another person's agenda: we are very much in the driving seat. In terms of brand communication, this has a profound impact on the language we use, the characters we build, the narrative we frame – basically everything needs to change because currently our research suggests that women simply do not see themselves reflected in much of the advertising they observe.

I find this incredibly exciting but also creatively it gives us a much bigger, more interesting canvas to explore, because crucially women want to be recognised and represented on that creative canvas for the women they are, not the women we assume them to be. In the next few chapters I'll start to describe what that means.

One of the big pitfalls as I see it in the new era of 'femvertising' has been the creation of advertising that simply hectors women: it presumes to know what feminism is (often a very narrow definition) and lectures women with a faux feminist manifesto. Having to listen to this is exhausting and often condescending: when will we stop telling women what to do? I don't need to prove I'm a 'strong powerful woman' with my purchases because I know I am one. I don't want a hyper-caffeinated feminist life coach. As a woman, I want what most people want, products and services designed and intuited to my needs.

I want to be seen and heard as a woman: if I'm buying a car, I don't want you to assume I'm the 'little lady' brought to the dealership to choose the colour; I know what happens under the bonnet, thank you. If I'm getting a mortgage, please don't by default put it in my husband or partner's name. If I'm booking travel tickets for the family, do not make the designated travel party leader the only male name on the tickets, because my money is just as hard earned, just as valuable and, if I'm the one spending it, that deserves recognition. I want equal visibility as a consumer and, moreover, as a human being. I want to feel significant, and for that you earn my loyalty: it really is that simple.

CHAPTER 2

· ·

The Dow Jane Effect and the Female Economy

'If Lehman Brothers had been "Lehman Sisters" today's economic crisis clearly would look quite different.' **Christine Lagarde**

They say that 'money talks', and it would seem that when it comes to what I'm terming the 'great female enlightenment' or, put more plainly, the growing recognition that women are not just stay-at-home consumers but powerful wealth creators, then the film world is one of the great exponents of this idea.

By way of illustration, witness Hollywood, purveyor of romcoms that would have us believe that grown women would fight over a wedding dress; that self-same institution is now alive to the idea of the female hero. An industry that has only ever parted with two Academy Awards in its entire history to women in achievement-based acting roles (i.e. active as opposed to passive) is alive to the Alpha Female. So, what exactly has prompted this volte face?

MONEY TALKS

In 2014, thanks in no small part to films like *Gravity* and *The Hunger Games*, female-led movies out-earned their male counterparts by a significant margin (30 per cent). Initially dismissed as a bit of an anomaly, this trend has continued unabated: in 2016 the figure was 16 per cent, and the female-led *Star Wars: The Force Awakens* took over $500 million in US box-office earnings alone; and in 2017 *Wonder Woman* became one of the biggest earning superhero films of our time: Female Capital once again. At the close of 2017, the top three highest grossing movies of the year had female leads: *Star Wars: The Last Jedi*, *Beauty and the Beast* and *Wonder Woman*. Thanks to our box-office earning potential,[1] studios are now fully embracing the idea of female superheroes, so you can put down that copy of *Bride Magazine* and maybe pick up *Martial Arts Illustrated*.

This is not just a trend isolated to Hollywood. Over on Wall Street we see the launch of the Barclays Women in Leadership Total Return Index; if you are savvy enough to have discovered that women on management boards generate typically stronger financial performances (up to a 15 per cent increase in profitability according to a global study by the Peterson Institute[2]) you can put your own money where your mouth is and invest in female-managed companies. On average, female-led hedge funds consistently outperform those managed by their male peers.[3] and a 2015 report by HFR with analysis dating back to 2007 revealed a consistent trend with female-led funds returning an average of 59 per cent versus an average of 37 per cent.[4] In 2009, in recognition of this 'Dow Jane effect', Naissance Capital, a global investment company, introduced gender diversity screening for investment funds to prioritise those with women on the boards.

Employing women in senior management doesn't only look good for diversity quotas, it yields financial returns. A Catalyst study across Fortune 500 companies revealed a direct correlation between the proportion of female directors and key financial metrics.[5] What proved surprising was the scale of the findings:

- 84 per cent return on sales
- 60 per cent greater return on invested capital
- 46 per cent greater return on equity.

The global study in 2016 from the Peterson Institute concluded the same thing, namely the fact that women in the boardroom deliver a direct impact on corporate earnings: once again, the Dow Jane effect.

In response to this 'female economy', Walmart has started to actively promote female-owned businesses via a labelling system, recognising through its own research that women are significantly more likely to purchase products made by women, citing quality as a key motivation. In 2014, Walmart reported that women-owned businesses were the fastest growing sector of their business. This is perhaps the tip of the iceberg: a 2013 study published by Amex revealed that in the US not only are women starting their own businesses at twice the rate of men, they are growing big businesses. Women-owned businesses in the $10 million plus category have growth rates outstripping their peers, perhaps contributing to the fact that 60 per cent of all personal wealth in the US is held by women.[6]

These are not disparate or isolated findings and do not appear to be a blip. This is a phenomenon and further evidence of the Dow Jane effect. In essence, we are witnessing the recognition of and response to a female economy, embracing the concept of women not only as consumers but as wealth creators in their own right, whether we're actively conscious of it or not. I'm not alone in this sentiment. From Ernst & Young describing women as 'the next emerging market' to Forbes describing us as the 'new global growth engine', the female economy has arrived. Notice Ernst & Young used the term 'emerging market', and that is certainly true. Many barriers exist to women realising their full economic potential. For all that female-run hedge funds may be more profitable, they are still few and far between, at around 3 per cent of all funds according to HFR research.

RISE OF THE FEMALE BREADWINNER

Women's financial empowerment is not limited to the City, and increasingly women are the major breadwinners at home. Liza Mundy, a *Washington Post* reporter and author of *The Richer Sex*, predicts that by 2025 more than half of US households will have a woman at the financial helm. From our own Women's Index research, in the UK and US, 24 per cent of women claimed to out-earn their spouse, with 50 per cent of all women describing themselves as the 'major breadwinner'.[7] This trend is not isolated to the Western world either. A Forbes analysis of Global Entrepreneurship Monitor revealed that countries where women were rising the fastest, as opposed to riding out a local trend, were found largely in the developing world, particularly in Brazil, India, Vietnam and the Philippines. In case you missed Hanna Rosin's controversial book *The End of Men and the Rise of Women*, published in 2012, this could be the decade for women.

WOMEN'S INDEX FINDINGS

We explored the area of financial responsibilities in our Women's Index research, and the findings certainly seemed to support the idea of women's increased economic empowerment. These were the key findings:

We are the breadwinners

Half of all women around the world are the major breadwinner at home, rising to 60 per cent in Brazil and peaking at 68 per cent in Thailand. We also witnessed a global average of 22 per cent of women saying they out-earned their spouse. This rose to one in three women in Brazil, Thailand and the Philippines, but only 5 per cent in Japan: given we talked to women in over 19 countries this is a very significant figure. Sit that alongside the film and advertising representation of women as unemployed or stay-at-home housewives, and one can see how ridiculous it seems.

We are proud to be a good provider

There was no sense of shame in their status as major breadwinner, no inkling that, given the choice, they would rather be at home filing their nails with a rich husband as provider. Far from it: nearly three-quarters of women globally said they were 'proud to be a good provider', and 73 per cent of women said they made the majority of household financial decisions, rising to 85 per cent in Brazil. We also observed, however, that the financial impact of motherhood concerned nearly half of all women worldwide, with this felt most profoundly in Asia Pacific, with 58 per cent sharing this concern, perhaps explaining plummeting birth rates. particularly in Japan.

We have ambition for the future

Linked to earnings potential we also explored the idea of ambition, and once again the findings supported the idea of an emergent and sizeable cohort of 'Alpha Females'. We found that 56 per cent of all women around the world claimed they were more ambitious than their significant other. Set against that global average, however, significantly more women in Thailand, Brazil, Egypt, Lebanon and India claimed to be more ambitious than their spouse: above 70 per cent across these markets.

We push hard: because we have to

What we observed was a strong correlation between ambition and sexual discrimination. Those countries where women were more ambitious were also the countries where sexual discrimination was most prevalent. In Thailand, Brazil, Egypt, Lebanon and India significantly more women claimed they experienced discrimination at work, with more than half of women in agreement, well above the all market average (40 per cent). This did not feel like a coincidence.

If work doesn't work for her, she works for herself

Another intriguing finding from the research was the link between experiencing gender discrimination at work and female entrepreneurship. Of those countries where significantly more women – more than the all-market average – experienced discrimination, the importance of starting their own businesses spiked. In Lebanon and Brazil, for example, home to some of the highest levels of gender discrimination in the workplace, more than 70 per cent of women felt starting their own business was important, relative to an all-market average of just over 50 per cent. So, companies that don't value their female talent are in danger of losing it to entrepreneurship. Why would you work twice as hard to get nowhere if you could do better working for yourself? More than 50 per cent of all women in our survey said they were pretty sure they were getting paid less than their male peers, doing the same job – powerful stimulus for being your own boss.

THE UNIVERSALITY OF ALPHA CHARACTERISTICS

In our study we defined alpha characteristics as not solely about ambition and drive, for example, wanting to get to the top of one's career, but also the degree to which career defined the self. What was extraordinary was the degree to which alpha characteristics were prevalent around the world. Of course, not all women had adopted feminism, and between one-fifth to a third of women around the world conformed to more traditional 'tribes' – the 'Nurturers' for example, for whom the home is centre of her universe, or the 'Spouse Focused' tribe, in which the husband is the centre of her universe. A surprising factor, however, was that traditional tribes were much less prevalent (around one in five women) in Asia Pacific, and much more prevalent (around one in three) in the Western World! This challenges all our assumptions of Western women being the most progressive and Asian women being the passive, doe-eyed homemakers. From what our data was telling us, this simply wasn't the case, with the exception of Japan, which proved to be different from the rest of Asia and traditional in many respects.

What was clear from our data was that women were for the most part not only more ambitious than their spouse, as claimed by 56 per cent of women in our sample, they were not content to wait at home for money to arrive on the table. We were witnessing the driver of the Dow Jane effect. These were women in charge of their own destiny, making the majority of the financial and household decisions: these were 'Alpha Females'.

ALPHAS ARE MOTHERS TOO

Dispelling yet more myths of age and life stage being reasonable predictors of behaviour, we ran a brief analysis to look at Alpha Females across social class, age and life stage. The results revealed there showed no correlation between age, social class, income, marital status or maternal status. None. So, the presumption that ambition is the preserve of the wealthy unmarried woman is entirely fictitious. Let me illustrate with an example, looking at the qualities of entrepreneurship. Of all those women who cited starting their own business as 'very important' in life, 53 per cent of mothers agreed globally, and 54 per cent of child-free women agreed: no significant difference. Equally 'being successful' was important to 79 per cent of mothers and 83 per cent of childfree women, so likewise not a significant difference between the two.[8]

Not only that, but if anything we saw a slight increase in the prevalence of alpha characteristics once women had children, so if anything being a mother only serves to sharpen the career and breadwinning drive. When you say that out loud, it seems so reasonable and logical, yet I have lost count of the arguments I have had over the years with clients wedded to the idea that no mother ever had ambition, for her children yes, but for herself, forget about it. The data I had on the table staring back at me suggested the exact opposite: a small but gratifying victory, with far-reaching implications.

RISE OF THE ALPHA FEMALE

So how does culture define the Alpha Female? Clinical psychologist Mansi Hassan described the key characteristics of an Alpha Female: 'Alpha women can be described as ambitious and career-oriented, emotionally self-sufficient, sexually expressive, confident and in many cases aggressive. They have strong personality traits which usually make them independent and easily successful. They are also high in confidence and in some cases more rational than emotional.'[9]

These values contrast sharply with what we associate with typically 'feminine' values or characteristics. In part, the role of nurture as opposed to nature bears influence. Traditionally from childhood boys are rewarded for their self-confidence, while girls are encouraged to take a less self-regarding approach to their development, to 'think of others' in preparation for motherhood: with the stay-at-home mum their role model.

This is changing, however; successive world wars propelled women into the workforce and while some returned to the home post-war, many did not; now, in the UK alone it's estimated that over two-thirds of women with children work at least part-time.[10] So we're witnessing the legacy of generations of working mothers instilling as role models a sense of ambition and competition in their daughters, and this self-belief and confidence is helping to inspire a new generation of Alpha Females. A study by the Harvard Business School found that daughters of working mothers were more likely to earn more and rise to supervisory level in their careers, and this trend held true for all 24 countries in the study.[11]

Young women are increasingly aspiring to higher education, and in the US women's university enrolment significantly outpaces their male peers.[12] In the UK, the latest UCAS figures point to a staggering gender gap on university entrants, with over 20 per cent more women applying versus their male peers.[13] Women's pursuit of higher education is not confined to the West: across key Gulf states and the Middle East, female university enrolment is tracking ahead of men. In Qatar, for example, there are roughly two female undergraduates for every male, while in China women account for 48 per cent of the university population.[14] Perhaps most surprising is the pursuit of STEM subjects among women in the Middle East: some 60 per cent of engineering students are female in the Gulf states, while in Iran 70 per cent of science and engineering graduates were women.[15] Iran also leads the world in the dramatic rise in scientific publications,[16] so it's not the case that women are the big fish in a small pond, making the pursuit of STEM subjects among women in the Middle East so impressive and harder to dismiss.

We in the West often flatter ourselves in our progressive and enlightened attitudes towards female empowerment and challenging of gender roles, so it's ironic that women studying STEM subjects in the US lags so far behind at only 30 per cent. In the case of the Gulf states, governments have recognised the economic contribution of an educated female elite and have subsequently used grants and incentives to facilitate further education. Equally, Iran has a rich history of supporting academic excellence predating the Shah era, no doubt reinforcing the importance of education.

THE SIGNIFICANCE OF MENTORSHIP

It's also more socially acceptable today for women to display pride and achievement in their educational attainment and career, and while there aren't enough there are more female role models and entrepreneurs for younger women to emulate, helping to foster innate ambition. Love them or hate them, the Kardashians are super-savvy businesswomen, Oprah Winfrey is the first black self-made billionaire, Shonda Rhimes a successful showrunner and TV mogul, Jessica Alba an actress turned entrepreneur. It's hypothesised that one of the factors underlying women's educational achievement within the Gulf states is the presence of more female role models as educators, since girls are taught by local female teachers as compared to boys, often schooled by male ex-pat teachers.[17] The theory would support the importance of female role models and female mentoring as key to women's development, and a study by the Harvard Business School found that women were more likely to achieve promotion and less likely to quit if they had female partners as mentors.[18] From our own research we saw that women recognised the value and significance of mentoring, with more than 80 per cent of women globally feeling it was important for women to step up as mentors to younger women in the workplace.[19]

DOES EDUCATION TRANSLATE INTO EARNINGS?

Education is only part of the story, and it's worth exploring whether education translates into earnings potential. Certainly, increasing women's access to education benefits economies; it's estimated that women's increased education over the past 50 years has contributed to 50 per cent of the growth within OECD countries.[20]Across the Middle East, women's employment and therefore earning opportunities still lag behind those for men, yet when we look towards say the US and UK we see a nuanced picture. While women may out-earn men at the start of their careers, factoring in career breaks and maternity leave, women's salaries in senior management often lag behind those of their male counterparts. In Britain, women earn roughly 26 per cent less than their male counterparts for management roles, with bonuses and other benefits also lagging.[21] The reason for the disparity in wages is often blamed on career breaks, but this becomes harder to justify when the disparity also affects pensions and bonuses. Analysis by the World Economic Forum demonstrates the global gender pay gap is increasing,[22] so entrenched attitudes surrounding women's value at work still persist.

THE MOTHERHOOD PENALTY

A frequent issue that's often used to explain the lack of career trajectory or equal pay for women is motherhood. The 'motherhood penalty' can affect women in several ways directly, indirectly or implicitly. Career breaks can mean that a woman leaves the fast track for maybe a year, and so she can lose out on the chance of promotion or working on career-building projects: she is simply off the radar.

Of all women surveyed in the Women's Index, 44 per cent said that, if they had to, they would consider postponing marriage and motherhood to focus on their career. This figure ratcheted up to 59 per cent in India and the high fifties across China, Brazil and Saudi Arabia. The motivation was quite simple. When we looked at the response to the question on whether child-free co-workers had more career opportunities, we saw that more than two-thirds of women across the same countries felt this to be true, and the reason was principally because child-free women were prepared to work longer hours. Mothers were also significantly more likely versus 'Not Mums' (57 per cent versus 51 per cent) to feel that they didn't have the same career and professional opportunities as men, and over 50 per cent of women in Brazil, China, India and Saudi Arabia were worried about the impact of motherhood on their finances: clearly these were cultures where combining a career with children was particularly challenging.

But there is the more subtle and pernicious idea, rarely openly articulated, that motherhood dulls a woman's drive: she loses her focus as a result of 'baby brain', so unconscious bias kicks in and women lose out on promotions because they may 'lack the necessary drive'. Note that I highlighted 'baby brain' as an 'idea' and not fact, unlike Paul Tudor Jones, a celebrated Wall Street hedge fund billionaire:

> As soon as that baby's lips touch that girl's bosom, forget it. Every single investment idea, every desire to understand what's going to make this go up or going to go down is going to be overwhelmed by the most beautiful experience – which a man will never share – about a mode of connection between that mother and that baby.[23]

THE BABY-BRAIN MYTH

The problem with these attitudes is that, aside from the fact they are prehistoric, is that 'baby brain' as a concept is perceptual – it *does not* exist, and we now have the evidence from neuropsychologists.[24] Researchers discovered that not only was 'baby brain' a myth, but equally motherhood, far from diminishing intellect, served to sharpen mental cognition and emotional intelligence. Dr Craig Kinsley of Richmond University, Virginia found that motherhood improved mental agility with enduring effects: 'The changes that kick in then could last for the rest of their lives, bolstering cognitive abilities and protecting them against degenerative diseases'.[25]

From our own research we observed that far from dulling a woman's drive, motherhood served to sharpen it, with three-quarters of women saying that having children had made them work 'harder and faster', and in a 'more productive way'. I would also go further to say that from what we observed women who were mothers were more likely to value their career; 76 per cent of mothers said that their work was 'very important and linked to their sense of self', compared to 70 per cent of 'Not Mums'.[26] Mothers were also more likely to claim that they had a more responsible job than their spouse: no baby brain here!

BABIES AND FATHERS: DISCUSS

The problem I have is that only women are ever subjected to the whole 'baby brain' myth – we never consider the impact of parenthood on fathers. It is as if fathers live a separate existence. The suggestion that a sleep-deprived new dad might demote work to second fiddle while he adjusts to and celebrates parenthood just hasn't entered public consciousness. Research by Ruth Feldman at the Bar Ilan University in Israel revealed that the experience of parenthood did impact a father's brain function, particularly the socio-cognitive functioning: so while it's less about direct hormonal impact, parenting does 'rewire' fathers' brains.[27] At the same time, while paternity leave is seen as a progressive acknowledgement of the role of fathers in parenting, it rarely seems to attract the same criticism to which women are subjected – namely the idea that paternity leave will rob the workplace of its talent at a critical moment, or the man will 'let's the side down'. While parental leave 'empowers' fathers, it frequently disempowers women. But maybe if more fathers actually start to embrace paternity leave, they will meet with similar eye-rolls from their superiors, and we will be equally disempowered as parents in the workplace!

MOTHERHOOD: THE BOTTOM LINE

A more frustrating factor in the 'motherhood penalty' is the impact of motherhood on salary. Here again, gender tells a very different story: data compiled by the TUC and IPPR reveals that while having children can propel a man's salary and promotional prospects, for women's careers it's almost the direct opposite: so babies present a 'motherhood penalty' but a 'fatherhood premium', with full-time fathers receiving up to a 22 per cent wage premium: so while you will labour away for nine months to produce the baby, don't bank on any financial advantage thereafter.[28]

As a culture, we are hardwired, through the images we see and the films we watch, to expect that childrearing is a woman's role, while breadwinning belongs to men, despite the irrefutable evidence to counter this idea: cultural consciousness hasn't caught up with the facts. Even more depressingly, recent research in the US suggests that as far as millennials are concerned, or at least millennial men, willingness to accept a female breadwinner is going backwards![29] Fewer than half of millennial men in the survey supported the idea of women working outside the home, compared to less than 30 per cent of millennial women, and the preparedness to embrace a female breadwinner shows steep declines since the 1980s. But then consider, for example, the steep decline in employment prospects for the American middle class – could this have anything to do with the fact that working women present more competition in the labour market? That same competition meant that the state effectively legislated housewife status for women in post-war America, and married women were forced to give up their jobs to make way for returning servicemen. This might seem outrageous in today's terms but, remember, this was barely 60 years ago. So, if the present conservatism sweeping the US intends to create a 'job for everyone', whether 'everyone' includes women remains to be seen, especially if the Donald Trump administration is successful in its bid to roll back employee rights – including, of course, those of working mothers.

PRODUCING CHILDREN AND PRODUCTIVITY

There is a glimmer of a silver lining. True to say, many women undoubtedly experience the impact of motherhood on their career trajectory, but there is a handful of exceptions. A surprising statistic is that the youngest ever female partner of a leading global law firm was promoted while on maternity leave and Marissa Mayer of Yahoo was recruited while pregnant. It would take rose-tinted glasses of jam-jar thickness, however, to proclaim that these lucky few are challenging the idea that motherhood kills careers, but at least it is evidence of enlightenment – acceptance that humans will at some point seek to breed and we just need to deal with it. Given that the 'CEO of home finance' is more likely than not female, and given the very compelling evidence that women in the boardroom benefit the bottom line, then a smart organisation should seek to embed female insight throughout its organisation: ultimately meaning more women as decision makers. It's funny how on paper that seems so obvious, yet to the corporate and communications world it's still such a revelatory concept, and a thumping clue as to why I wrote this book.

THE ONLY THING WE HAVE TO FEAR IS FEAR ITSELF: OR IS IT?

One key attribute that defines all Alpha Men and Women is confidence. And while confidence is often socially conditioned into men, for women it doesn't come so easily, or perhaps isn't as socially acceptable. How many times have we heard women described as 'bossy', 'shrill' or my personal favourite 'feisty'? These adjectives are gendered, and not in a good way, they are specifically used to describe female assertion in the pejorative sense: the result is women have less permission to be assertive. I can recall many occasions on which I have been told I come across as too strident, or to be 'less angry', or that I might be perceived as 'shrill'; these have never been comments made by women, and no, I never heed this advice. When I know that being a woman isn't going to be an impediment, to stop me or others like me from fulfilling my dreams, then I'll stop pushing, but only then.

What can also hold women back from high achievement and entrepreneurship is lack of confidence and, more specifically, the fear of failure. The Global Entrepreneurship Monitor (GEM) concluded: 'Perceptual factors that reflect optimism, self-confidence, and reduced fear of failure are important predictors of women's entrepreneurship.' Typical characteristics of entrepreneurs show little deviation between the sexes: individuals with a high tolerance for risk, self-belief and optimism. The key differentiator is confidence and fear of failure: women are typically much more afraid of failure.[30]

We saw evidence of women's corrosive self-doubt in the Women's Index data. When we quizzed women on perceptual barriers to their success, more than 40 per cent cited themselves as 'their own worst enemy'; this peaked to more than half of women in Asia.[31] Women in India were much more likely to cite cultural values, or their family or spouse, as the main barrier to their success, but this did not deter them; more than 70 per cent of Indian women were confident they would be successful in life, making what we call the 'Mumbai Millennials' bold and fearless in the pursuit of their goals.

FAIL FAST: JUST NOT IF YOU'RE A WOMAN

If you read the business press or have attended a few marketing conferences in your lifetime, a soundbite you will have frequently heard is that true entrepreneurs will 'fail fast'; in short, they will be unafraid of getting things wrong, it won't deter their progress, but crucially they will learn from it. One important nuance to the fear of failure among women as distinct from men is the concept of 'permission' to fail: you can only 'fail faster' if it's OK to fail in the first place, if it doesn't derail your whole career. Because when women 'fail fast' it's usually career suicide: they fail fast and they fall even faster. It's often cited that if a woman fails she 'let's the side down': we fail for the whole of our gender, and it's serves to fuel the sceptics proving that women aren't 'up to it'. No such prejudice exists for men: if he fails, he simply dusts himself down and starts over. He can dismiss it to bad luck. There's the old adage that women wait to be 100 per cent qualified for a job before they apply, and men only 50 per cent. I don't believe that, or not in the way the data is presented. I think *employers* wait for a woman to be 100 per cent qualified, since there is unconscious bias that she's a risky bet – men not so much. We see this pattern repeated time and time again: we watch while our underqualified male peers somersault through the career ranks and we plod along, treading water. And not just in the business world. In the film world, this same unconscious bias prevents female directors getting work, whereas their underqualified male peers direct big-budget movies, often with no prior experience. Slated CEO Stephan Paternot characterised it as the 'trust gap'.

The problem with being a 'trailblazer' for your sex is that being the first to do something attracts attention, and there's always something to prove. The flipside is that there's something to disprove too: a woman's failure can have a consequence for her gender, and can close doors and keep them shut for longer, serving to pile on the pressure. Researchers at Yale University, led by Victoria Brescoll, discovered that culturally we are far more critical of leaders when they make bad judgements if they are in an unfamiliar role for their gender, so women managers in typically male sectors have much farther to fall if they make a mistake, and a considerably harder landing. This rule works for both sexes, but the innate problem is that men have a much wider sphere of management territory.[32] So the upshot here is that women wanting to break into a male career field have to make almost zero bad decisions if they want to be accepted. Fair? Not really. Little wonder so many women might decide the ends just don't justify the means; who wants to live in constant fear of failure? Consequently, we see an exodus of women in the corporate world in their late forties and early fifties, and those same women starting their own businesses. Speak to any management recruitment consultant, and they will all shake their heads at the rate of dropout among older more senior women: and why would you not take your experience and use it for your own advantage if you could?

FEAR CAN BE POWERFUL

Let me go out on a limb, however, and suggest that fear of failure may not be such a bad thing after all. Maybe fear of failure can be a good thing, in the same way that fear of dying in a car crash makes us (mostly) drive in a sane and responsible fashion, regularly checking for hazards. Imagine if this were an economy and not a car. Linked to the fear of failure is the acceptance or pursuit of risk and here, while hormones play a significant role, it's not as black and white as one would expect.

A recent study of male market traders in the US revealed that as testosterone levels increased, coupled with successful trades, this in turn generated a surge of testosterone, what they termed the 'Winner Effect'. The 'Winner Effect' is a state of overconfidence or invincibility and can result in a heightened tolerance to risk and even impulsive behaviour or deliberate risk-taking in order to fuel the sensation, which could result in potentially damaging decision-making behaviour.[33] What researchers observed in the study was that, as the afternoon progressed, male trading behaviour became riskier, more volatile and this impacted on profitability: they lost money. Unfortunately, the study only focused on the male brain, but it would prove interesting to understand whether female traders were subject to the same hormonal behavioural traits. The implicit suggestion here is whether the impact of more female traders would be greater market stability, leading Christine Lagarde to make her quip about the 'Lehman Sisters'. In fact, in the six years to 2013, hedge funds run by women delivered a 6 per cent return, compared to those run by men, which ran at a loss,[34] seeding the idea that women are the better investors, at times more cautious and level-headed. In an article in the *Financial Times*, Stephen Foley points to behavioural studies that suggest the idea that women are more level-headed, more risk averse and play the long game, making for steadier gains.[35]

The idea of women's 'steady hand' is used in part to explain women's predominance within the Indian banking sector, where eight out of the top ten banks are headed by women. In fact, India's female-led banks control some 40 per cent of India's assets, which marks India out as the most progressive country in the world for the status of women within the financial sector.[36] To understand such a startling phenomenon, you have to know what cultural factors are at play. There are some key practical reasons, for example extended families often facilitate easy access to childcare, and culturally the entrenched class (caste) system means that being part of the social elite overrides gender barriers in India. It's the particular set of values that women bring to management, however, that have secured their advancement within the Indian banking sector; alongside their loyalty, it's their caution, structured approach and teamworking that have opened the boardroom doors and kept them open. 'Women tend to be more conservative, more structured, more careful about money, good leaders and better team players,' according to Swati Piramal, vice chair of Piramal Enterprises.[37]

Equally women can engender trust and inspire other women, reassuring investors after the Lehman Brothers crisis. It was ICICI's CEO Chanda Kochhar's status as a mother that assuaged fears. 'We now feel comfortable because we are hearing you in person, as a mother,' said investors, and equally young female students in India are inspired: 'I never thought the banking industry was male dominated because I could see Chanda Kochhar lead such a big bank ... Chanda is my inspiration.'[38]

A BANK RUN BY WOMEN: FOR WOMEN

Such is the impact of women in India's financial sector and the desire to address women's lagging economic empowerment in 2013 that the first bank dedicated to women was opened. Despite women's entry into the boardroom, only 26 per cent of women in India have a formal relationship with a bank.[39] The ICICI bank, however, prioritises the financial empowerment of Indian women as it recognises that this could lead to significant, wider benefits to society.[40] It offers concessionary rates of interest for women, together with financial literacy classes, training and development in order for women to become income generators and in turn benefit their communities – elevating other women from poverty.

ASIAN ALPHAS: THE TIGER WOMEN

Of course, no discussion of the female economy or Alpha Females would be complete without turning our attention to Asia because behind every tiger economy there's a tiger woman. This is not something we normally associate with Asia or the typical docile Asian female stereotype, but the fact remains that modern Asian women are shedding the homemaker stereotype to form an economic powerhouse. With a third of CEOs in Thailand being female and 34 per cent of all senior management positions in China being held by women, they are proving to be a significant contributor to the region's prosperity.[41]

The 'Asian Alpha' is educated, emancipated and ambitious. She wants to define her destiny herself and she has no plans to settle down into marriage any time soon, despite the hopes of her parents and grandparents. In fact, we witnessed in our Women's Index data that Chinese women were the least likely to cite their mother or grandmother as their role model; they are also among the most likely to be prepared to postpone marriage and children in order to focus on their careers.

What makes the Asia Alpha distinct from her Western Alpha Female cousin is that she often faces very intense pressure to marry, and is more likely to choose a celibate lifestyle. It's still largely culturally unacceptable to cohabit before marriage, so Asian Alphas are largely single and childless.

In a region characterised by the submissive role of women, a new wave of super-ambitious women seems particularly counterculture. These women have an appetite for success – average isn't good enough, they want to get to the top. Today's Chinese professional women are even more ambitious at work than their American counterparts; 76 per cent of Chinese women surveyed in 2011 by the New York-based Center for Talent Innovation said they 'aspire to top jobs' versus 52 per cent of Americans. Chinese women employed by multinational companies frequently work more than 70 hours a week. In fact, over 50 per cent of Chinese billionaires are women, and women hold 34 per cent of all senior management positions. In a country where, according to our own Women's Index research, nearly one in four women believe that being a woman is an impediment to achieving their full potential, ambition isn't optional if you want to succeed, it's mandatory.

This dynamic is not confined to China as almost a third of all CEOs in Thailand are women, and Asia is the region with the highest ratio of female to male CEOs in the world.[42] Not only are women rising to senior management positions in Asia, they are reaching not millionaire but billionaire status: China now has more self-made female billionaires than any other country in the world. These women's meteoric rise to the top often starts from humble beginnings and is testament to the vaunting ambition of the Asian female. Zhang Xin, a former factory worker, built her empire in real estate and boasts 3 million followers on Sina Weibo (China's Twitter); high-end restaurant mogul Zhang Lan slept next to a pigsty as a girl; Peggy Yu started out as an interpreter and secretary for a boiler company to become the owner of Dangdang, one of China's biggest online book retailers and the equivalent of Amazon.

What unites these women in their success, beyond a 'Western' education in entrepreneurship, is their values of optimism, courage and drive. In a region often noted for its conservatism, these women display the killer combination of energy and acceptance of risk in the pursuit of success. As Luo Yun, marketing chief for Zhang Lan's South Beauty restaurant empire, says of Zhang, 'She has great courage to do something bold and innovative. And the results often prove that she is right.'[43] This chimes with our own research, which revealed that 50 per cent of Chinese women aspire to be 'aggressive' as a core female trait; no other country came close to this result with the one exception, Taiwan, with 49 per cent of women.

To a degree, the Asian Alpha is a product of the one-child policy coupled with 'tiger parenting'. We saw in our research that Chinese women were significantly more likely to prioritise education during childhood over 'friendships and fun'.[44] In an age of only children, if a family's one child is a girl, parents have little choice but to groom her for long-term success. As Yang Yuli, who works as a producer for the BBC in Beijing, has it, 'it no longer matters if you are a boy or girl; you are the only person responsible for [your] family's future'. From our Women's Index research, the idea of 'education as a necessity' was almost universally accepted by some 98 per cent of Chinese women, but perhaps more intriguingly 91 per cent of Chinese women felt that 'one can get farther in life on street smarts than book smarts' (i.e. being savvy in the real world rather than academically advanced). No other country had such forceful agreement with this idea. The importance of 'street smarts' in China perhaps reflects the importance of 'who you know', not just 'what you know', in a country characterised by a powerful and influential social elite.

The new 'equality' in parenting has meant that girls are pushing ahead academically, with their parents' support, and outperforming the boys in university entry exams, with the numbers of women achieving the top scores as high as 60 per cent in some provinces.[45] We witnessed in our Women's Index research that throughout their teenage years, Chinese women prioritised education as their number-one priority, far more important than being healthy, happy or making friendships: the women of no other country had such single-minded educational tunnel vision.

It could be theorised that the increasing Westernisation of Asia and access to global media has served to broaden the horizons of the modern Asian girl. Whereas once she might have aspired to be a wife and mother, she now recognises that she can carve out a self-determined future for herself, and she's aspiring to more than her mother or grandmother.

Key to her freedom is financial independence, especially in China where the cost and access to fundamentals like healthcare is still a significant cause of bankruptcy, and we witnessed in the Women's Index data one-third of Chinese women citing financial independence as the most important life priority. Kate Ba, a PR in Beijing, commented, 'My generation are just now starting to become managers, and in the future I think we'll see more women as presidents and CEOs, far more than in my mother's generation.'

THE LEFTOVER LADIES

While China and other parts of Asia might have embraced capitalism and economic empowerment, there are still traditional cultural values that serve to undermine a woman's progress. Despite their ambition and new-found financial freedom, many young women still live in fear of becoming a '*sheng nu*' or 'leftover lady'. Typically, most women are expected to be married by their twenty-fifth birthday, which affords them little time to focus on their career. This was borne out in our Women's Index data. China was the only country where marriage appeared in the top five measures of success, and this was to the exclusion of 'happiness', which didn't make it into the top five, and speaks to the cultural importance tied to marriage.

Since the culture in China is for women to marry up or 'hypergamy', as women vault up the career ladder they find their pool of marriageable men is far smaller, and the pressure to find a suitable partner can feel intense. China's government-backed 'Women's Federation' has the following advice for the 'leftover ladies':

Pretty girls don't need a lot of education to marry into a rich and powerful family, but girls with an average or ugly appearance will find it difficult. These kinds of girls hope to further their education in order to increase their competitiveness. The tragedy is, they don't realize that as women age, they are worth less and less, so by the time they get their MA or PhD, they are already old, like yellowed pearls.

Perhaps then it's not surprising that China now ranks number three in the world for cosmetic surgery procedures, as the pretty girls snag the best husbands, and from our Women's Index data, a startling one in ten Chinese women, more than in any other country, cited 'being attractive' as the most important life goal. Equally 63 per cent of women in China felt they could use their femininity as a means of power and influence, significantly higher than the all-country average. Perhaps this goes some way to explain why the China women's national football team are dubbed the 'Steel Roses', for the combination of femininity applied to ambition.

There are signs of change, however, and financial and emotional emancipation are slowly evolving the Asian marriage model, and perhaps in future this will see Asian women embrace marriage as equal partners, as opposed to being an encumbered spouse. The disintegration of North Korea's economy has confronted its women with new pressures and problems as they struggle to feed their families. But for some, at least, their growing economic contribution has brought an unaccustomed say in domestic affairs and a new assertiveness. 'Men can't make enough money to run the family so it's women's job now,' said Lee Young-le, who trades food on the Chinese border. 'It's the mother who pays for school for the child, who dresses the child and feeds the child. Men want women to obey but when the basis of everything is money and eating, you can't say anything.'[46]

THE FORMIDABLE FACTORY GIRLS

It's important to point out that the Asian Alpha doesn't just exist in the wealthy urban areas: 'alpha' values are not the preserve of the educated elite. Women in rural communities are also taking up the mantle of economic empowerment, and in her book, *Factory Girls*, Leslie Chang concluded that Chinese rural women were more ambitious than their male peers and were 'more motivated to improve themselves and more likely to value migration for its life-changing possibilities'.[47] These women are leaving rural communities to work often 13-hour days in China's gargantuan manufacturing industry, sending money and presents home to their families and in turn spreading wealth into often neglected Chinese provinces. Given their relatively low pay and crippling hours, not to mention spartan working conditions, one could be forgiven for perceiving them to be the exploited working class: but this is at odds with their self-perception. 'In their own eyes they are proud, resourceful, energetic risk-takers at the cutting edge of a social revolution,' states Leslie Chang.

In this sense, we see women in Asia as wealth generators but also the conduit for the distribution of wealth and prosperity through the region. Equally, whereas factory girls were employed once for their 'docile' and compliant nature, a shortage of supply compared to the relentless manufacturing demands (despite a 110 million strong labour force) has shifted the balance of power into the hands of the workforce, with strikes and collective bargaining helping to improve working conditions. In Guangdong, most of the strikes, according to the *China Labour Bulletin*, were among largely female workforces, describing them as 'some of the most active workers posting information online about strikes and protests, and in seeking out legal assistance for problems at work'.[48]

Financial empowerment can come with a heavy price, however, and many Chinese migrant workers suffer serious health issues caused by working in factories polluted with toxic dust and chemical fumes, particularly within those factories producing textiles, shoes and toys. It can only be hoped that the increasingly empowered workforce is successful in addressing health and safety issues, in line with international standards.

JAPAN: AN OUTLIER OF TRADITIONAL VALUES

Once again, though, there are cultural and societal factors at work to keep women in the home. A key drawback for a woman's progression in the corporate world in Asia is the disproportionate burden of family care resting on her shoulders in addition to her day job, with male participation in the home traditionally low. She may also have elderly parents to care for, as the responsibility typically falls to the wife. The so-called 'double burden' often results in women leaving employment or resisting promotion. This is particularly true in Japan, and the hostile work culture – inhumanely long working hours and lack of acceptance of working mothers – means that true empowerment for women in Japan is some way off. Japanese women were least likely in our research to feel 'It's never been a better time to be a woman', with only 43 per cent of women subscribing to feminist optimism.[49] We saw reflected in our research not only the almost non-existent incidence of 'Asian Alphas' in Japan but equally a very high incidence of what we call the 'Insecure Self-doubters', women who have no expectation of success in life, who experience high levels of self-doubt and insecurity.

EMBRACING THE ASIAN ALPHAS

While Japan is the exception to the rule, what we see in our research is the existence of a dynamic and highly entrepreneurial Asian Alpha, and the more enlightened companies in Asia are doing everything they can to retain their female talent. In Japan, Google provides its female employees with taxis to get them home safely after dark. In India, pharmaceutical company Boehringer Ingelheim allows young female employees to bring their mothers on business trips to avoid the cultural disapproval women sometimes face when travelling alone. In South Korea, the government provides incentives for companies to build childcare facilities, and as a result up to 30 per cent of companies do. Infosys has a satellite office in the middle of Bangalore where new mothers can work without travelling to the suburban main campus, cutting their daily commute in half. The company's Women's Inclusivity Network offers a one-year childcare sabbatical as well as the option of working part-time for the following two years. The part-time option has in-built flexibility, enabling employees to work either half days or a few full days per week. In India, where it's not unusual for an applicant to need parental approval of a job offer, Ernst & Young holds a regular Family Day open house to demystify the workplace.[50] These are innovative and forward-thinking workplace solutions for a region we think of as conservative and often culturally 'set in its ways': if only the West was more progressive!

It's not just employers who have recognised the value of female talent. Increasingly brand owners are starting to recognise the spending power of this new cohort. Retailers in China have woken up to the fact that young affluent women are some of the biggest luxury goods consumers, with luxury car brands in India starting to actively target wealthy young women with female-friendly customisations.

Amrita Banta, managing director of Agility Research and Strategy, concluded from the company's online survey of 560 affluent 18- to 35-year-old women across six Asian markets, 'The affluent Asian female has certainly become the next big consumer segment for brands to focus on.'[51] Indeed, the survey revealed a wealthy yet increasingly independent woman, with 38 per cent considering luxury travel alone.

This self-determinative streak was also confirmed in a Starcom MediaVest study entitled 'WOMEN' and focusing on China, which indicated that an increasingly ambitious and economically empowered woman in China was deserting traditional life choices such as marriage and motherhood, and likely to prove the most influential force for change in the region. In our own Women's Index study, even though only a relatively modest 14 per cent of Chinese millennials want to 'challenge the status quo', this was more than twice the all-country average.

WOMEN'S SECOND LIFE AND BOOMER ENTREPRENEURS

In discussing the female economy and Alpha Females, it would be easy to assume that this new financial empowerment is the province of the young, increasingly well-educated woman or the millennials, who seem to dominate every headline. This is to underestimate women in the second and third phase of their lives, because whereas once upon a time a woman got married, had children and settled down, the life script, as discussed, doesn't work that way anymore for many women. We are witnessing women who may have married in their twenties divorcing in their forties and fifties and starting over.

These women are challenging preconceptions of age as a predictor of life-stage and behaviour, and they don't intend to disappear silently into the background. The designer Diane von Fürstenberg is an iconic figure for the 'second lifers': 'Once Diane hit 50, she entered a period of complete confusion, frustration but, ultimately, rejuvenation. She bought back and restarted her business, moved it into a huge office building in the Meatpacking district of Manhattan, and remarried, becoming the poster child for women over 50 who are reinventing themselves with style.'[52]

Perhaps Diane is not unique. Research has revealed that the boomer and the baby-boomer generations are among the most entrepreneurial. In the US, entrepreneurs aged between 55 and 64 years old stand at 23 per cent of the total compared to 14 per cent in 1996, and perhaps most surprising is the fact that high-tech start-ups are twice as likely to be created by the 50-plus generation.[53] Aligned to the study was the finding that boomers were more comfortable than their younger counterparts in risk acceptance, which certainly contradicts the idea that with age there comes a creeping conservatism.[54]

In the UK, Ros Altmann, who was director general of the over-fifties group Saga, said: 'life is really changing for the over-60s and for many it's the start of the next phase of their lives, not the end of their life as people in the past were often led to expect'.[55]

THE FEMALE ECONOMY: WHAT THIS MEANS

What is true and inarguable is the emergence and proliferation of a female economy, influenced by women not just as consumers but as wealth creators and managers. This is a global trend, not confined only to the West, but prevalent in East Asia and India, for example, and spanning strata of society from the educated elite through to blue collar 'factory girls'.

The emergence of a financially empowered woman has a societal ripple effect. What characterises 'high-net-worth' women, for example, is their sense of social responsibility aligned to their investment decisions. Equally economists observe that for every marginal dollar a woman earns, 90 per cent is invested back into her family,[56] so when women prosper, whole communities prosper.

Women feel far more strongly than men about the social, political and environmental impact of investment decisions, and their actions reflect a desire to invest time, money and energy in companies and causes that support their values.[57] A desire to deliver a social impact through wealth creation is observed to influence female entrepreneurship in the first place more often than men, and can prove more important than wealth generation in itself.[58] Research also reveals that women feel a greater responsibility to support their immediate and extended family, even if it's to their own detriment: 56 per cent of high-net-worth women compared to 46 per cent of men stated their need to protect their family financially.[59] This is a phenomenon echoed among all women around the world, as reported by UN Women and the World Bank, as women's increased control over household spending frequently benefits children.[60]

The intrinsic link between economics and wellbeing could underline why more women are being attracted to the finance industry, at a time when two of the world's most powerful financial institutions are controlled by women: the Federal Reserve (Janet Yellen) and the IMF (Christine Lagarde). Yellen explained her interest in economics: 'What I really liked about economics was that it provided a rigorous, analytical way of thinking about issues that have great impact on people's lives … Economics is a subject that really relates to core aspects of human well-being.'[61]

For all this success, there is still a long way to go. Women at a global level still lag behind men in economic activity, possession of assets and earnings. It is estimated that if women achieved gender equality by 2025, the global GDP would experience an uplift estimated to be around $28 trillion.[62] Now that surely has to be worth aiming for.

WHAT THIS MEANS: KEY TAKEAWAYS FOR BRANDS

I don't think I'm overstating the facts here when I say that women are the most powerful economic force globally in terms of being consumers but also wealth creators. In a time of financial turbulence, if there was more awareness or active engagement with this fact then perhaps we would see more concrete action, not just intent, in relation to women's empowerment. Both within this and the next chapter, there is solid evidence that should convince many business owners immediately to hire and promote more female talent, to pay closer attention to the retention of female talent – particularly as women get older and, as the data suggests, more effective. The evidence underlines the need to stop dismissing motherhood as an awkward inconvenience and accept the reality that it is a prism through which women's ambition and drive are only heightened. Women in your workforce represent a powerful catalyst for growth.

Welcome to the female consumer

If there is any imperative for brands and marketers to truly understand women as an audience then the size and scale of this growing female economy have to be the most persuasive argument yet. It would be very unwise, to put it lightly, for any organisation not to even consider the business potential of this audience.

Since Female Tribes and latterly Female Tribes Consulting were set up, a number of businesses built on the foundations of a male consumer audience and, perhaps more frequently, a male management team have approached us, alive to the idea that continuing to have a sustainable business model exclusive of this audience was impossible. Consider, for example, the automotive industry, for decades designed, engineered and serviced through a male lens, yet now in the US more women have driving licences than men. Until very recently, cars were designed using a crash-test dummy with a male torso, with the result that women were 47 per cent more likely to be seriously injured in the event of a collision.[63] The use of a female torso only became a statutory requirement in 2012. Yet the situation remains that collision and, in particular, whiplash protection design is still configured for men, even though women are 30 per cent more likely to suffer whiplash injury due to their lighter torsos.[64] Women walking into car dealerships have long been treated as invisible, or irrelevant to the car-buying decision, yet, as our Women's Index data points out, women make the majority of household and financial purchasing decisions, meaning that maintaining the status quo in this regard is no longer acceptable or good business practice.

Stop designing for men: 'adapting' for women

In harnessing the female audience, it is essential for any business and for any marketer to consider, in the light of women's economic potential whether they are doing enough to attract and service the female audience. Aligned to that question, I would ask whether products and services designed with men in mind are then 'adapted' for women, or whether they are truly, fundamentally designed through a female lens. Those businesses who can truly say that they design through a female lens, in my experience, are in the minority.

If you're a car maker, for example, look at your retail environment. Is it welcoming to women, or does it signal that women are very much a minority? No female sales representatives are a big giveaway here. In the case of collision safety, don't just look at crash-test dummy design, think about pedal size and position (we have smaller feet) or the fact that pregnant women drive too, yet seatbelt design has yet to really adapt to this revelation. Frequently women have to try and accommodate the seatbelt around their baby bump and hope for the best in the event of an accident. Shouldn't a car dealership be able to offer a service that adapts the seatbelt to ensure optimum protection? And how do most car dealerships make their profit? Through finance and after-sales service. I rest my case.

In the case of financial services, little has been done to attract a female audience with specifically designed products: taking into account, for example, that women live longer and are often paid less, and therefore need a different model when it comes to pension provision; or the fact that we may take career breaks to care for elderly parents or have children, which means that mortgage design could offer in-built flexibility. There are innumerable examples. The point here is that attracting a female audience goes way beyond a pink sales brochure or token woman on camera: it is fundamental, and it begins with female insight not assumption.

The era of the female entrepreneur

The entrepreneurial drive we witnessed among women across the world in our Women's Index data was impressive. Of all women surveyed, 54 per cent cited starting their own business as important in life, with one in four prioritising this as 'very important', demonstrating that women are just as entrepreneurial as men. Consider that if you're hiring for your own business. In the UK women-led businesses are described as a 'driving force' of the economy, generating some £15 billion in sales revenue in 2016,[65] and 67 per cent of women-led businesses are in the technology sector, again confounding stereotypes that female-run businesses must all be small-scale hairdressers and cakemaking enterprises.

As a financial service provider, choosing to invest in and support a female-run business represents a smart investment opportunity, so it's worth examining how you can make it easier for women to access venture capital. Consider, for example, the questions that you are asking of a female entrepreneur compared to her male peers: are you excluding her as an investment opportunity from the start? Are you examining her business plan in terms of potential for failure as opposed to potential for growth? It's estimated that if the UK achieved equivalence with the US in terms of female entrepreneurship, £23 billion would be added to the UK economy.[66] The evidence from the PwC Crowdfunding report indicates a high degree of unconscious bias when it comes to investment decisions, and a bias that doesn't favour female ventures is actively damaging the UK economy.[67] Therefore, it's worth undertaking a review of criteria and decision-making, and having equal representation on panels to consider how to challenge this ingrained behaviour. And if you're a woman and an entrepreneur reading this, it makes sense to consider crowdfunding as a means to secure capital for your business, as it seems that you'll be more successful in the short term. Perhaps reappraise your investment targets, since crowdfunding data reveals that female entrepreneurs seek more modest investment capital than their male peers.

Given the growth and healthy outlook for female entrepreneurship, business-to-business suppliers and support services should consider prioritising women-led start-ups, if for nothing else than seeing it as a smart opportunity: the data presented implies that women-run businesses present a huge opportunity and the source of a sustainable business model.

It's time we all adjusted our view on what entrepreneurship looks like, because the evidence suggests it's female.

CHAPTER 3

The Leading Ladies – Women and Leadership

'In the future there will be no female leaders. There will just be leaders.' **Sheryl Sandberg**

The last 50 years have marked unprecedented progress for women around the world particularly in the realms of leadership. While Hillary Clinton may not have become president of the US, there are plenty of female precedents of which to be proud. In Britain, Theresa May is the second female British prime minister and Nicola Sturgeon is first minister of Scotland, and across to Europe, German Chancellor Angela Merkel is arguably the most powerful figure within the EU; Park Geun-hye is the first female president of South Korea, while Christine Lagarde, head of the IMF, and US Federal Reserve Chief Janet Yellen influence the world economies: these are the new leading ladies of our time.

Stepping aside from the world of politics, women are rising through the ranks to command battalions, lead intelligence operations in the CIA, and set new standards of sporting achievement and scientific discovery. It's no longer the case that they are content to enjoy silent influence 'behind every powerful man'; increasingly women are leading from the front: in high visibility.

What is it about women as leaders that distinguishes them from men? Why the sudden propulsion and are there particular qualities that define female leadership? According to Christine Lagarde, the recent economic crises have propelled women into the 'front line', highlighting Iceland for example as a case study: 'The country essentially went down the tubes. Who was elected prime minister? A woman. Who was called in to restore the situation with the banks? Women. The only financial institution that survived the crisis was led by a woman.'[1] Lagarde's perspective is that it's women's composure, 'sense of responsibility and great pragmatism in delicate situations' that renders them up to the task of crisis management.

There is evidence to suggest, certainly in the turbulent political climate globally, that women are often preferred as a 'safe pair of hands', and so like the women leading the Indian banking sector, it's our cool head that propels us forward. A study by Northwestern University concluded 'when troubled nations elect women to the key national leadership office their economies experience a significant rise in GDP compared with their male counterparts', and female leadership drives the greatest growth among those nations with more ethnic diversity.[2] This suggests that we are the more inclusive leaders, or maybe having been the outsider we are more aware to include those who may have felt disenfranchised: let's face it, it's a feeling we should know well. This idea was endorsed through our research, as 70 per cent of women said that female leaders make a work environment more inclusive and collaborative.[3] It's the qualities of female leadership, namely a democratic, participative style, that seem to favour women, valued in times of turbulence. The Northwestern University researchers concluded 'when people perceive a threat and need to change their environment, they prefer female leaders', perhaps explaining the current predominance of female leaders emerging after the Brexit storms in the UK.

That's not to say that all female leaders have the qualities of inclusivity and liberalism: there is increasing representation of women within the far-right movement across Europe, and Marine Le Pen in France is one such example. Female swing voters form a key powerbase, so the far right often use fear of the impact of immigration from Islamic nations on women's rights as a persuasive argument towards increased nationalism and isolationism. And if that argument sounds familiar, let's not forget it was educated white female voters that helped propel Donald Trump into the White House. What the far right and nationalists play well to is an anti-establishment, anti-career politician sentiment, and they seek to court the disenfranchised. It's important to remember that low income earners, those without higher education and those with part-time work are among the first to fall during an economic downturn: and many of those will be women.

PUBLIC SECTOR VERSUS PRIVATE SECTOR

While women are assiduously and quietly climbing the ranks of public office, in stark contrast we see women's progress in the corporate world stalling. The 2016 FTSE Female Board Report revealed that female representation on corporate boards is sliding backwards, with only 25 per cent of FTSE 100 companies achieving female board representation and at the most senior levels of management female representation plummets to 10 per cent.[4] The US, meanwhile, is no exception with Catalyst analysis of the S&P 500 reporting that women hold 19 per cent of board seats, static since 2014, and the percentage falls to 15 if you look at the S&P 1500.[5] Yet, normally, the 'dynamic' corporate world is the trailblazer.

The gulf between women's political leadership and corporate leadership feels particularly unjustified when one considers the weight of evidence that demonstrates women-run companies perform better. In 2015, Quantopian analysed investor returns over a 12-year period for female-run companies benchmarked with S&P 500 companies, concluding that those with women at the helm generated significantly higher returns.[6]

There is also a significant body of evidence pointing to women as the more efficient leaders, particularly as they get older. In a global study of nearly 16,000 leaders, it was women who were perceived overall as more efficient by a factor of 2.7 per cent. This might not sound like much, but the research identified that as women mature their superior efficiency versus men rises, peaking among the 55 to 60-year-old cohort with a 9 per cent lead for women: so, like a fine wine, women get better with age.[7] Efficiency was measured across 16 management competencies, and while women excelled in the predictable feminine or 'nurturing' behaviours, they also excelled in the areas of 'taking the initiative', innovation, integrity and drive for results, those values more closely associated with masculine leadership traits. The results also confound a few more female management myths when one looks at women's efficiency across the more typical male disciplines such as engineering and IT: it's women who are more effective.

The results, as good as they are, make one want to weep because if women are so efficient as leaders, surely companies should be on a mass recruitment drive. But then, perhaps it's part and parcel of the struggle for equality that serves to heighten women's performance: the idea that as the underdog they have to work twice as hard to get noticed, with an innate sense of having something to prove, with no room for error. If this sounds familiar to you, it's an example of the unconscious bias women have to counter if they are to succeed, and numerous studies now exist highlighting how far it pervades culture.

UNCONSCIOUS BIAS AND RECRUITING: LEADING YET LAGGING BEHIND

In one experiment across US university science faculties, staff were required to screen applications identical in all respects – apart from gender. The study identified that within the science faculties, male candidates were favoured and more likely to be rated as 'better qualified', and tellingly participants proposed a higher starting salary for male candidates: remember, the only difference across these applications was gender.[8] So perhaps women work harder because they believe they have to in order to get the same opportunities as men, and considering the facts, their assumption is correct.

We saw evidence of overt gender bias experienced in the workplace in our Women's Index data. Of all women surveyed, across every country, 40 per cent claimed to experience gender bias or sexism at work on a regular basis, with 45 per cent feeling they were held back professionally just because of their gender. The idea that their gender was thwarting them professionally was most prevalent in Lebanon (73 per cent), China (63 per cent), Saudi Arabia (63 per cent) and India (54 per cent).

Gender didn't just affect professional opportunities, it impacted on their paycheques, with 54 per cent of all women surveyed reporting that they felt underpaid compared to men performing their equivalent role, and just over half of our sample reporting that it felt harder as a woman to ask for a pay rise.

Of course, the bias that serves to hold women back starts early, with 44 per cent of all women in our survey claiming that even during their education they still weren't in receipt of the same opportunities as men, with nearly two-thirds of women in Brazil and Saudi Arabia subject to this dynamic. If overcoming adversity prepares you for leadership, then no wonder women make highly effective leaders.

Obviously, as we have seen, part of the 'problem' for women is the motherhood issue, but the damage can be felt even if a woman doesn't have children as many employers are conditioned to think that women's most productive years are pre-children and this impacts on salary expectations: the idea being that employers won't invest in your career if you're going to 'go off and have children'. I have had female friends retell this almost word for word when they reported back on their salary negotiations, one even regretting wearing her engagement ring to the meeting. Once again, the numbers don't lie: when you look at salary data, women typically earn more than their male counterparts in their twenties but crucially earn less than their male peers in their thirties, with a tipping point around the age of 35, which coincidentally is when many women are having her first child in the UK according to the Office for National Statistics.[9] That is surely no coincidence.

HOW TO BREAK THE CYCLE: GETTING A LEG UP

If we're going to help women climb up the greasy pole towards leadership then quotas are a great imperative for change, and an idea I would strongly support; within our agency, for example, during the creative hiring process we now mandate that at least one candidate has to be female; we also mandate that a woman has to be on the interview panel, serving to temper that unconscious bias because creative departments within most agencies are heavily staffed by men.

Quotas alone aren't enough, and I am a firm believer that it is incumbent on everyone to do their bit to nurture and support female talent, and reassuringly the women in our survey also recognised the need for women to support each other in the workplace. Across all countries, 84 per cent of women said it was important for women to step up as mentors for other women, with 82 per cent in agreement that it's important for women to help other women advance in their careers. There was almost universal agreement with this sentiment among women in Brazil and China, so, in the countries where women experience the most gender bias, they are more likely to stick together and support each other. We also observed that regardless of age women recognised the importance of mentoring and supporting other women in the workplace, and this was uniform across generations for all countries.

While on the one hand this universal female advocacy is positive, offering the sense of a supportive sisterhood, one can also read this as evidence that women of all ages recognise how tough it is as a woman, that she needs all the help she can get. I choose to see this as proof positive that the female 'Bitch Boss' or 'Queen Bee' stymieing the prospects of other women is by and large a work of fiction: in the real world, we are prepared to give our peers a leg up.

While women may encounter many challenges in the workplace, as we have touched on, and in the political sphere there is still by no means equal representation, women are forging ahead particularly in Africa and Latin America, two of the regions where you may least expect such progress.

THE AFRICAN POLITICAL CLASS: FORGING CHANGE

Africa is now home to an active, vocal and energised female political class, intent on progress. When we think of Rwanda, for example, we often think of a war-torn, ravaged country, with women brutalised and worse in the name of civil war. Today, however, Rwanda boasts more women in parliament than almost any other country in the world, with 64 per cent of the seats held by women. And while demographics and quotas have played a role, and Rwanda's conflict wiped out an entire generation of men, leaving women as 70 per cent of the population, something more significant is at work.

AFRICA: A TIME FOR ECONOMIC AND SOCIAL PROGRESS

Africa is poised to enter a period of unprecedented economic growth as the world looks to harness Africa's rich natural resources, with South

Africa, Nigeria, Angola, Ghana and Ethiopia among the most vibrant economies. The members of the old political class – typically male, 70 years or over and conservative – have been slow to embrace social or technological change: but adapt they must, as this will be vital to the future prosperity of the continent.

It's easy to overlook but Africa is a relatively youthful continent in terms of demographics, with the UN reporting that 85 per cent of the population are under 45 years of age,[10] so arguably the male political old guard will have little in common with the electorate. Enter stage left a new generation of educated and ambitious women, dedicated to engineering change for the good of their nations, and presenting the idea of change to a younger, more globally aware voter. According to Lindiwe Mazibuko, former opposition leader in South Africa's National Assembly, 'Africa is in the midst of an economic boom. If this development is to be stable, we need new ideas and a younger elite. And, of course we need far more women in positions of leadership.'[11]

To put a sense of scale to female political participation in Africa, the fact that in 11 African countries women have attained 30 per cent representation in the lower houses of parliament is nothing short of remarkable, especially compared with the US where women hold just 19 per cent of seats in Congress. In South Africa, women hold 42 per cent of the parliamentary seats and there are signs that female candidates will also participate in the next presidential election; in Senegal women hold 43 per cent of the parliamentary seats and a recent prime minister was a woman; and Liberia and Malawi have had female presidents.

Given that women face the most poverty and economic disempowerment in Africa, perhaps it is not surprising that it takes women to mobilise change. Arcane property laws often prevent women even getting a foot on the ladder towards financial betterment, so, for example, in sub-Saharan Africa women produce about 80 per cent of all food products, yet own 1 per cent of arable land.[12] Little surprise then that upon her election Joyce Banda, a former market trader who was Malawi's president in 2012–14, swiftly sold her predecessor's luxury limousines (a fleet of no less than 60 Mercedes) and private jet, shrugging off the move by saying, 'I'm already used to hitchhiking.'

Upon election Banda was quick to pursue economic reforms but also to put in place legislative freedoms, lifting the ban on homosexuality. Indeed, her own experiences shaped much of her policy reforms, and she credits her drive towards female financial empowerment (founding microfinance initiatives for women in rural areas) as being the result of her experience in an abusive marriage. In fact, in this respect women are well placed to empathise with the most disenfranchised parties within society, a factor no doubt key to their popularity. In India, UN research revealed that the number of drinking water projects in female-led councils was 62 per cent higher than those with male-led councils, again illustrating that women have a keener sense of urgency when it comes to improving the living conditions within their communities.[13]

In many African countries it has been women who have fought to bring about change for the better. In the Democratic Republic of Congo, it has been women who are campaigning for peace, forming grassroots movements and petitioning for change. Neema Namadamu, founder of the Maman Shujaa Media Centre, promised 'we the women of Congo will not be quiet until real peace is upon us'. Perhaps it's no coincidence that those nations where women have achieved the most significant political representation are those nations emerging from prolonged periods of conflict. As part of the peace process and rebuilding efforts, women have recognised the opportunity to assert their voice. In some cases, the legacy of conflict has also provided them with a strength in numbers relative to men, making social exclusion much harder to perpetuate. In Rwanda, as mentioned, the wiping out of a generation of men meant that women assumed the role of community leaders and financial providers. In fact, in many cases the peace process itself has emerged thanks to the campaigning of women's groups. For example, in Sierra Leone it was the prolonged and determined campaigning by women's networks that created momentum behind the peace process, engaging both sides of the warring factions in order to create dialogue. Certainly, involving women in the peace process has been proven to hasten an end to conflict. Research carried out by UN Women revealed that by their inclusion the probability of a lasting peaceful resolution was increased by up to 35 per cent.[14] It's also suggested, however, that women's involvement in peace negotiations has enabled them to witness the impact of their influence, thereby motivating more women to mobilise and get involved in the political sphere.

In many of the African nations, gender quotas have proved successful in driving change. For example, in Uganda, every constituency has to have at least one female MP, a paradoxical nod towards female empowerment in a nation that only recently banned the mini-skirt. While the enforcement or even enshrinement of quotas as part of electoral policy has met with resistance and legal challenge, they have undoubtedly opened doors and accelerated the pace of change in terms of female representation, and quotas have provided the necessary imperative to force change among a sometimes-reluctant establishment.

But it's also African women themselves who have worked assiduously to drive and shape change, in many respects leading and not following the Western world: for example, at the 1980 World Conference on Women in Copenhagen, the African female delegates arrived armed with draft policy proposals, based on their own research: a fact to which very little credit is given. Perhaps as a reflection of the way in which the old stereotyped narratives still prevail, the women of Africa often receive little credit in terms of the way in which progress is being driven from within: this really needs to change.

WOMEN'S INDEX: SOUTH AFRICA, HOME TO THE AMBITIOUS LEADERS

Analysis of our Women's Index data confirmed the sense of social responsibility felt among women in South Africa, with 92 per cent feeling it was important to work to improve their community around them, set against a global all-country average of 75 per cent. South Africa also had the highest proportion of women citing this as the 'most important' life priority, with more than one in ten women in agreement, again significantly higher than the all-country average. We also questioned women about the values they aspired to as a woman and it's fair to say that the qualities of leadership were unique in their popularity among South African women. Nearly two-thirds aspired to be a leader and, with the exception of US women at 53 per cent, no other country came close; this was nearly double the all-country average. South African women were also much more likely to aspire to the values of leadership with the most aspirational qualities of contemporary femininity being ambition, confidence and determination, with all values ranked markedly above the all-country average. Putting to one side 'ambition', which saw a ten-point drop from South African millennials to baby-boomers, all other 'alpha' values were universal to all age groups. It was clear that South Africa was home to women determined to be their own leading lady, the empowered subject of their own lives and not the passive participant.

In looking to Africa, we can learn much about the importance and benefits of female political and social engagement, because viewed through the prism of the political enfranchisement of women, it's Africa that perhaps presents the 'developed world' and the West 'the developing world'.

Africa is not the only region where women have significant political agency, though, and it's worth turning our attention to Latin America –

home to 'machismo' but also home to an equally powerful 'leading lady' or 'alpha' tribe, who I have termed the 'Latina Matriarchs'.

THE LATINA MATRIARCHS

We tend to think of Latin culture as macho and inherently chauvinistic – good at keeping women in the kitchen. The region is experiencing diverse cultural change, however, and this is having the effect of opening doors for women. More women are in employment than ever before, and they are getting access to the corridors of power, demonstrating that the Latina Matriarch's influence extends far beyond the home. In fact, the Latin America–Caribbean region, once a 'cauldron' of machismo and gender inequality, has historically elected more female leaders than any other region in the world.

We often assume that life for women in Latin America must be much tougher because of the entrenched macho culture and discrimination – the region 'leads' the world in domestic violence. In more impoverished countries, it's much more likely that women are the ones who will be poor, with less access to education and welfare. The region is experiencing a sustained period of change, though, which is leading to the social and economic emancipation of women, and it's a move partly attributed to the increasingly left-wing leanings of the prevailing governments. To quote Hugo Chávez, Venezuelan president from 1999 until his death in 2013, 'true socialism is feminist'. By way of example, in Cuba literacy is 100 per cent; 65 per cent of all university graduates and 50 per cent of all doctors are women; and women represent 43 per cent of deputies in the National Assembly, among the highest percentages in the world.

In Bolivia, the election of Evo Morales in 2006 marked an influx of female representation in the cabinet, leading to the implementation of progressive female-centric programmes. Crucially, female representation at the heart of government policy and legislature has forced the tide of change within the region,[15], and today women account for one in four legislators in Latin America.[16]

While the crude statistics of political representation tell one story, we shouldn't overlook the *qualities* of women's leadership in public office, and in particular their attention to improving life on the home front and an almost forensic line of sight on quality of life in grassroots communities.

Women are keen providers of community development, in their role as social pioneers, to quote Brazil's former president Dilma Rousseff: 'In my country, women have been fundamental in overcoming social inequalities. Women play a central role in our income distribution programs. It is they who manage the resources that allow families to invest in the health and education of their children.'[17] While heavily criticised, Brazil's Bolsa Família (Family Allowance) programme has recognised this dynamic, and provides income support to women within the household, conditional on their children participating in education and welfare programmes such as immunisation. The programme has been so successful in lifting families and children from extreme poverty that it is being adopted across Latin America.

Dialogue and cooperation between women's movements and the legislature, with regular conferences and forums, have facilitated the prioritisation of women's interests within the Brazilian nation with the creation of the Special Secretariat of Public Policies for Women. Equally, investment in women's education and a particular focus on sustainability has enabled Brazil to become number one in the world for women in STEM and innovation;[18] a fact few people would know or even expect within a country that still struggles with endemic inequality and high levels of domestic violence, affecting up to one in three women.

THE LEGACY OF FEMALE ACTIVISM

Is the spectre of charismatic women as leaders or agents of change really a new phenomenon? If we delve into the region's history, the archetype of the powerful female leader is enmeshed in Latin American culture and stretches back to the twelfth century with the legend of Xochitl, the Toltec Queen. It's recorded that in the 1700s it was women who took up arms to fight Spanish rule in both Peru and Colombia, and women played a frontline combat role in the battle for Mexican independence in the early twentieth century, something for which precious little credit is given. During this period, women from all backgrounds participated in the cause from practical support roles, to developing and distributing propaganda through to armed combat. The renowned Margarita Neri led a force of more than 1,000 soldiers, and *soldaderas* or female soldiers were a powerful emblem of the cause. 'La Adelita', one such woman immortalised by a folk song, has become a synonym for any woman who fights for her rights.

EDUCATION AND EMPOWERMENT

Women are not just participating in the political arena in Latin America: their participation in the labour force combined with increasing levels of education are undoubtedly a driving force in prosperity. In the field of education girls are catching up, with enrolment levels reaching parity and girls outperforming boys in secondary and tertiary education.[19] Data from the World Bank has indicated that women's participation in the workforce in Latin America is responsible for a 30 per cent overall reduction in extreme poverty.[20]

While it's true to say that women are taking a more active role in the economic growth of Latin America, it's not a totally rosy picture.

Women's salaries still lag behind men across the region: they are better educated yet lower paid, which sounds horribly familiar and consistent with the rest of the world, and in the more highly skilled, senior positions, the wage gap rises to 58 per cent.[21] In our own research we observed high levels of claims of workforce discrimination among women in Brazil.

Undoubtedly access to reliable and lawful contraception methods has liberated women by virtue of smaller families and self-determination in family planning, giving women more power to control her own destiny. Access to the pill and sex education are key instruments in freeing women to participate in education and the workforce, although Latin America still has one of the highest teen-pregnancy rates in the world. The increase in female labour force participation in Brazil, Argentina and Mexico over the last 20 years is significantly greater than other countries, and now more than 50 per cent of women in the region are in employment.[22] A consequence of women's participation in the workforce is greater school enrolment for children: the World Bank has drawn a direct correlation between dependence on female income and school enrolment rates across Latin America, since school attendance provides valuable free childcare, with all the attendant educational benefits.[23] The report observed up to 25 per cent higher school enrolment rates for families dependent on female income as compared to families reliant on male income: so again we see another important legacy effect of women's workforce participation. Equally, access to education and employment is helping to reshape the horizons of young girls; according to the Center for Talent and Innovation in New York, 59 per cent of university-educated Brazilian women describe themselves as very ambitious compared with 36 per cent of their US sisters.

THE LATINA MATRIARCH WANTS TO SHARE HER SUCCESS

Important distinctions exist between the Latina Matriarch and her Western cousin, the Alpha Female. Firstly, while women in Latin America might be striving for equal opportunities, there is a sense of collective responsibility: she wants to improve the welfare of the community around her. In our Women's Index research, we observed that Brazilian women were much more likely to recognise the importance of helping other women advance in the workplace, with 92 per cent of Brazilian women supporting this idea compared to an 82 per cent global all-market average.[24] Women in Brazil were also significantly more likely to feel that women should have a louder voice culturally, with nine out of ten women in our survey in agreement, and they were significantly more likely to prioritise working to improve their community around them. The Brazilian alpha doesn't want success for herself, she wants to create a ripple effect in her community.

We also observed that Brazilian women are highly entrepreneurial, not just compared to Brazilian men: three Brazilian women start a new business to every four Brazilian men,[25] and it's important to observe that, after sub-Saharan Africa, the women of Latin America show the highest entrepreneurial activity in the world.[26] Again, perhaps this is symptomatic of the familiar pattern that a workplace culture that still penalises women is the stimulus for greater entrepreneurial activity: why struggle against the system when you can be your own boss?

PROGRESSIVE YET TRADITIONAL

The paradox for the Latina Matriarch is the degree to which, on the one hand, she strives for equality but, on the other hand, the degree to which she asserts traditional values, another example of 'soft power'. To quote former Mexican presidential candidate Josefina Vázquez Mota, 'I am a woman, I am a housewife, I am a government official, I've twice been government secretary, I've been leader of a parliamentary group, I am an economist.' She may be a powerful political player, but she must still be seen as the matriarch of the household. We see this dynamic reflected in the fact that women in Latin America still bear the burden of the household responsibilities regardless of their working status. For example, Mexican working women still clock up on average 33 hours of housework per week, compared to an average of 3 hours by their husbands.[27] Little surprise, therefore, that Michelle Bachelet, twice president of Chile, was dubbed *Madre* (Mother), as she was still seen as a domestic figure.

There is an observable dynamic apparently identified by researchers at Utrecht University that if men feel emasculated by their wife in the breadwinning stakes they 'assert their masculinity' by dodging the housework,[28] so many women are not 'imagining' the fact that he doesn't do his fair share. On the upside, it probably means you are doing well in your career if you're doing most of the ironing!

If we are going to explore female leadership and its many facets, and specifically the idea of women 'leading from the front', we shouldn't ignore women leading 'on the front line': the idea of women in the armed forces and security forces.

WOMEN ON THE FRONT LINE

In the American Civil War, women had to cross-dress in order to take up arms, but now women are taking a much more active and visible role in the armed forces. The realities of war have propelled women to the front line, seeing them participate in active combat. In the US women make up 15 per cent of the armed forces and, in a landmark decision, women in the army were allowed into combat roles at the end of 2013. Some 280,000

US women have served in Iraq and Afghanistan.[29] Canada, Germany and Australia already allow women on the front line, in Norway women have been allowed to perform combat roles since the 1980s, and women comprise up to 34 per cent of the Israel Defence Force. In Pakistan, although there were already 4,000 women in Pakistan's armed forces, in 2013 Ayesha Farooq became the first female pilot in the air force to be combat ready.

At the most elemental level, placing women in frontline combat makes them both creators and takers of life, and it's hard to predict what the psychological impact will be, or whether the impact of combat will be different for women as opposed to men. Limited evidence exists, but a study into the effect of combat among military healthcare providers concluded that post-combat women exhibited greater incidence of damaging drinking behaviour versus men.[30] In terms of trauma experienced, military sexual trauma (discrimination/harassment) and separation from family were cited as among the key contributors to stress.

Women serve a very valuable role in armed combat, however, which is yet another example of Female Capital. Studies looking at female combat performance in Israel observed that women exhibit superiority in the areas of discipline, motivation, maintaining alertness, management and organisation, shooting and weapons use.[31] Research conducted by the Massachusetts Institute of Technology and Carnegie Mellon revealed that far from damaging morale, the presence of women in battalions could improve the cohesion and collective intelligence of the group, the hypothesis being that women lend the group enhanced 'social sensitivity', i.e. the reading of emotions.[32] While women in combat bring obvious practical and intellectual skills, they can also exert a powerful impact on morale. The 600 female Peshmerga solders within the Kurdish army fighting ISIS may only have been a small proportion of the military force numbering around 150,000, but they struck a very particular fear among

Islamic State fighters based on the belief that a man killed by a woman will not receive his 72 virgins in paradise.

Joining up used to be the way for young boys from socially deprived areas to get a trade and better themselves; typically, women are more likely to exist in poverty so a career in the armed forces likewise provides access to a better life, but also empowerment and the type of responsibility and self-actualisation that might otherwise be denied to them.

For some women, entry into the armed forces reflects not a pragmatic choice but a deeper, more profound calling: the desire to defend one's homeland and return with honour. Serving one's country also reflects the way in which women think outwards: the desire to improve the community around them, especially prevalent in women's peacekeeping efforts. Could it be that women enlist to end wars and not start them? Whatever the case, we witness a valuable contribution made by women in the military.

In recognition of this, the US Marines together with JWT Atlanta developed the first dedicated female recruitment campaign, 'Battle Up', as part of the Marines' commitment to achieve 10 per cent female representation by 2019. The campaign focuses on the qualities sought for the service, namely strength, not just physical strength but mental and moral strength, irrelevant of gender. The campaign features Captain Erin Demchko, who serves with the III Marine Expeditionary Force, having served in active combat in Afghanistan.

WOMEN INTELLIGENCE OPERATIVES

Women are not just taking up positions on the front line in combat, they are also taking on highly influential roles in the intelligence services. In 1991, in response to complaints of discrimination, the US Central Intelligence Agency commissioned 'The Glass Ceiling Study', which concluded perhaps unsurprisingly that sex discrimination existed within the walls of the CIA. What followed was an expensive class action suit, serving to raise at least the financial stakes for the achievement of gender equality. The resulting reforms have led to the gradual liberalisation of CIA recruitment beyond male, white Ivy Leaguers to embrace a more diverse workforce and, crucially, the recruitment and promotion of women among its ranks. From the founding of the Bin Laden unit at the CIA in December 1995 onward, female analysts played a key role in the hunt for al-Qaeda's leaders. In fact, a paper entitled 'Inroads' written by a female operative, was to prove a highly influential guide in the hunt for Bin Laden as dramatised in Kathryn Bigelow's movie, *Zero Dark Thirty* (2012).

The founder of that unit, Michael Scheuer, explained the value and contribution of women to the service, saying that female analysts 'seem to have an exceptional knack for detail, for seeing patterns and understanding relationships, and they also, quite frankly, spend a great deal less time telling war stories, chatting and going outside for cigarettes than the boys. If I could have put up a sign saying, "No boys need apply," I would've done it.'[33]

In some senses, the domestic perceptions and underestimation of women can play to advantage in the field of espionage, with women more able to slip unnoticed 'under the radar'. Melita Norwood, a British-born Russian spy, spent her entire operational life undetected, as few suspected a middle-class grandmother as a KGB kingpin. Melita was perhaps one of the most significant agents of the Cold War,[34] a Che Guevara tea mug was perhaps the only clue that she was not the usual *Archers*-obsessed 'little old lady', that and bulk-buying the *Morning Star*. Melita was described as 'the most important female British spy ever recruited by the KGB', and one could equally put her gender to one side to dub her 'the most important spy' because for nearly 40 years, under the codename 'Hola', she passed on nuclear secrets to the Russians, and it's alleged that her efforts contributed to Russia's acceleration of their nuclear programme.[35]

AGE AND GENDER: THE PERFECT INVISIBILITY CLOAK

Melita had the perfect cover, particularly in later life as part of the generation of 'women of a certain age' who become largely invisible to society: a fact that hasn't gone unnoticed to the security services. It's reputed that MI5 has been utilising numerous mothers' blogging sites, for example Mumsnet, to recruit female spies, motivated not just by their ability to evade suspicion but also their emotional intelligence.[36] So, if you are considering a career in espionage or crime, being a 'little old lady' is your invisibility cloak. Melita was not the only example. Doris 'Diamond' Payne, an international jewel thief and 85-year-old African American 'sweet old lady' who resembled 'Mrs Santa Claus', has a multi-volume Interpol file that makes Jason Bourne look lazy; and in 2011 Detroit was being regularly pillaged by the 'Mad Hatters', a gang of elderly female fraudsters with a penchant for millinery. Again, being part of the 'invisible' generation was the perfect guise, and the geriatric gang's crime spree went on undeterred. Thanks to the heist movie genre that teaches us what most crooks look like – male, usually good looking, hunting in packs to a funk-jazz soundtrack – women fall to the bottom of the list of suspects.

Yet if the heist movie has a blind spot when it comes to female criminal masterminds, popular culture has been largely dismissive of female intelligence agents, painting them typically as 'honey-trap' operatives, the 'Mata Hari' trading sex for information, completely ignorant of the high functioning skills they possess. Yet, according to Tamir Pardo of Mossad, their ability to 'suppress their ego in order to attain goals' renders them excellence field operatives, in many cases superior to men.[37]

THE PEACE PROCESS

Women aren't just gaining leadership positions in combat and espionage: female participation in peacekeeping operations has gained significant relevance over the last decade, through the intervention of the UN Security Council in this issue, recognising that women often experience conflict differently to men, and women are often subject to sexual violence as part of armed conflict. From its own research, the UN recognised that if local women are involved in peace process negotiations lasting peace is significantly more likely to be achieved.[38] The fact remains, however, that women are woefully under-represented in formal peace negotiations despite their frequent activism – in the period from 2008 to 2012 women were signatories in only 2 of the 61 peace agreements.[39] This serves to perpetuate the idea that women are the passive victims and not the empowered instruments of peace, which serves nobody well. In Colombia, for example, it was the mediation of female representatives from both the government and rebel group FARC that helped secure a peace accord to end over 50 years of violent conflict, securing the release of hostages and lasting ceasefires. In Northern Ireland, it was women representing the human impact of 'the Troubles' that supported peace negotiations, and female politician Mo Mowlam who oversaw the signing of the Good Friday Agreement in 1998.

In promoting women to prominent positions in peacekeeping, this lends women and girls formal advocacy, which is often denied. In the words of Ellen Johnson Sirleaf, president of Liberia in 2006–18, 'What a woman brings to the task is the extra sensitivity, more caring. I think that these are the characteristics that come from being a mother, taking care of family, being concerned about children, and managing the home.' Also supporting the importance of women in the peacekeeping process, research at the University of Minnesota drew a direct correlation between gender inequality and the likelihood of civil war.[40]

What we can conclude is the importance of gender equality for the establishment and preservation of peace, but also in the peace process itself. In August 2014, Major General Kristin Lund, a Norwegian with over 30 years' military experience, became the first female commander of a UN peacekeeping force: a step forward for women in the quest for lasting peace.

WOMEN AND LEADERSHIP: DISCUSS

Throughout this discussion of female leadership, we witness leadership as a complex and diverse idea, not just derived from the qualities of 'alphas' but also through more traditionally 'female' qualities such as 'social sensitivity'. Increasingly, it seems that society is starting to embrace the idea that a good leader is not a man or a woman behaving as a man, and that women, and more specifically the innate values of female leadership, have enormous value. The fact is that for a business to succeed in the modern knowledge economy, it requires diversity of ideas and this can only come from a diverse workforce, because a limiting culture of unchecked 'group think' can emerge from organisations in which everybody looks, thinks and behaves according to one model.

It's a sad fact, though, that across many industries, economies and political landscapes women lag far behind, for often very complex reasons. It's no longer enough to put women's lack of leadership roles down to career self-editing, the 'opting-out' syndrome, where women take their foot off the pedal to concentrate on family. In fact, US research demonstrated that as women travelled through the management ranks, their interest in achieving top management status *doubled*, rising from 16 per cent to 31 per cent, with 83 per cent interested in rising to the next level at work.[41] What is startling, though, is the entrenched perception that a woman's childrearing 'duties' will limit her application to her career, and this assumption exists among both men and women, underlining firstly that childcare is still viewed as a woman's responsibility, but also why the frequent question of 'how do you combine motherhood with that stellar career?' is so damaging.

Returning to women as leaders: while a US military study concluded that the best leaders are often borderline sociopaths,[42] perhaps the rise of women into leadership will serve to introduce more diversity into the criteria of what we perceive constitutes 'good' leadership. Diversity in leadership can be good; diversity can work against that potentially damaging 'group think' phenomenon as identified in military studies, that results in the unquestioning yield to authority or 'excessive commitment'.[43] and history is littered with examples of the dangerous and inhumane behaviours resulting from unquestioning and excessive commitment to authority.

As we have witnessed in the many fields of female leadership, women can bring to bear their intellectual capabilities but also a greater sense of perspective, and a reminder of the community impact of decision-making. But to gain more female leadership, one theme consistently reappears: the need for role models. More female role models in leadership positions will beget more female leaders in the future.

WHAT THIS MEANS: KEY TAKEAWAYS FOR BRANDS

The fact remains that with very few exceptions there is a paucity of female representation across the boards of most companies, global or local. Organisations are missing out on the wealth and productivity of female talent. This isn't just an empty argument based on quotas to make up the numbers and fulfil an altruistic goal of social inclusion: women in your organisation make you more money.

Hire more women

I could be facetious here and just say three words: hire more women. To be honest, whichever way I dress this up, if you read this and you're not thinking that you need more women in your organisation, perhaps you are not interested in organisational efficiency, shareholder returns or the building of a more sustainable business model. Endless studies point to the fact that building a more diverse culture and including more women, not just on the office floor but in senior management, pays dividends, literally. Yet somehow the facts don't seem to stick and have not brought about wider awareness. It is only by creating precedents and publicising female leadership more that we will start to create change and make a dent in the unconscious bias that pervades business and management culture.

I appreciate that it's not always that easy to hire female talent on demand. Firstly, one has to create a culture that attracts the desired talent, but that assumes all talent comes from outside and this ignores the development and retention of existing talent. Therefore, it's important to identify the stars within your organisation, and it's really important to look beyond or challenge how you assess these 'stars' in the first place – because unconscious bias can hide them within your appraisal criteria, and can cloud your judgement when it comes to zeroing in on the high potential candidates. More than once in my career, I have openly challenged appraisal and performance criteria, arguing that it rewarded more 'masculine' behaviours, assuming these to be the de facto drivers of efficiency, yet ignoring 'feminine' behaviours, just as effective yet different. I suggest that anyone in a position of power or participating in performance reviews pays attention to the criteria and challenges bias if it exists.

Greater management efficiency

As we have seen from the research, by including women in your workforce, you benefit from their management competencies, which generally improve with age, contrary to popular belief. Equally, from our own data, we also witness that parenthood makes women *more* productive not less, which is true to my own observations, and I would hope should challenge the common myths as to the value of working mothers within an organisation.

A workforce that includes women also serves to disrupt the often toxic 'group think' that can often pervade an organisation with too many like-minded people: the monoculture. Group think can render companies slow to adapt to change, make them unquestioning of past behaviours and slow to challenge future assumptions, all death to the kind of dynamism and adaptability now required for survival. Monocultures mean that we are also slow to seek new opportunities, to embrace diversity or new audiences within our consumer base, for that read 'women'. Because a simple way to gain female insight is to hire women.

Create a culture that values Female Capital

If you want to attract and retain female talent, it's essential that you demonstrate that you perceive the innate value women bring beyond just a superficial position of 'making up the numbers'. What this means is embracing the cultural change or flux that might go hand in hand with hiring more women, and I'm basing this on an assumption and position that most organisations are more male-dominated – certainly at the senior levels. This doesn't mean that your office is going to be flooded with windchimes and pot plants, that it's going to be all touchy-feely because, as we have seen, women excel at the more 'typical' masculine or 'harder' management competencies as well as the softer skills. Creating a culture that values women and Female Capital means, and I look towards the likes of Silicon Valley, intentionally disrupting the often-toxic masculinity behaviours, boys' club or 'bro culture'. Here are some suggestions for how this can be achieved:

- Include at least one woman on interview and appraisal panels.
- Consider blind recruitment – to screen out gender and unconscious bias.
- Actively hire and promote women to senior management, and make them visible both internally and externally.
- Truly embrace flexible working patterns for parents (notice that I say 'parents' not 'mothers' – again highlighting the importance of language, and the fact that we shouldn't assume childcare is just a woman's responsibility).
- Create mentorship programmes enabling senior women to nurture younger female talent.
- Scrutinise your social policy – are you running the equivalent of a boys' drinking club? If every social event is after hours, you are potentially excluding parents.
- Look at your pay and remuneration policy: is there a gender pay gap, are you rewarding the right behaviours, do you even recognise the 'right' behaviours?
- Have a maternity and paternity policy and not a motherhood penalty – this is often the trigger for losing female talent.

So much of the above might seem like common sense, but it's surprising how many organisations pay lip service to valuing female talent, and so the changes are short lived, the intentions lack conviction and the old behaviours and cultures perpetuate. Equally, when I say 'actively' promoting women and hiring women in an organisation, we often have to become more intentional, since the temptation is to hire in one's own image or to recruit through friends and associates, which means more of the same. Part of the problem in hiring female talent into creative departments has been that we tend to recommend from a pool of talent we already know, people we may have worked with before, and in a mostly male creative department that means hiring more of the same through the 'friends network': you have to work harder to recruit more diverse talent.

There's also the fact that women are often, and this can be quite unconscious, viewed as a risky bet: we have to prove our worth or have much more extensive experience to be considered over a male candidate: men are hired on potential, women on experience. This dynamic means it takes women much longer to climb the ladder, and this is the area where we have to challenge our behaviours and biases, and the questions that we ask at interview.

In my experience, which includes having worked for a boss who truly believed in Female Capital, once an organisation really tunes into and starts to believe in the intrinsic benefits of Female Capital, effecting the above changes becomes easy, and you can literally feel the difference it makes.

CHAPTER 4

· ·

The Change Makers and Female Pioneers – Mothers of Invention

'If you want something said, ask a man, if you want something done, ask a woman.' **Margaret Thatcher**

Of all the many injustices wreaked on women, not least the right to control a TV remote, it is the lack of representation in culture for our achievements or, more specifically, our legacy in shaping world progress that frustrates me the most. Our exclusion not only serves to rob women of their place in history, it suggests that bravery, intelligence, vision and risk-taking, so essential to the spirit of pioneering, are inherently male characteristics. One could be forgiven for thinking it redundant to even explore the field of female achievement. When it comes to history, it is definitely *his*-story. It is not just our wrinkles that are airbrushed: some 60 per cent of women in our Women's Index study felt that female achievement had been removed from history.[1] In fact, the word history is derived from the Greek *histōr* for a wise man, so should women's invisibility really prove so surprising? Little wonder then that more than three-quarters of women in our survey said they wished they had seen more female role models when they were growing up (or I presume, at least know that female role models existed). Fortunately, I have always enjoyed proving doubters wrong, and so I set off to discover the rich legacy past and present of female pioneering, and to demonstrate the fact that it is not a male domain.

In truth, recent discoveries are starting to challenge the way we regard women's contribution to civilisation and our assumptions of traditional gender roles. The analysis of DNA from a burial site in 2017 has now concluded that a famous Viking warrior was in fact female,[2] and new research has revealed that women were the nomads in ancient Britain and a force for civilisation, serving to spread culture and 'technology' with them on their travels, while the menfolk stayed at home.[3]

These new revelations about women's role in the world also extend to far more recent times. Did you realise, for example, that what we know as the 'environmental movement' was founded by a woman? Rachel Carson's pivotal book, *Silent Spring*, drew the world's attention to the impact on nature of modern pesticides, and set into motion our great environmental awakening back in the 1960s, while Al Gore collected the 2007 Nobel Prize. And speaking of the natural world, it might surprise you to discover that supporting Charles Darwin's work on natural history and evolution was a silent team of not less than ten women botanists, naturalists and discoverers making significant but uncredited contributions to his work. It's also theorised that Albert Einstein's first wife, Mileva Marić, co-authored the theory of relativity.

There are many formidable females in the field of astronomy, dating back even to early Greece, but for more contemporary examples in the 1920s there's Annie Jump Cannon, who devised the method by which we classify and catalogue the stars and celestial bodies; Henrietta Swan Leavitt pioneered a measurement system for interstellar distances; and we owe the Hubble Telescope to the work of Nancy Grace Roman, whose work in developing orbital telescopes helped astronomers understand how stars form and develop.

Once I started researching female pioneers, I was falling over the wealth of examples, and I think we can safely conclude that over the centuries women have played as big a role in understanding how the world works and furthering scientific theory as men.

Yet why had I not heard these names before? But perhaps that's the point, I had to track these women down: knowledge of them wasn't brought to me. When I studied Chemistry to degree level, so often I felt like an imposter in the laboratory, with numerous textbooks wheeling out the names of venerated scientists – all male, yet virtually no women of note: it didn't exactly encourage me, and we scratch our heads wondering why so few women study STEM (Science, Technology, Engineering, Maths) subjects. In the case of Einstein, the correspondence between Mileva and her sister reveal a brilliant scientific mind, and extensive collaboration with Albert, yet it was he who took the credit, and it is Einstein who is the de facto icon for scientific brilliance, etching into our minds the idea that the face of genius is white and male. There is also no doubt in my mind that this bias will have influenced so many hiring and admissions decisions and awards perpetuating women's exclusion, and this is precisely why we need to change the narrative around achievement to include women and people of colour to create a much more diverse picture of what scientific genius, or indeed any genius, looks like.

THE COMPUTER GIRLS: WOMEN IN STEM

While women do get some credit for the more female-centric inventions of our time, for example the first brassiere (Herminie Cadolle) and the first Barbie Doll (Ruth Handler), the field of technology was and is still is perceived as a male domain, and that is something that should be challenged. Consider that the inventor of the first algorithm was the improbably named Ada Lovelace, so arguably the first computer programmer was not a white male Harvard graduate, but a fiercely intelligent nineteenth-century mathematician, and the only legitimate child of Lord Byron.

Building on the idea of women in computing, it was a woman, Dr Grace Murray Hopper, who led the team inventing the first computer software for business, and we have the Hollywood actress and inventor Hedy Lamarr to thank for GPS and Wifi, based on her early work in radio communication systems. Hedy and her co-inventing partner George Antheil patented their system in 1942, but it took until 1997 for her work to be properly recognised with the Pioneer Award from the Electrical Frontier Foundation. Hedy's characteristically laconic response was 'It's about time.'[4] I could go further to say that often the only credit women get in the field of technology is when Kim Kardashian's latest dress or lack of dress 'breaks the internet'. In reality, it's women's work that underpins what we know today as the World Wide Web, for Radia Perlman's work on spanning-tree protocol (STP) is the foundation of 'network bridges', i.e. 'the net'. Yet once again it is a man, Tim Berners Lee – self-proclaimed 'inventor of the World Wide Web' – who takes the credit. Radia herself has always been keen to emphasise that the inception of the internet was the result of collective thinking, of many individuals and not one person. It is a pity more people don't share this philosophy.

WOMEN: THEY COOK AND CODE

Funnily enough (I keep telling myself it's funny so I don't get quite so angry), back in the early dawn days of computing, when coding was thought to be a 'clerical job', women dominated the sector. In copies of *Cosmopolitan* magazine from the 1960s there are articles such as 'The Computer Girls' positively urging more girls to get into the industry and outlining the many opportunities.[5] Funnily enough the article breezily acknowledges that if a woman was 'really ambitious' she could 'go into the professions and compete with men, usually working harder and longer for less pay. How little has changed.

There were legions of women in NASA, for example. They were the so-called 'human computers' and many of them were African-American women, as now dramatised in the film *Hidden Figures*, a box office hit in 2016–17. And we have a woman to thank for the first Apollo moon landings, for it was Margaret Hamilton's code that got the astronauts to the moon, and then safely home again. Margaret was an early pioneer of what we now know as software. She was also incidentally a 'busy working mum' – her daughter would often camp out at the labs while she quietly worked. Margaret's software company, Hamilton Technologies, is still going strong to this day.

UNCONSCIOUS OR CONSCIOUS BIAS?

If women were so instrumental in technology, how on earth did they get edged out? The theory is that as the industry grew, there was the active 'marketing' and professionalising of the sector in order to attract more prestige (and funding). Along with the professional associations and formal training bodies, personality questionnaires materialised, which deliberately 'masculinised' the profession through the screening questions, and so women were gradually and perhaps deliberately sidelined.[6] A department populated by women looks like a typing circle, after all, but if it is populated by men ... hey presto, we have 'software engineers'. The abysmal irony is that women apparently make the better coders: a study by GitHub demonstrated that women produce better, more accurate code with fewer rejections but their code is only judged to be more accurate when it's submitted anonymously: basically, if the code is known to be produced by a woman it's often rejected.[7]

In fact, in our Women's Index research we witnessed first-hand the result of this 'masculinisation' of technology because, despite the fact that technology has been an empowering force for women – a sentiment expressed by over 80 per cent of our global sample – a little more than one in three women felt that technology was made by men for men.[8] The sense of exclusion was writ large, with 70 per cent of women feeling that there weren't enough women in the technology industry: and they were right. What was perhaps most telling was the fact that women in the Middle East and Asia were much more likely to feel a sense of exclusion from the industry: 44 per cent of women in Asia Pacific felt tech was designed through a male lens, rising to a staggering 95 per cent in the Philippines, with the sentiment shared by 52 per cent of women in Saudi Arabia and 66 per cent in Lebanon.

So, an industry pioneered by women is arguably now an industry that serves to exclude them, and it's not just through design, judging by the stories of sexual harassment spilling over from Silicon Valley. The masculinisation of the industry has created a culture but also a belief system that refuses to accept women's contribution. Witness the Google employee recently fired for expressing the opinion that women just aren't suited to STEM, suggesting that 'Differences in distributions of traits between men and women may in part explain why we don't have 50 per cent representation of women in tech and leadership.'[9] How little he knows about history, or make that 'herstory'.

In contrast, in the Middle East there is reason to be optimistic: it's estimated that some 25 per cent of start-ups in the region are helmed by women, and one reason hypothesised is that as an industry new to the Middle East, there is much less of a sense of 'male ownership' serving to exclude women, so it's more meritocratic.[10]

SISTERS IN STEM

When it comes to women's scientific legacy, at least in some areas of science, we are starting to give a few women the credit they deserve. For example, Rosalind Franklin's research leading to the discovery of DNA is gaining recognition, but equally there are still glaring omissions: Lise Meitner is possibly a name unheard in the physics classroom despite her work leading to the discovery of nuclear fission – and the Nobel Prize went exclusively to her male colleague, Otto Hahn, who failed to credit her – so let's not wheel out the Champagne and canapés just yet.

Equally I'm not sure we should be so grateful for the paucity of namechecks when so much of our contribution to science and innovation is still either wrongly credited to male scientists, typically the husband, or simply wiped from the records. The phenomenon is so prevalent it has even acquired its own name: 'The Matilda effect',[11] which describes the conscious or unconscious bias at work in the scientific community against female researchers. I say 'conscious' based on the writings of Angela Saini, whose book *Inferior* uncovers what she characterises as 'ferocious' gender wars in almost every branch of science, and should serve to remind us of the need for more gender equality in the scientific world.[12]

Perhaps tellingly, as women we're not immune to gender bias, and in our Women's Index study 61 per cent of respondents felt there were some subjects that were 'more appropriate' for women to study, and this ratcheted up to 78 per cent in Asia Pacific. Yet intriguingly or perhaps encouragingly we don't seem to take our own advice, and when we looked at college or degree study, 56 per cent of our sample had studied a STEM subject.[13]

In the meantime, I think we should all be lobbying anyone prepared to listen for the stories of women in STEM to be told, but we can also tell these stories of awesome women ourselves. Post stories of awesome female scientists on Facebook, tell your sisters, your daughters and your friends, spread the word, thanks be to social media. If we were the frontrunners in the creation of the internet, let's use it to publicise our magnificence. Because I ask myself, would it be so quite hard or 'revolutionary' to get more girls to study STEM subjects if they were aware of the rich legacy of women in technology? Doesn't it make you just a little bit angry the way the 'idea' of getting girls into STEM subjects presented as a new 'phenomenon' and that to increase the numbers we have to 'feminise' it in some way for our daughters to put down their Barbie dolls? Take, for example, IBM's ill-conceived 'hack a hairdryer' campaign, the idea being that to get ladies into the technical world they had to speak in a language women would understand. So, girls were invited to 'hack' a hairdryer and enter their inventions into a competition. Things did not end well: women didn't so much hack the hairdryer as hack up the idea, forcing the campaign's termination by serving up the scorn it deserved.

Even a cursory review of literature reveals that women have *always* had an interest in STEM subjects, pointing to a history of achievement – they just rarely received the proper credit for their achievements and that would discourage most people, wouldn't it? Let me put it in 'feminine terms' you'll understand: you bake your best friend a cake every day, and they prise it from your hands without so much as a word of thanks and eat the cake silently in front of you. At some point, you will stop baking cakes. The point I'm making here is that giving people credit is a huge incentive, it makes them feel valued and most importantly recognises their achievements. Allow me to suggest, therefore, that instead of 'feminising' science and technology or feeling the need to 'sell' it in some way to girls – a condescending suggestion that we wouldn't otherwise be interested – the best way to encourage girls to enter the field is to spend a little time celebrating the *female role models already in existence*, which would have the effect of making STEM subjects a male *and* female pursuit: give women the credit they deserve, and adding some wry truth to the phrase 'mother of invention'.

If the future of the world, the future of pioneering resides largely within the tech world, we need to urgently recruit more women into the tech industry, because at the same time their exclusion has powerful and far-reaching consequences. Our Women's Index Data was a great reminder of the degree to which technology has set her free, whilst 84 per cent of women globally felt that the world was a better place due to technological advancements[14], 82 per cent felt technology had empowered them, rising to 92 per cent in India and China. Equally 72 per cent of women felt that technology or social media had given them a voice, and let's face it, women's voices are some of the first to be excluded or ignored. Technology serves a powerful role not just as a tool for progress in itself but in facilitating social progress through connection, so 84 per cent of women felt that technology had made them feel like a global citizen and served a key role in connecting them to friends or family; this sentiment was keenly felt across women in the Middle East. So, we see that technology will be a powerful force in fuelling not just progress itself but social progress, and women need to have equal access to derive equal benefits.

THE SOCIAL PIONEERS

Pioneering takes many shapes and forms, and as well as the scientific and technological pioneers, I want to consider the 'Social Pioneers', that is to say women seeking to 'do good' or make the world a better place. Florence Nightingale, Emmeline Pankhurst and Melinda Gates have one thing in common: they're the social pioneers or change makers of their generations. Whether it's women's emancipation, healthcare or charitable endeavour these women have driven and led social change. In our Women's Index survey more than 70 per cent of women globally felt it was important to work to improve their community or the world around them.[15]

Perhaps one of the effects of being conditioned to think about your responsibilities in the world explains why women tend to be the bigger givers when it comes to social causes; women donate on average

50 per cent more to charity versus men;[16] they also become much more personally involved in shaping how their money is spent. It's not just wealthy women that we are talking about, women of all income brackets are more philanthropic,[17] and what distinguishes women from men is their desire – on their way up – to give something back to members of their own community, to bring them with them. In our Women's Index study 84 per cent of women globally felt it was important for women to step up as mentors for younger women.[18]

The Social Pioneer is a global phenomenon and has its roots in a history of female philanthropy. In one sense, it could be argued that, historically, women otherwise culturally denied a formal means of employment turned to philanthropy to provide them with a means of purpose, to leave their mark on the world. And when often one's only source of wealth was derived through inheritance or by marriage, what woman of means would not want to help those less fortunate through providing financial or educational support or healthcare, or more cynically have a library, a hospital, or a museum named after her? After all, she wasn't going to get credit elsewhere. In the US, for example, Smith College was founded in 1871 by Sophia Smith, and the Museum of Modern Art (MOMA) was co-founded by Lizzie Plummer Bliss, women whose kindness and foresight have left an indelible mark on culture.

The history of female philanthropy often implies wealthy wives engaging in charities to idle away their time, spending their husband's money, but in some ways that diminishes their achievements.

Some of the biggest philanthropic institutions we know today were founded by women, for example, Save the Children (Eglantyne Jebb), the National Trust (Octavia Hill) and the American Red Cross (Clara Barton). Baroness Burdett-Coutts of the Coutts banking dynasty was one of the greatest philanthropists of the Victorian era and pioneer of social housing. Coutts married her 29-year-old American secretary, William Bartlett, at the age of 67, and unusually it was William who adopted her name of Burdett-Coutts upon marriage, which from all accounts was a happy one and tells us something about her reverence for social convention. She was a pioneer in every sense!

Lest we risk focusing solely on wealthy white socialites, it's important to recognise the origins of female philanthropy and social progress as a global and multiracial movement. African-American educator and activist Mary McLeod Bethune founded Bethune–Cookman University; Rosa Parks is perhaps best known as one of the key founders of the American civil rights movement; and Katherine Johnson was a fearsome mathematician and 'human computer' whose work was intrinsic to the success of the NASA space programme, and her name is now immortalised in the Katherine Johnson Computational Research Facility at Langley. Marie Van Brittan Brown, an African-American nurse, designed safety and security systems that paved the way for modern security systems, while Madame C. Walker (real name: Sarah Breedlove) was a philanthropist and entrepreneur who revolutionised African-American haircare, dramatically improving the quality and tolerability of the products, and in the process financially enabled and mentored thousands of women like herself. She would go on to become America's first female millionaire.

Today, we are entering an era of more 'self-made' women, with female millionaires and billionaires now much less unusual. Enabled by their improved access to education and rising financial power, there are more women philanthropists than ever before, using their newfound financial independence as a force for good, emphasising the common thread between women's entrepreneurial activity and their philanthropic activity. According to Donna Hall, president of the Women Donors Network in the US, women are naturally more predisposed think of their community: 'Women are more comfortable working in community, making decisions together, pooling resources and leveraging their collective impact than men.'

Of course, the flipside is that 70 per cent of those people living in poverty around the world are women and children, so by mobilising women to help other women we are creating a force for social change – if women are lifted out of poverty so are their children.[19]

The rise of the female Social Pioneer is not just confined to the wealthy Western world. *Forbes* magazine reported in 2010 that the top four philanthropists in India were all female, with Rohini Nilekani donating over $40 million to supporting healthcare, clean water and microfinance projects in India.

What is significant about female philanthropists is that they engage those around them for counsel and to drive awareness of their endeavours and engaging the community. They also seek more diverse ways in which to make their contributions, for example, giving to circles, trusts and community projects. Women also tend to get more personally involved in their charitable endeavours; whereas men may use them as a strategic tax break, women want to see and shape the results of their donations.[20]

The *WomenCount: Charity Leaders 2012* report shows women are thriving in the voluntary sector, with 32 per cent of directors of the UK's top 100 charities are female when the organisations are ranked by income. That's double the 15 per cent of women on the boards of FTSE 100 firms in the private sector. The report also found that 17 per cent of charities are chaired by women, compared to just 1 per cent of FTSE 100 companies.

Women have the financial resources and the influence to bring about social change, and when they do, they act in such a way as to deliver impact that's community wide.

Part of a woman's socialisation is to think outwards and consider the needs of others, and so she's more likely to gravitate towards brands that share her outlook and philosophy.

SPORT AND SOCIAL PROGRESS

Philanthropy is not the only way to make an impact, and though it may seem less obvious, sport is a great tool for social progress. For women, sport is the great equaliser because sporting achievement is truly meritocratic: it's no respecter of class, wealth or, in many senses, even gender, and plays a vital role in laying the foundation for developing women's capabilities. A United Nations report points out that 'the participation of women and girls in sport challenges gender stereotypes and discrimination, and can therefore provide a vehicle to promote gender equality and the empowerment of women and girls. In particular, women in sport leadership can shape attitudes towards women's capabilities as leaders and decision-makers, especially in traditional male domains.'[21]

In fact, research in 1991 concluded that half of girls who participate in sports 'experience higher than average levels of self-esteem and less depression'.[22] What's interesting to note is that while sports participation has a beneficial effect for young girls, the benefits are more profound as women get older. Research has recently drawn a direct link between the effect of sports participation and employment prospects, increasing the likelihood of employment by up to 40 per cent among 25 to 34 year-old women.[23]

Participation in sports also teaches a younger woman that it's OK to be competitive, and will equip her with skills and behaviours that will mean she's more likely to get further in education and her career. So, sport not only equips her with physical confidence and self-esteem but also undoes much of the traditional social conditioning for girls to play nice and make way for the boys. Sport encourages women to compete, to develop an aggressive streak or appetite for winning that may serve them well in the workplace.

One organisation that has recognised the value of female sports participation is Standard Chartered Bank, which, in partnership with global development charities, created its 'Goal' programme in 2006 to empower adolescent girls through sports training and life-skills education; it aimed to influence the lives of 100,000 young women by 2013. Goal currently runs in China, India, Jordan, Nigeria and Zambia.

BEHIND EVERY GREAT FEMALE LEADER: A SECRET SPORTING SIDE

A great example of this dynamic was discovered during our work on co-creating *Her Story: The Female Revolution*.[24] The four-part documentary focused on women changing the world, and our episode on leadership featured some of the most prominent women of contemporary times, for example, Dalia Grybauskaite, president of Lithuania, Chhavi Rajawat, first female sarpanch or mayor of Soda, her village, and Christine Lagarde. While these women hailed from very different backgrounds and cultures, they shared the same qualities of quiet determination, fearlessness and an inner strength. What we later discovered through our research and interviews was that almost to a one, they had a secret sporting passion, a physical pursuit that served to equip them with that inner fortitude. Chhavi was an equestrian, Dalia a black belt in karate, and Christine a former fencing champion. What intrigued us was the fact that while these sports fuelled women's alpha personalities, they talked about them in a very different manner to male alphas: they were quieter, much more low key in their pursuits. While Dalia may possess a black belt, you will never see her staging a show fight in the same way that Vladimir Putin seeks to demonstrate his mastery of the martial arts; yet Dalia is the woman who quietly but firmly stood firm against Putin's political demands. Perhaps it's on the sports field where women can quietly hone their inner strength that will serve them well in the world at large.

CLOSING THE PERFORMANCE GAP: THE SUPER ATHLETES

Perhaps historically women in sport were easy to dismiss, burdened as they were with the postulated dual handicaps of a naturally less competitive nature and a more fragile physiognomy. The 2016 Olympics, however, served to showcase the new breed of female 'super athlete' with record numbers of female Olympians (45 per cent), and of the 19 new world records set, 10 were achieved by women, suggesting that young women are more competitive and physically agile than previously thought, and making female sporting prowess much harder to ignore. Take, for example, Olivia Quigley, who defied stage-four cancer to win two gold medals at the 2015 Special Olympics World Games; Uzbekistani gymnast Oksana Chusovitina, still in Olympic competition in her forties; Serena Williams, who won the 2017 Australian Open while eight weeks pregnant, and without dropping a set; and American Simone Biles who, still in her early twenties, is the most decorated gymnast, male or female, and an elite athlete despite her humble beginnings in foster care. Oksana has a teenage son, and a gymnastic career older than most of her peers. By rights she should be sitting on the sidelines or coaching instead of on the beam, yet Oksana and her ilk are breaking all the rules and conventions of sport to deliver world-beating performance standards.

One feature of the last Olympics was the promotion of women in boxing, countering many cultural taboos. In fact, many young sportswomen are closing the gap between male and female performance standards. According to Lance Armstrong, the worst fate for a male athlete was getting 'chicked', i.e. beaten by a woman. Women, however, are catching up on the sports field, particularly in the endurance sports. Chrissie Wellington, the British Triathlete, comments, 'We are narrowing the gap between men and women, and showing that anything truly is possible. We are raising the bar and giving the men a swim, bike and run for their money.'

In truth, there is mounting research that suggests endurance sports favour women's bodies. Yes, we have smaller muscles, but our muscles don't tire as fast, according to Sandra Hunter, professor of sports science and specialist in female physiology at Marquette University Milwaukee, which coupled with our higher proportion of body fat sustains us over the course. This is why in sports such as climbing, men and women are equal.[25]

Equally in tennis and swimming women are closing the gender gap in terms of physical performance standards. Author David Epstein points out in his book *The Sports Gene* that there is only a 6 per cent gulf between the fastest male swimmer and female swimmer in the 800m freestyle[26] and in tennis Serena Williams' fastest serve is faster than that of many male competitors.

But it's not just their physical performance that favours women in endurance sports. As revealed by an extensive marathon study, women are more proficient in pacing themselves. To quote the study's author, Jens Jakob Andersen, 'men may be more likely to adopt a "risky" pace where an individual begins the race with a fast early pace (relative to their ability) and this increases their likelihood of slowing later'.[27]

In baseball, meanwhile, we witnessed in 2016 the signing of two female players, Stacy Piagno and Kelsie Whitmore, to Sonoma Stompers, the first time since the 1950s that women have played in major league baseball. While their appointment passed with relatively minor publicity, make no mistake that this is significant both for women and for girls growing up watching the sport: they have a few new role models as inspiration.

To quote Nawal El Moutawakel, 1984 Olympic gold medallist, 'Sport is one of the best tools for social change because it is a large part of cultures around the world and reaches into every socioeconomic class of society ... serve as a medium of communication and empower women to improve themselves and their communities.'

IS AGE JUST A NUMBER FOR FEMALE ATHLETES?

Another interesting feature of women's growing sports participation is the number of women participating at competition level way outside of the 'normal' age bracket. Whilst Oksana Chusovitina, the forty-year-old Olympic gymnast, is one such example, she is by no means the oldest. Johanna Quaas, now in her nineties, is according to *Guinness World Records* the 'oldest gymnast in the world' and still competes in her native Germany, albeit at amateur level. Meanwhile, Mieko Nagaoka is a Japanese swimming champion, and despite her years (she's over a century old) has her sights set on the 2020 Olympics; Ernestine Shepherd is an award-winning American bodybuilder in her eighties; Mary Hanna is an Australian Olympic equestrian in her sixties; and the environmentalist Dr Sylvia Earle is a world-renowned scuba diver in her eighties. While one can observe this is a demonstration of our increased longevity as women, perhaps it's a sign that our drive and our passion don't diminish with age.

One consistent quality observable in these older female athletes is the sense that they are using their activity, and perhaps 'physical activism', to inspire others, to give something back – it is less of a selfish pursuit. So, while younger women may use sport to inspire and unleash their inner alpha, older women are using it to mobilise communities. Sylvia Earles has spent her entire career spanning more than 60 years using her scuba diving to explore the oceans and campaign, drawing attention to dying marine ecosystems and inspiring a whole new generation of female scuba divers and environmentalists: yet another example of women's propensity to think outwards.

COMBAT SPORTS EMPOWER THE DISEMPOWERED

Sport can prove a potent force for social change, and for women denied freedoms and disenfranchised in all other aspects of their lives it serves an important role. Witness the growing sporting participation within the Muslim world. Afghani sprinter Robina Muqimyar trains in Kabul Stadium, once reserved for public executions. 'This is important. The women in Afghanistan will know they can do anything, if there is hope in the heart,' she said. 'Standing on the track, I will feel like a winner.'

Elsewhere in Afghanistan the sport of choice is boxing. Halima Sadat, 16, says she sees boxing as helping prepare her for a career as a lawyer: 'I want to fight corruption and go after people who take bribes and who violate our rights,' she says. 'I want to make sure that powerful men don't get away with committing crimes.'[28]

Continuing the theme of sport as a great liberator, increasingly women in Iran are participating in sports as a means of empowerment, redressing the power balance that society at large seeks to take away, with sports such as karate and kung fu enjoying increased participation among young women, and the latest trend is parkour. Nooshin, a councillor for Iran's welfare organisation in the city of Hamedan recognises the value of combat sports for women in the region, 'Do you think it's coincidence that more women are taking karate and kung-fu classes? Women, especially young women, are learning about their rights and fighting back.'[29]

Sport and athletic achievement can have a profound impact on women's fortunes and self-esteem. For these young women are not just participating and competing for themselves but for their sisters and their community, and while they may face more cultural, religious and social barriers to their participation, they feel the rewards are worth the effort.

SPORT AND LEGACY EFFECT

Sport for women is about more than just looking good or losing weight. In our research, more than 70 per cent of women said they would rather be described as 'strong' than 'sweet',[30] and we see a new more muscular vision of femininity emerging. Observe, for example, the cult of the 'revenge body', with entire Instagram communities and even a TV show devoted to getting a ripped body in the wake of a relationship breakup. It is interesting to see that women post-breakup are not looking to disappear, or to mope quietly, they're actually increasing their physical presence – a revenge body is an assertion of physical power, and this is new.

For any sports brand marketing to women or girls, it's worth considering the profound social impact that sport can play as a facilitator of cultural and social change. Teaching young women that it's OK to compete undoes ingrained social conditioning; it brings out the alpha personality, the type A, and enables women to push themselves forward without embarrassment or compromising her femininity: the Always brand's 'Like a Girl' campaign is a case in point, reframing the expression 'run like a girl' from a pejorative term to a means of pride. This confidence and self-worth will serve a girl well through education but also throughout life, and pay dividends through her career. Equally, Sport England's campaign 'This Girl Can' has been transformative in democratising sport for women, breaking down barriers to participation and dramatically increasing women's involvement.

Despite female athletes still receiving lower earnings than their male peers, women's sports are at last starting to attract more media coverage, boosting audiences, and in time will gain more sponsorship funding. From our research, 76 per cent of women wanted to see more coverage of female athletes.[31] The Women's World Cup attracted a British audience of some 12 million viewers in 2015, a 100 per cent increase on the previous championship. From our Women's Index research, we saw the cultural legacy of seeing women athletes compete and win; three-quarters of women said that when they see a woman win a medal it inspires them to believe they can follow their dreams,[32] so increasing women's participation in sports, and increasing the media coverage and attention, feels particularly important in order to yield that cultural ripple effect.

Perhaps we may in time see women achieve equal pay in the sporting world – one of the last bastions where there appears to be a rationalised construct to justify the earnings gulf between men and women. This relates to ratings and sponsorship, and in tennis it's the fact that women play fewer sets – we are paid per serve, it would seem, not according to the level of entertainment or skill. It's an important issue because the pay gap implicitly sends a message about women's value in the world. This was endorsed in our survey, in which 82 per cent of women who said that when they hear a female athlete isn't paid as much as men, it makes them feel that they are not valued as a customer or viewer.[33]

WOMEN CHANGING THE WORLD BY DESIGN

As we have touched on, a desire to change the world – the spirit of pioneering, of inventiveness and invention – is not wholly confined to the male brain; leaving one's mark on the world is not exclusive to the male sensibility. Our accomplishments may have been sidelined, overlooked in the history books and missing from the awards ceremonies and the Nobel Prizes, but that doesn't diminish the fact that they do exist. Only now, like social archaeologists, there is something of a movement to uncover the stories of these women, to excavate and exhibit their achievements for the inspiration of future generations.

It is critical to the world that we have more women in innovation and STEM, since women view the world through a slightly different lens, and we need this perspective when it comes to design and utility. Let's start with a more trivial example that nonetheless shows why this is important.

Around about 18 or so years ago, early on in my career, I was working in marketing for a frozen food company. In my first week on the job, as part of my induction I was marched down to the packaging department. There I met two male packaging engineers who had been trying to crack the code of easy-open packaging for a frozen gateau for around two years, maybe more. They had gone through endless designs and prototypes, costing thousands of pounds in machine tooling and man hours: all deemed failures. It was an important project since 'easy-open' packaging (for that read a plastic carton that doesn't render serving the gateau akin to a Lucille Ball skit) would represent a competitive advantage and therefore a price premium, i.e. we could charge more, and when every penny mattered the engineers needed to crack it. I figured it out in less than ten minutes because I had been personally opening cake cartons and figuring out my own easy-open method for many years. I drew up the design, took it down to the engineers and, with the look of cold sick registering on their faces, realised I was onto something: the design was duly prototyped and patented. Had I been smarter, I would have quit right then and there, taken my design to the patent office and laughed all the way to the bank. But my respect for duty and compliance and a relative lack of arrogance – perhaps because of my gender – meant that I wouldn't have dreamed of taking credit for the idea. The point is that neither of those male engineers had ever opened a cake carton as part of their domestic lives and, putting gender stereotypes and household division of labour issues to one side, the bigger problem was that they had never thought to ask someone, most likely a woman, how she opened a cake carton: so, what could have taken ten minutes took two years.

A more sobering example is the fact that women are significantly more likely to die from heart disease as the diagnostic algorithm or symptom recognition for heart disease is based on a male body and women experience symptoms differently.

There is a growing body of evidence to suggest that the lack of women in scientific research both as study participants and researchers has actively served to undermine or actively damage women's health, as there has been a failure to distinguish between disease aetiology or drug responses based on gender.[34] As proof positive of this theory, a recent study published in *Nature Human Behaviour* has highlighted the significance of women in medical research as, having studied over 1.5 million papers, they observed a pattern that when research teams included one female scientist or more, gender became an important part of the study.[35] This is particularly significant when one considers that male and female physiognomy and hormonal profiles are different, indicating different responses to drugs and different disease progressions. It's also true that women have their pain overlooked more frequently by male doctors, which undoubtedly led to the finding in 2017 by the UK clinical watchdog NICE that women on average spend between four and ten years and have numerous GP appointments before endometriosis is diagnosed.[36] I should point out that endometriosis, a gynaecological condition, can cause agonising pain and left unresolved can lead to infertility. Little still is understood about endometriosis, and without more women in medical research it's likely that this situation will only perpetuate.

Let's look at another field: sports shoes – how many decades have we been wearing trainers? For those same decades a female trainer was simply a male trainer shrunk to 'fit' a woman's foot, the old 'shrink it and pink it' approach to design. This approach neglected the fact that women's feet are not just smaller in length, they are different in many respects including width and arch placement, and our ligaments may loosen with our hormonal cycles (particularly during pregnancy), making it much easier for women to sustain an injury. Hence for many of those decades, women's trainers have not been fit for purpose. Yet despite the numbers of women competing in endurance running, going to gyms and flinging themselves across Tough Mudder assault courses, only in 2017 have we been met with a trainer designed specifically and ergonomically for a woman's foot, witness Adidas Pure Boost X. Given that women are half of the population, why has this taken so long? Why, you might also want to ask, was the Apple Health app launched without the inclusion of a menstrual tracker when women's hormonal cycles are so fundamental to their health and wellbeing or physical state?

You may also care to question why Dell chose to launch a laptop with an inbuilt calorie counter. Or why Nikon chose to launch a newly designed camera with 50 of the world's 'top photographers', and not one of them a woman.

The answer to all of these questions is that the world is still designed through a male lens, and that needs to change, urgently. This is why we need more women in design and in STEM. Not only that, but we need to celebrate the achievements of women in science and design to degender the disciplines: just think what we could invent in the world with more women. A different perspective yields a different result.

WHAT THIS MEANS: KEY TAKEAWAYS FOR BRANDS

When it comes to women, one could argue that it's our unique perspective that makes us the better inventors in the first place for, as the givers of life, the begetters of future generations, we have more invested in the concept of legacy and making the world a better place for our children.

We are also conditioned to think outwards, so perhaps the 'responsibility' mindset is also a useful stimulus for women's pioneer spirit. Just look at the women of Greenham Common, who for nearly two decades raised public consciousness around the existential threat posed by nuclear armaments through their programme of civil disobedience and peaceful resistance. It is hard to imagine quite so many men content to weather such basic living conditions (especially as many of the protestors had young children to care for) for quite so long – but then women do have one asset when it comes to provoking change: we're used to being patient. Women's activism recently came to the fore again. The Women's Marches of January 2017 were the largest mass protest of their kind – women marching peacefully to imprint on the public and political consciousness: we're watching, and together we are powerful.

Women think about legacy

It is my experience, and this is demonstrated through our research, that women think about and are motivated much more by the idea of legacy: their children, their children's children, their friends' children and their communities. It should be therefore little surprise that women are the great social pioneers, be it in the smallest way: there is the oft-quoted fact that for every marginal dollar a woman earns she will invest 90 per cent back into her community. She is a one-woman ripple effect, and I would urge brands to think about how powerful that is. If women make the majority of consumer purchases, perhaps it's no coincidence that Unilever has concluded that purpose-led brands generate 30 per cent more growth,[37] and the Millward Brown Global BrandZ study looking at the most valuable brands concluded that those with a clearly defined purpose had grown revenue three times faster over the past 12 years.[38] By 'purpose' we mean 'making life better' for the user. And while not every brand needs to commit to making the world a better place, to quote Howard Gossage from the

Mad Men era, 'if you're in the business of advertising, hopefully it inspires you to use your talents to enrich people's lives in some way'.

At the very least, given women's legacy in the environmental movement and desire to improve communities around them, in future brands are going to be much more closely scrutinised in terms of their environmental credentials or sustainability, and much more likely by women.

Design through a female lens

For brand innovation and service design there are some very clear lessons to be learned: firstly, the idea of design through a female lens, and what this really means. If you want to design for women, it feels pretty smart to employ women in design, not just to know 'what women want' in the most superficial sense, but to experience and see the world as women: if women make such great pioneers, you would surely want some on your team. A great example here is healthcare as women may experience symptoms differently or different symptoms, and they may describe them in a different way. They may not use the same language, so you need to make sure you have women involved in your study design and diagnostic algorithms (basically the diagnostic decision tree of questions). Perhaps most fascinating is the recent Harvard study that concluded that patients of female doctors have longer life expectancies; the researchers hypothesise that this is in part due to the fact that female doctors spend longer with patients, ask different questions and adhere to protocols, another example of what that female lens can deliver.[39]

A second and obvious but overlooked point is that physically and hormonally, men and women are not the same. Take, for example, skincare: men have more body hair, they sweat more and have a different skin pH, but have these differences been fully explored in the design of, say, sunscreen? The answer is no, not yet. Truly designing for women can mean fundamental changes to your product DNA, which might sound scary, but think about the potential rewards and competitive advantage.

Empowering through technology

Here's another thought to consider: if technology is such a powerful force for women both in empowerment and social connection, have you fully harnessed this idea? Are you providing services or brand utility that serves the brand, or that serves your audience? By this, I mean serves a human need. Consider how you can embed women in the design process and, at the very least, if you need any coding, ask a woman to do it. While we see clear evidence that tech can empower women, there is also demonstrable evidence of the darker side of technology. In the case of domestic violence, for example, a survey by Women's Aid revealed the prevalence of tracking devices and apps used by aggressors to monitor and control women's movements, affecting 41 per cent of women in the survey.[40] Given that one in four women in Britain are victims of domestic violence,[41] and one in three on average in the rest of the world, it's little surprise perhaps that so many women in our Women's Index study suggested that technology was designed by men for men, which points to the importance of putting more technology design in the hands of women.

Brands and social change

Brands and services have the potential to create powerful cultural ripple effects, to be a force for good and positive social change if we choose. Since its launch, Sport England's 'This Girl Can' campaign has achieved remarkable progress in narrowing the gender gap in sporting participation, from some 2 million to just over 1.5 million,[42] creating a positive legacy both in terms of women and girls' physical fitness, but also their sense of confidence and, for girls, their likely educational attainment. Meanwhile, Always's 'Like a Girl' has not only boosted brand purchase intent by over

50 per cent, it has changed perceptions around the language we use: doing something 'like a girl' is no longer the pejorative it once was, a view shared by 70 per cent of women and 60 per cent of men who had seen the campaign, which achieved 90 million views.[43] Here is a case of a brand literally changing culture. The old Benetton campaigns of the 1980s challenged our attitudes towards racism and HIV, and their philosophy of making 'Clothes for Humans' underlines a powerful statement of social inclusivity, so often absent from the fashion industry and perhaps the world at large.[44]

Achieving cultural change doesn't have to be in the form of grand campaign gestures or brand posturing, but through small acts, through intelligent and sensitive design, through purposeful action and work that we do every day. Consider, for example, the social change achievable if mortgage products were to offer in-built payment holidays for parents having children, enabling them to take proper maternity and paternity leave. Brands can change the world: it just requires a little imagination and a spark of ambition. Try asking yourself, if I don't create change, who will?

CHAPTER 5

· ·

Motherhood Reimagined

'I don't know why women need to have children to be seen as complete human beings.' **Marisa Tomei**

One of the biggest 'revolutions' currently within the 'developed' world and illustrative of the end of the 'life script' is the impact on motherhood, and it's a relatively recent phenomenon. Motherhood has changed fundamentally over the past decades, not just in terms of the fact that we're delaying motherhood, or increasingly working while childrearing, but also the intense scrutiny focused upon motherhood, for example through the cult of perfection, the 'Yummy Mummy', 'Tiger Mother' and competitive parenting. It used to be the case that you became pregnant, had the baby and then got on with it: not anymore. These days there's a whole media-storm of scrutiny obsessed with when you have your child, how you have it, how you'll parent, when you drop the baby-weight, etc. This specific scrutiny perhaps unfairly seems to focus on the mother; fathers seem to be able to pass under the radar unnoticed. All too often conversations about childcare or parenting assume that it's a woman's responsibility, and as a society we have been slow to change.

IT PAYS TO WAIT

There's no doubt about it, in the developed world we are having children later: many of us are seeking to postpone motherhood. In 1970s Britain, women's average age at the birth of their first child was around 26 years, today that stands at 30 years;[1] in the US women's age at the birth of their first child has increased from 22 years to 26 years in the same period.[2] To illustrate the scale of change. it's worth noting that in the UK more women in their forties are having children versus women in their teens, for the first time.[3] As I sit here writing this, I am pregnant with my first child, at the age of 45, so the themes I will discuss here have a personal resonance.

Obviously, with the advent of the contraceptive pill, women have been able to assert choice over their reproductive destiny: if and when they will have children and how many. This has undoubtedly been one of the biggest tools for, if not quite gender equality, then female agency: one can draw a direct link between reproductive rights and economic empowerment. Birth control can help break the cycle of poverty: referring to the economic impact of birth control for African Americans, Martin Luther King Jr highlighted back in the 1960s that it promotes 'fair opportunity to develop and advance as all other people in our society'.[4] In fact, US research conducted in 2007 concluded that a narrowing of the gender wage gap could be attributed to delayed childbearing for women and linked to higher probability of university completion.[5] Similar studies also suggest that access to contraception can be directly linked to the 30 per cent increase in women in skilled careers from 1970 to 1990,[6] and a gain of nearly $125,000 in lifetime earnings for those women who delayed parenthood to their thirties.[7] So it literally pays to wait, and not just for women – consider all that additional taxable income. Delaying motherhood is a trend we witness not just within the US and UK, but across Europe and parts of Asia, particularly Japan and China.

THE LATE STARTER

The 'Late Starter' is the 'poster girl' for this trend: a woman in her late thirties or early forties doing what women used to do in their twenties, namely getting married and having children. Of course, these days, certainly in the West, marriage doesn't necessarily precede childrearing. I call her the 'Late Starter' after hearing women refer to themselves as such, but equally because, after all, who wants to be labelled an 'older' mother, infirm and over the hill: at least the medical term has thankfully evolved from 'geriatric mother' to perhaps the slightly less-damning 'woman of advanced maternal age'.

But let's not get too carried away with our newfound reproductive freedoms, because instead of being rewarded for the contribution we make to society thanks to many more tax-paying years, the Late Starter mother gets more than a little flack. The same cannot be said for Late Starter fathers.

Contemporary media is fond of suggesting that the Late Starter is a 'victim' of the 'success penalty', a rather condescending explanation for women embracing motherhood later in life. The key narrative of the 'success penalty' is that her selfish pursuit of education and career has penalised her through making her delay becoming a mother or wife and, implicitly, finding 'happiness'. There are two key problems with this particular narrative, firstly the fact that it excludes the idea of choice. The sense that women may *want* to delay motherhood is anathema, because it assumes that all women must want to be mothers. The result is that a successful empowered woman is repackaged as a tragic victim of her own (selfish) success, in a desperate quest to find a 'baby-daddy' before it's too late. The second problem with this idea, and what the often-screeching headlines fail to point out, is that marriage rates are falling for everyone and we're often single for longer, and while educated women may marry later, data suggests they are more likely to have happy marriages that last.

The other narrative that surrounds the Late Starter mother is the idea that she is placing undue stress on the healthcare system through being geriatric *and* pregnant, with the associated risks of preterm labour, birth complications and birth defects. What this narrative fails to accept is that the health and weight of a mother are equally significant in the overall outcome of a pregnancy. Being overweight, for example, increases the risk of birth complications and defects; a mother with a BMI of 40 or over has a 37 per cent increased risk of having a child with birth defects.[8] Similarly, overall health and lifestyle. and whether one smokes or drinks excessive alcohol, are all factors in pregnancy outcomes: age is only part of the equation. Sadly, that fact fails to make for good headlines. Within the popular press, it seems to be the idea that a woman can *choose* to have a baby later that attracts the most attention and criticism: perhaps we're uncomfortable with the idea of women and choice. Certainly, the new wave of conservatism creeping across the US and impacting on reproductive freedoms would seem to reinforce this view, with the suggestion that contraception does not constitute essential healthcare under new reforms.

STARTING LATER: A GLOBAL TREND

Delaying motherhood seems to be something of a global phenomenon, certainly within the developed world. From our own research, 12 per cent of women outside of Asia gave birth to their first child aged 35 or over, rising to 16 per cent of women across Asia Pacific.[9] In the US the birth rate among over 35s has doubled, while in Asia the average age at marriage has dramatically increased, and by implication the age of motherhood has increased alongside this trend, since few children are born in Asia outside of wedlock (only 2 per cent in Japan in 2007). To add a sense of scale to this phenomenon, 20 per cent of live births in the UK are to women over 35 years old, and in the last ten years there has been an 84 per cent increase in women giving birth in their forties,[10] with women even waiting until their fifties thanks to IVF treatments and assisted conception.

So just how did Mommy Dearest get to be so old? A number of disparate phenomena collide to create the 'Late Starter' tribe. Possibly the most influential dynamic is that many women are choosing to stay in education for longer in a bid to get ahead in their careers, and ultimately starting to erode the gender pay gap. From our Women's Index study, 44 per cent of women globally said they would consider postponing motherhood to focus on their careers, rising to 52 per cent in Asia Pacific, with many countries' responses in the region significantly higher. In Thailand, for example, 68 per cent of women would put education before children; the outlier was the more traditional Japan at 31 per cent.[11]

The Organisation for Economic Co-operation and Development estimated that, by 2015, 72 per cent of all graduates would be women, and for every year spent in education, that's a year a female is not likely to be pushing the baby stroller. In many developed nations, she'll also finish university with a sizeable debt to repay, meaning she's compelled to maximise her earnings potential to make a dent in the student loan repayments. Given that children cost money and the reality of the gender wage gap, not to mention the cost of childcare, she is likely to do maximise earnings before she thinks about starting a family. Certainly, in the UK, the rising cost of housing has put the brakes on starting a family. In 2015 a government housing bill reported that a median London rent consumed 43 per cent of the income of a two-person household, and a study by the European Bank for Reconstruction and Development concluded that a 10 per cent increase in house prices leads to a 1.3 per cent fall in the birth rate.[12] Certainly we observed evidence of the financial burden of motherhood in our data, with 44 per cent of women globally concerned as to how motherhood would affect them financially, rising to 58 per cent in Asia Pacific.[13] In fact, two-thirds of women across many countries in Asia Pacific were worried about the financial impact of motherhood, compared to one-third in the UK and US.

There are also cultural factors – particularly the urbanised 'modern' cities, where both the intensive working patterns and the high cost of living serve to disincentivise 'settling down' – that serve to propagate the Late Starter. Witness that this tribe is more prevalent in these cities as opposed to the 'country' or less urbanised cities. When we looked at maternal tribes in the US, we identified that the Midwest was home to significantly more 'traditionalist' tribes, for example 'Nurturers' and 'Spouse Focused' women for whom home and family was the centre of their universe, than the rest of the country.

In New York, the spectre of Late Starters is likened to the extension of the collegiate lifestyle, with women and men existing in a prolonged state of 'young adulthood'. Alyson Jon, New York artist and blogger, explains:

> New York City lifestyle is like a prolonged college-life. Young adulthood lasts for however long you want it to. Every time I go on Facebook, I see that someone else at home in the Midwest has gotten married/having a baby. When I go home for Christmas I'm always asked about my plans about settling down. I mention those things here in the city and it's met an attitude of 'but we're doing so much more with our lives.' Mothers at 25 are treated like welfare cases; 'How can she have a child so young!'

Much has been discussed in the media about the marriage prospects of better educated women. And among some commentators the theory persists that the higher a woman's education the more difficult it will be to find a suitable marriage partner, since women will not want to 'marry down' or she may perceive that society or a male partner doesn't accept the new female-breadwinner relationship model.

LATE STARTERS OR LEFTOVERS: ASIA

Culturally it's much more acceptable for women to 'marry up', i.e. the idea of 'hypergamy', especially in Asia, but 'marrying down' is much less acceptable: 'Women these days aren't going to marry just anybody,' says Junko Sakai, whose *Howl of the Loser Dogs*, a book about single career women, that has sold more than 300,000 copies. In part, there's a subtler dynamic at play here too, since 'marrying down', particularly in Asia, also carries the risk of marrying into a less liberal and more traditional culture that might be much less accepting of a woman's financial independence. It's unlikely that many self-determined young women climbing the career ladder will want to tie the knot knowing that, with the toss of the confetti, a curtain will be drawn across her professional life, and she must retreat into the home and kitchen.

To understand the plight of the Late Starter in Japan, you need to understand the Christmas Cake joke: 'Japanese women are like Christmas cakes: if they surpass the 25th (Christmas day or their birthday), they'll be difficult to dispose of.' Marriage has certainly lost some of its allure for Japanese women. Japanese government statistics reveal that, over the past decade, the portion of Japanese women age 25 to 29 who have not married has surged from 40 per cent to 54 per cent (compared to 40 per cent for US women of the same age).[14] The percentage for women age 30 to 34 has increased from 14 per cent to 27 per cent, and this has a profound effect on fertility since, in Japanese society, there is still intense cultural stigma around single mothers, in some cases making it harder for them to even secure accommodation since many landlords shun single parents. From our own data, some 76 per cent of Japanese women without children said they were either opposed to the idea of having children or undecided, almost twice the global average of 44 per cent.[15] According to the Women's Index Study, the most popular reason for not wanting children in Japan was because women hadn't found a partner, with 45 per cent of childfree women citing this as a reason, almost double the global average of 23 per cent,[16] and given only 2 per cent of children in Japan are born outside of marriage, no partner almost definitely means no children.

The trend is having a profound impact on public policy, with the government worried that the implied drop in the birth rate will lead to a top-heavy society. In a nation already struggling to care for an ageing population, this has disastrous long-term implications both economically but also practically – who will care for the elderly? Researchers at Tokyo University have even designed a Doomsday clock to count down to the day the Japanese population will become extinct! To put this into perspective, the birth rate now stands at 1.29 per woman compared to 2.13 for the US. This is a record low for Japan, and has led to some regions offering subsidised IVF treatments in a bid to swell the population. Despite governmental efforts to incentivise parenthood, for example by providing childcare facilities and improving maternity leave, it's still failing to address the fact that women just aren't getting married.

At the same time, a generation of Japanese men are opting out of the traditional macho breadwinner role. The *soshokukei danshi* (grass-eating or herbivorous men), a term coined by commentator Maki Fukisawa, seek security in a life without dating, sex or marriage. It's estimated that up to 60 per cent of Japanese men aged 20–34 years display characteristics of the 'herbivores'.[17] This is startling when one considers the way in which Japan has been a traditionally macho society or warrior culture, and therein perhaps lies the problem with this societal diagnosis. Perhaps the *soshokukei danshi* are simply Asian 'metrosexuals', displaying less 'alpha male' characteristics rather than signposting a bigger social malaise. Remember, this is a country where gender roles are so ingrained that it's only recently women have been allowed to train as sushi chefs, having been held back by the cultural belief that women's warmer body temperature (code for menstruation) leads to poorer quality food.

Typically, Asian marriage places enormous responsibility for the home and care-giving on the wife; couple this with the ageing population and she may find herself caring for the home, the children and elderly parents, and this is incompatible with a full-time job without some sharing of responsibility.

It would seem Asian men have been slow to catch up, spending on average around 24 minutes a day on the household chores in Japan and 48 minutes in China, compared to 107 minutes for men in Denmark.[18] As a result, financially independent women are questioning the benefits that marriage will bring. And, as mentioned, it would also appear that the burden of housework rests more heavily on a woman's shoulders if she out-earns her spouse, who may seek to reassert his masculinity by avoiding participation in the household chores – perhaps not the best recipe for a happy and equal marriage. Meanwhile, governments are struggling to adapt to this change in societal make-up and values. In a desperate bid to see the elderly not fall into neglect, China has recently passed a law forcing parental visitation: the 'Elderly rights law', passed in 2013, compels children to look after their parents' 'spiritual needs' and 'never neglect or snub elderly people', but in reality it was vague in setting out the terms of the policy.

US LATE STARTERS

In the US, the Late Starter dynamic is reported to be most pronounced among African-American women, according to the US Census: African-American women aged 35 to 44 are the only group of American women of child-bearing age with lower rates of marriage than men of the same race or ethnicity, with commentators fearing the terminal decline of marriage in the black community. This decline has been attributed to the rise of higher education among women of colour. But is this just propaganda, 'punishing' women for seeking to better themselves or discouraging them from the pursuit of career?

If we dig a little deeper into the statistics all is not what it seems, and a few interesting facts emerge. A new US study by Dr Ivory Toldson of Howard University and the Institute for Social Research tells a slightly different story: among all ages, 43 per cent of African-American women have never married compared to 20 per cent of white women, but recut the data and look at women of 35 or older, and only 25 per cent of African-American women have never married.[19]

So African-American women are marrying later, but they're still marrying. The study also concluded that, contrary to the headlines, educated African-American men were more likely to marry educated African-American women: so, education is not the barrier to marriage that some journalists might suggest.

CHILDREN AND CAREERS: THE BRUTAL TRUTH

Sadly, many women also feel that having children curtails a career and earnings potential, arguing that you're more likely to be hit by a comet than snag a promotion or pay rise when you are pregnant or on maternity leave, and very few exceptions serve to disprove this assumption. When women return to work after having a baby, they also feel they wear the invisible mantle of 'Working Mother', by implication dulling the formerly bright star of a stellar career, and from our research we saw that 58 per cent of women globally, rising to 66 per cent in Asia Pacific, felt their childfree co-workers were given more career opportunities.[20] In truth, the facts tell an even more depressing story. A 2017 UK study by career coaches Women

Returners revealed that while more than a third of women fully expected to assume a more junior position on resuming work after a career break, the reality is a little starker; a study by PwC concluded that three-fifths of professional women were welcomed back with a more junior or lower paid position.[21] How's that for a 'welcome back'? What PwC also highlight is that the underutilisation of this professional talent is costing the UK economy some £1.7 billion in lost tax revenue and spending power. So, while women themselves feel that they will be judged as work shy, or lacking in commitment, and they will be given the unwanted jobs and the dead-end accounts, and will be treading water professionally for many years to come – all true – they are a high-potential workforce, hugely valuable to the economy, and if employers were more enlightened as a society we would all reap the benefits. But as the world stands today there are very good reasons to invest time and energy on maximising one's earnings and career 'equity' before going on maternity leave.

Within the workplace, the Late Starter is likely to have worked her way into a valuable senior position, and unless we wake up to later life pregnancy some employers are still going to be blindsided when their senior female talent shows up pregnant aged 42.

If companies want to retain valuable female talent they will need to think more laterally about ways in which they can accommodate her changing needs, and not write off a woman just because she decides to have children. Sadly, it's only ever women who are asked, and by implication burdened, with the question of 'how you combine a career and children'. In fact, 88 per cent of women in our study were frustrated with the fact that working women were assumed to be the primary parent by default.[22] It's only ever women who are grilled on their choice of when and how they intend to return to work, blind to the fact that increasingly men want to take a more active role in parenting and fathers may need career breaks too. In London, building on the success of 'City Mothers', 'City Fathers' has recently been set up to serve the needs of parents in the Square Mile, dispensing information, support and advice. Making it easier and more acceptable for working fathers to request paternity leave will free women from sole parenting duties, enabling both partners to participate more equally in career and parenthood.

LATE STARTER MOTHERHOOD: THE FACT AND THE FICTION

With women settling down later, they are having children later. The rise of the older mother has attracted significant media attention over the past decade. As previously discussed, mainstream media has struggled to accept and embrace this phenomenon, with numerous studies and headlines trumpeting the risks of mortality/birth defects and general doom. While the negativity persists, more enlightened research, perhaps fuelled by a realisation that we're living longer, is starting to quietly challenge the hysteria.

Older mothers, it would seem, can provide a number of benefits for the child (beyond, say, an encyclopaedic knowledge of 1980s music). In a study from the National Institute of Child Health and Human Development (NICHD) in the United States, researchers concluded that older parents were more financially stable, had more patience and time to play with their children, and stuck to less traditional childrearing roles.[23] Researchers concluded that older parents 'tended to plan ahead and be even more careful about diet and exercise to make sure that they were in the best physical condition they could be to take care of their children as long as possible', so perhaps the Late Starters are not such a burden to the healthcare system after all. Equally, a 2016 study demonstrated that children born to mothers of 'advanced maternal age' have a greater cognitive ability.[24] while another study suggested that older mothers adapted to parenting more easily and were more relaxed with their children.[25]

Perhaps influenced by the negative stereotyping in the media, attitudes of their colleagues and families or simply due to their specialised needs, older mothers are learning to stick together and communities devoted to educating, supporting and lobbying on their behalf are emerging. For example, OlderMum.co.uk, AllTheMoms.com and Mumsnet all have dedicated Late Starter forums, and work to dispel many of the myths and prejudices surrounding 'Elderly Primigravida' (medical-speak for pregnant and getting on a bit).

Late Starters need to actively challenge the myths because judging from the rise in fertility among the over forties, this is not a phenomenon that's likely to change anytime soon.

In her 1991 book *Backlash*, feminist writer Susan Faludi attributed the visceral media response to a conspiracy of holding women back in order to protect jobs for the boys. With women confined to the kitchen and their careers curtailed in favour of motherhood, there would certainly be less competition for men in the labour market. Where once this might have felt like mild hysteria, it seems statistics have been 'manipulated' or rather framed in such a way as to persuade women they will have to choose between career and 'happiness', when the truth is that as a society we are all settling down and marrying later, certainly in the developed world. Propaganda is also used to persuade women into expensive fertility treatments before they are really necessary, with a significant emotional cost.

In my own experiences of speaking to midwives and doctors, there was a received wisdom that any baby born to a woman over 40 must be the result of IVF; yet thousands of babies are born to over 40-year-olds in the UK, and squaring this with the woeful success statistics among IVF clinics for women in this cohort, the numbers just don't add up: so, where are all these babies coming from? I looked on mother's forums, for example Mumsnet and NetMums, and the anecdotal evidence of women conceiving naturally in their forties was plain to see. Yes, some women are not so lucky, but then this applies to women across many age groups. The 18 per cent rise in abortions within the past decade among women in their forties, as reported by BPAS (British Pregnancy Advice Service), suggests that current medical advice and popular wisdom surrounding 'later life' fertility may need to be adjusted, since over 40 per cent of those women seeking abortions had not been using contraception, having been persuaded that they were infertile.

So maybe it's time for a more objective discussion on women's reproductive choices; perhaps we need to be alive to the fact that there are women who actively want to delay motherhood, or for whom career and motherhood are dual priorities and feel they shouldn't have to choose. This is about giving women the choice to make informed decisions (informed through facts), not demonising them for asserting their right to choose, and most importantly not seeking to manipulate or force women's hand through the misuse of statistics. We're living longer, we're healthier, we're having children later, so let's just deal with it.

MOMMY DEAREST AND PERFECT PARENTING

Of course, we couldn't discuss the idea of motherhood without lifting the lid on the whole 'cult' of parenting itself, and in particular the quest for perfection and competitive parenting. We have a whole industry and knowledge economy geared around the cult of parenting. Equally I should observe that the cult of parenting is perhaps better represented as the cult of motherhood, since much of the industry's attention focuses solely on women, telling us what to do, how to do it and when to do it, lest we become anything less than 'the perfect mother'. Comedian Ali Wong, observing that her partner merely had to show up for scan appointments to be lavished with praise, nailed the inequality of parenting standards perfectly: 'It takes so little to be considered a great dad, and it also takes so little to be considered a shitty mom.'[26]

One of the most polarising figures within this whole culture is the 'Tiger Mother'. Is it just me or does the phrase Tiger Mother bring you out in a cold sweat? I am relieved to say I did not have a 'Tiger Mother'; 'eccentric mother', yes, but thankfully that meant I escaped having a robotic parenting automaton. So, who is the Tiger Mother?

THE TIGER MOTHER

Battle Hymn of the Tiger Mother is a book by Amy Chua published in 2011, and reveals what we already suspected: Asian mothers are relentlessly ambitious for their children. From our own data, we observed that women in Asia were significantly more likely to put education as a 'top priority' during childhood and early teens; 58 per cent of women in Asia Pacific, compared to 48 per cent in the rest of the world.[27] A Tiger Mother is characterised as a strict disciplinarian who devotes herself to raising her children to achieve high standards of education, overseeing every aspect of their development. What's interesting is that while the Tiger Mother is lauded and applauded in her native Asia, in the West her cousin, the 'Helicopter Mother', is derided and criticised for her controlling ways.

According to Chinese culture, those people born in the year of the tiger are 'powerful, authoritative and magnetic', and Tiger Mothers are a force with which to be reckoned.

If Amy Chua's memoir is in any way an accurate portrayal of the Tiger Mother parenting experience then it paints a rather exhausting picture of a mother who seeks to micromanage every aspect of her child's upbringing, refusing to accept anything other than excellence from her child. From our research we observed that while 17 per cent of women across Asia Pacific could be described as a 'Tiger Mother', they were most prevalent in Vietnam (30 per cent), China (22 per cent) and Japan (20 per cent).[28]

What appears to be the most polarising facet of the Tiger Mother, beyond their uncompromising attitude to their child's attainment, is the all-consuming emphasis on education in preference to play. Chua's eye-watering narrative relays a childhood of no play dates, no sleepovers, no free thinking and crucially no fun. Again, our data reinforced this view, and we observed that those countries with the most 'Tigers' were least likely to prioritise 'friendships and fun' during the childhood years. One is left to ponder what indeed constitutes childhood.

It's hard to consider the rise of the Tiger Mother in isolation of the Tiger economies, and not be in awe of the prospect of an über-educated 'master race'. What then for the rest of us, and for our children?

In contemporary Western educational culture, increasingly fearful of allowing children to compete and embracing the idea of 'good enough', one could argue that we are in danger of encouraging mediocrity or denying our children the opportunity to realise their full potential. Arguably, a good education is the foundation to success, it opens doors and affords choice, while a bad education confines. Perhaps more importantly, high educational standards breed the indigenous talent required for the economy, the next generation of innovators, entrepreneurs, doctors and politicians. In December 2010, the results of the Programme for International Student Assessment, or PISA, tests were announced. The US was outside the top 20 in most subjects. To quote Arne Duncan, US Secretary of Education, 'The United States came in twenty-third or twenty-fourth in most subjects. We can quibble, or we can face the brutal truth that we're being out-educated.' To highlight the point, Chinese children came first in every subject area.

In Asia, the advent of Tiger Mothers has created an interesting cultural ripple effect; one such example is the rise of 'Super Tutors' or 'Tutor Kings' and 'Queens'. Self-styled Super Tutors are child tutors who have embraced publicity, cleverly marketing themselves to elevate their status to that of pop stars among the Tiger Mother cohort in Asia. Anxious Tiger Mothers compete to secure their child a place among their classes to elevate their child's grades. The hunger for educational excellence has elevated the most celebrated tutors to millionaire status, even leading to TV shows for some.

The tutoring phenomenon is spreading across Asia, and in South Korea it's estimated that up to 90 per cent of primary-school children attend tutoring schools.[29] Further evidence of the erosion of childhood in the quest for academic over-achievement.

What distinguishes the Tiger Mother from the Western 'Helicopter Mother' is the fearless way in which the Tiger Mother prepares her child for the tough outside world. The Tiger Mother is from the school of hard knocks and she doesn't want her child thinking life's a breeze. Sociologist Hilary Friedman comments in her 2013 book *Playing to Win: Raising Children in a Competitive Culture*: 'Competitive parents recognize that no matter how great you are, you are going to face adversity at some point in your life. If you learn how to deal with that at a younger age, and in a safer environment, that's a good thing.'

In contrast the Helicopter Mother seeks to protect her child from failure and the harsh outside world; omnipresent, she exists to watch over her child's development, stepping in when problems occur. Some commentators would claim that this behavioural pattern denies children the opportunity to think for themselves or problem-solve, and that once they leave the nest they may feel ill-prepared to face the adversity of the outside world.

Our response to this parenting phenomenon is determined by the degree to which parental involvement is accepted culturally. In Asia the Tiger Mother is lauded, she's an emblem of a culture based around achievement and excellence. It runs deeper than this, however, for the Tiger Mother is arguably another reflection of an Asian mother's feeling of duty to her family in giving over her own needs to the all-consuming responsibilities of marriage and home: in this way, the Tiger Mother's role is one of dutiful servitude – she is raising the next generation for the benefit of her family but also her society. In this sense, while we see the Tiger Mother alive to the realities of competing in an ever more dynamic world, she's something of a traditionalist in her self-sacrifice for the greater good, which is perhaps why culturally she gains more acceptance and even admiration. In Western society, the Helicopter Mother meets with less approval and some derision for her 'controlling ways', and there is much less of a sense of duty or the collective good associated with her drive; often she's just dismissed as another selfish 'pushy parent'. It's clear, however, that the same maternal desires and aspirations for their child motivate both the Tiger Mother and the Helicopter Mother, even if the outcome is not the same parenting style.

THE DARKER SIDE OF TIGER PARENTING

Growing up with tiger parents can also have its darker side due to the suppression of choice and free will. Tiger children are often channelled into the socially acceptable 'status' careers, doctor or lawyer being the frequent choices. We observed some signs of this in our Women's Index data. Women in Asia Pacific were among the most highly educated in our sample next to women across the Middle East, with 48 per cent of women in Asia Pacific having achieved a degree compared to 27 per cent in the rest of the world.[30] When we looked at degree subject, however, it was clear that an interest in the subject was much less likely as a driver in Asia compared to the rest of the world. Preordained career choices stifle the more creative child – what tiger parent will seek a future for their child as a struggling artist or actor? Tess Gerritsen, a writer and child of tiger parents, reflects: 'I've heard from too many Asians whose dreams of careers in the arts were thwarted by their parents. One 45-year-old computer engineer wrote me, mourning the fact he was now too old to pursue a fashion career. "I have only one life, and I'm spending it at a job I hate. Because it's what my parents wanted for me."'[31] Thus a whole generation of children risk a destiny of a successful but unfulfilling future. In this sense, it's worth paying some attention to considering to what degree 'over-education' and intensive schooling risks stamping out free thought, an essential part of a child's development, and the way in which cloistered tutoring may impact on a child's socialisation: a more destructive legacy of the Tiger Mother.

It would appear that the tiger phenomenon has its detractors. Some economists and educators recognise that the impact of intensive parenting can stamp out creativity and lateral thinking. According to the *Economist*, 'This is now seen as a competitive disadvantage in what are often called "knowledge economies", where innovation and inventiveness are at a premium.'[32] Equally, in Asia the Tiger Mother may not be universally embraced, Singapore Prime Minister Lee Hsien Loong launched an attack on Tiger Mothers in a speech in late August 2012 to mark Singapore's national day: 'Please let your children have their childhood … Instead of growing up balanced and happy, he grows up narrow and neurotic. No homework is not a bad thing. It's good for young children to play, and to learn through play.'

What unites mothers across all cultures is the desire for the best for their children. What constitutes 'the best' is where the division lies. It's no longer safe to assume that all Asian cultures embrace the intensive parenting styles of the Tiger Mother, and the signs are that there's increasing dissent in Singapore and Vietnam, for example, and a move towards a less controlling and more facilitating model of parenting.

In our discussion of 'motherhood reimagined', it's also worthwhile considering those women who have decided to postpone motherhood indefinitely, and the way in which society is adapting to the idea of women 'who are not mothers', because this is a worldwide phenomenon. Since 1960 the global fertility rate has halved, standing at 2.36 births per woman in 2015.[33]

THE CHILDFREE

While the attention devoted to parenthood and parenting is now such a phenomenon it has reached almost cult status – and in 2015 the global baby-care product market was estimated to have a value of $62 billion with healthy signs of growth[34] – parenthood is not to every woman's taste. Such is the all-consuming attention to parenting infecting social media that it has prompted something of a backlash, with the creation of sites such as 'Shut the F**Up, Parents' and apps such as 'Unbaby.me', a nifty tool that replaces baby pics with pleasing kittens or cars. They may be flippant, but they are a symptom of the fact that not everyone buys in to the whole parenting thing. Not every woman will only feel she's complete once she's added to the gene pool, and there are plenty of women who see themselves not as 'childless', which literally implies they are 'lesser' mortals, but 'childfree': to them 'having it all' does not include a baby.

In the US, the low birth rate is unprecedented, even compared to the Great Depression; in Italy, up to 25 per cent of women will never 'go forth and multiply'. From our own data we observed that globally 12 per cent of women could be described as members of the 'Child Free' tribe, i.e. childfree and not intending to have children anytime soon. This figure crept up to 14 per cent in Asia Pacific.[35] While the childfree were populous in Hong Kong (24 per cent), Japan, Taiwan and Singapore (all around 18 per cent), there were significant numbers in Australia (18 per cent), US (17 per cent) and UK (16 per cent), illustrating how prevalent this phenomenon is.

If delaying parenthood is politicised, then eschewing it altogether has the potential to become even more contentious, with some economic and religious pundits seeking to blame all of society's woes on those 'selfish' enough to forgo children, a view endorsed by Pope Francis: 'The choice not to have children is selfish.'[36] In his searing book, *What to Expect When No One's Expecting* (2013), Jonathan V. Last attributes America's economic implosion to the declining birth rate, and points to increasing higher education as a key culprit, claiming that it 'dampens fertility in all sorts of ways. It delays marriage, incurs debt, increases the opportunity costs of childbearing, and greatly increases the expense of raising a child'. This doesn't exactly read as support for women in education, and it is difficult to gather how he links women's higher education to the greatly increased expense of raising a child.

While serving as prime minister of Australia, Julia Gillard's childfree status prompted intense criticism by fellow politicians, with suggestions of her being 'deliberately barren'[37] (because that is most definitely a sin) and leading a government that 'lacks experience in raising children', so drawing a direct correlation between her lack of children and parliamentary competence. The attacks went further, with former Labour Leader Mark Latham suggesting that 'Anyone who chooses a life without children, as Gillard has, cannot have much love in them,'[38] so no children: no empathy. That doesn't necessarily chime with my experience of the world thus far. A stark contradiction of this assertion is the fact that the childfree are more likely to bequeath money to charities.[39] From our own research, we cut the data between mothers and childfree women and saw that there was very little difference in attitudes. Childfree women are not a separate selfish breed, and 'working to improve one's community' was prioritised as important in life among three-quarters of mothers and childfree women alike.[40]

It's striking how this criticism – the idea that you cannot be a fully functioning, feeling adult until you've been 'with child' – is reserved for women: there seems to be a 'special place in hell' for the childless 'spinster'. A recent *Daily Mail* headline summed this up perfectly: 'How the rise of childless women could change the face of Britain: Rampant infidelity. A struggling economy. Meltdown for the NHS. And shorter life expectancies.'[41] I'm only surprised they didn't attribute global warming to the obviously feckless childless woman.

Is it any surprise therefore that women who are deliberately childfree should seek to redefine their status within society? Especially when 'hard-working families' are the special interest of most political parties to the exclusion of any other demographic.

Trawling back through history, parenthood has not always been a concept enshrined by religion. The Shakers were a notable example known to frown on the idea of procreation, preferring instead adoption into their communities; interestingly, they also subscribed to the idea that men and women were equal under God, whom in their theology was both male and female. The Skoptsy, a secret sect in Russia during the Tsarist period, practised routine castration of men and mastectomy of women, in atonement for the perceived sins of Adam and Eve: which is possibly taking the idea of 'childfree' a little far.

It took until the 1970s, with the ripple effect of birth control access, for childfree organisations to gain profile, with the foundation of the National Organization for Non-Parents in the US, the international No Kidding social club and, more recently, the NotMom organisation, founded in 2012 by Karen Malone Wright. NotMom aims to connect, support and empower women who have sought not to pursue motherhood. Their first summit, held in 2015 in Cleveland, USA, attracted nationwide coverage, and has run annual seminars since its inception.

While in some cases childfree women seek to connect and organise, high-profile women and celebrities celebrating their own 'childfree' status publicly help to propagate the idea of chosen childlessness as a 'good thing' within popular culture, recent examples being Kim Cattrall and Cameron Diaz.

A frequent bugbear of women in the Child Free tribe, beyond the media criticism, is their cultural invisibility, which is certainly true where brands are concerned. Happily, childfree women are hardly a popular trope in movie culture, and childfree women are usually painted as either damaged, jealous of their parenting peers or gripped by a fear of their biological clock. We witnessed this frustration within our study, with 93 per cent of women saying they want to be recognised beyond whether or not they are a mother, and some 80 per cent of US women saying that society needs to accept that childfree women can be fulfilled.[42]

Women were highly critical of the financial services industry, for example, for ignoring their particular needs, as reported in a recent research report: 'as a single woman I often feel that financial service institutions are not interested in my business. They want people preparing for kids.'[43] Yet women without children are likely to have a higher disposable income and arguably make faster buying decisions given they don't have the needs of a family to consider, and pose a potentially lucrative target for finance, luxury, travel and retail fashion.

THE GOLDEN MISSES AND THE HEDONISTS

For Asian women, education has removed much of the financial if not cultural imperative to marry: educated Thai women are significantly less likely to be married young, with one-fifth still single in their forties compared to one-eighth among their less-educated peers.[44] It's a dynamic we observed in our Women's Index study: on average 28 per cent of Asia Pacific women were single, set against a global average of 21 per cent; by country, the figures were 41 per cent in the Philippines, 35 per cent in Singapore, 32 per cent in Taiwan and 26 per cent in Thailand, contrasting sharply with the UK at 16 per cent.[45]

Perhaps part of this reluctance to marry is that a traditional Asian marriage offers women little freedom or independence. In some areas of South Asia, wives may not even take their children to hospital without getting their husband's permission; equally Chinese legislation passed in 2011 means that property purchased before marriage belongs upon marriage to the purchaser – there is no sense of shared ownership. Given that it's traditional for a wife to live in her husband's home upon marriage, it's been dubbed the law that has the power to make divorced Chinese women homeless,[46] and what smart, educated woman wants that?

The so-called 'Golden Misses', a revision of the 'old misses', is the Asian version of the Child Free tribe. Given the emphasis on education and career in Asia – no doubt the product of tiger parenting – many of these misses are 'golden', i.e. independently wealthy as a high-earning elite with a sizeable disposable income. It's projected that the population of Chinese Golden Misses living in cities is around 9 million,[47] and these independent, high-earning women hold a significant influence over the economy. It's estimated that by 2020 the female economies in India and China will be worth $5 trillion.[48] While the Child Free tribe is largely ignored in the West, in Asia the Golden Misses are highly visible, given their disposable income, taste for consumerism and high-end luxury, because without a family or a husband to worry about they can focus on indulging their expensive tastes. It's estimated that in Tokyo, for example, 94 per cent of women in their twenties own a Louis Vuitton bag.[49] The more prominent Misses have their own social followings: these are the all-important social 'micro-influencers' that marketers in the region need to be alive to, because if husbands won't court them, brands will. This phenomenon is particularly prevalent in South Korea, with aspirational 'Doenjang girls' their less wealthy followers. The 'Doenjang girls' derive their name from their assiduous coffee-drinking, studiously following the iconic brands favoured by the Golden Misses, and Starbucks are said to have profited from this micro-culture within a culture. Some commentators point out that the endless coffee-drinking replaces meals, meaning the Doenjang can save their money for their all-important trophy purchases: food not being one of them! But then nobody said this consumer culture was healthy.

WHAT THIS MEANS: KEY TAKEAWAYS FOR BRANDS

While having children or choosing to be childfree are becoming increasingly charged issues, with the politics of parenthood still falling into women's domain, we can observe at least that motherhood is becoming more diverse as a concept. For all the increased scrutiny and industry around parenthood, thankfully we can all accept there is no one blueprint these days. That said, too many of the motherhood models focus on the quest for perfection, a standard that is not applied to fatherhood, where 'good enough' seems to prevail. It's also worth pointing out that the represented ideal of motherhood within marketing communications and advertising all too often presents the woman as the primary parent, in her twenties and the stay-at-home kind, i.e. the 'Stepford' stereotype. This can feel very alienating, particularly to those women who are the Late Starters, since women who postpone childbearing are more likely to adopt a less traditional parenting model.

Equally, women who have eschewed children should feel more included in the cultural dialogue. What the Child Free and the Late Starter illustrate well is the idea that motherhood is no longer (if it ever was) all-consuming for women: for many women it is not the sole preoccupation, and for an increasingly large cohort it may never materialise as a reality.

We are childfree for longer

A key message here for brands is that not all women want to have children, and at the same time not all women want to have children straight away. This means that women are childfree for longer, and they may or may not become Late Starters, which implies that women in both of these tribes will have a high disposable income, and a longer focus on her career and herself: much like the men that represent marketers' usual default audience. It's far too simplistic to think about women as either career-hungry alphas or stay-at-home mothers when they can be both or neither. As a further consequence, this means that once women do have children, their entire being is not consumed by parenthood: the woman is still an individual in her own right, something which many brands overlook, and she still has her own needs and desires. One of the key causes of depression among women when they do become mothers is their loss of identity, since the minute a baby is born, all attention focuses on the child and the woman becomes invisible: at the school gates you are 'Jimmy's mother' and you relinquish your sense of being.

In our work on the Bepanthen Nappy Care Ointment brand, we addressed head on the insight around identity loss, and created Bepanthen 10th Month, an online platform devoted to women in their first few weeks of new motherhood, or the 'tenth month' of pregnancy'. The platform dispensed advice and knowledge for women, not as mothers, but as women recovering from childbirth, the individual woman within the mother – addressing their needs and not the child's. In the first week of launch, the film we created generated over 4 million views in Brazil, which tells you everything about the need for such a platform.

Tune in to the Late Starter

Instead of admonishing her, we could embrace the Late Starter and open our eyes to the specialised needs of mothers in their late thirties and forties, who are likely to be concerned about preserving their future health, wellness and having the energy to care for their brood.

As mothers, having achieved a higher status in their career and education, they may well prove to be more demanding and discerning as consumers – and while this isn't an argument to patronise younger mothers while we talk up to the Later Starter, we should recognise the diversity within the maternal audience, and the fact that a woman's role of mother does not define her wholly. It's advisable to recognise the woman beyond the mother.

Late Starter mothers may also seek to return to work faster than their younger peers, given their likely career focus, so it's very reasonable to assume that, cash-rich and time-poor, they will lean much more heavily on service providers, particularly those promising on-demand personalised offerings, and will make many of their purchases online (I speak from experience).

Understand the local parenting culture

Brands specifically aimed at parents and child development would do well to tune into local parenting culture so as to understand the prevailing attitudes, and should harness opportunities to align themselves to influencers or agents of change. The baby-care markets are hugely influenced by parenting culture, and parenting culture is dynamic and open to change. Here, Friso is a great example of a challenger mentality. Recognising a re-evaluation of tiger parenting, Friso, a challenger brand in the infant formula market, identified an opportunity to align itself to a new parental movement. Mothers in Vietnam, increasingly frustrated with being pressurised to raise the next Einstein, sought to re-embrace childhood for their offspring, affording them precious time to be children and play: pursuing the role of facilitator and not educator. Instead of leveraging its nutritional properties in mental development, Friso instead positioned its benefits around immunity: the idea being that Friso enabled mothers to let their child play and roam free, safe in the knowledge that he or she was protected. Friso became a champion of 'modern motherhood', an emblem of freedom not just for the child but for the mother too.

There's also another opportunity to empathise with the maternal audience in recognising how tough it is to be saddled with the pressure of raising the next prodigy, and this could be the lone brand voice that really touches a nerve and generates engagement: because it's tough being a tiger.

Court the Child Free audience and Golden Misses

While the baby-care market might be booming, the smarter luxury brands in Asia have woken up to the prospect of the Golden Misses: single, highly educated, high-income women. The fact that the Child Free and particularly their Asian cousin the Golden Misses are unencumbered by dependents means that they have the power to control their own lives and have only themselves to consider: this gives them the potential to lead a relatively hedonistic lifestyle, and it explains the boom in the luxury goods market in the region. This audience is a prime target for luxury travel, beauty and cosmetics and cosmetic procedures (I don't judge!) – China ranks number three in the world for cosmetic surgery, and the Korean aesthetics industry is booming. Equally, luxury automotive brands are starting to wake up to this lucrative audience, and it's reported that one-third of Audi buyers in China are female.[50] Audi has achieved this by courting the right female influencers to optimise the brand's prestige status, and by offering tailored features and customised models, for example, compact models to adjust to women's more petite frame. This is a highly discerning audience and their social following and status is key, therefore personalisation is important and being the first to acquire the latest design or limited edition is highly motivating. It's also worth pointing out that the punitive working-hours culture in Asia means that although the Golden Misses have money to burn, the same cannot be said for their time. Therefore, brands must consider their online presence, and how they can create a seamless browsing-to-purchase experience. They could reward their audience with unique 'backstage' access, such as virtual changing rooms that enable the user to virtually try before she buys. These are all ways in which to court a Golden Miss.

Aside from indulging their rampant consumerism, financial services brands should be alive to the Child Free and the Golden Miss, enabling her to plan responsibly for her future, which may or may not include a husband or children. Encouraging her to invest her money wisely will enable her to protect the lifestyle to which she is accustomed. Given women live longer, particularly in Asia, and the importance of financial independence to this audience, financial planning and an investment strategy are critical, yet the industry has been slow to respond. In a global BCG survey, some 71 per cent of women were unhappy with their financial service provider.[51] Courting a female audience means more than just launching a rose-covered credit card: yes, a bank in Asia actually thought this constituted 'marketing to women'. High net worth women have different investment priorities, they are more goal oriented, they are more interested in wealth preservation, and they invest in more tangible assets, for example, art, property and luxury goods.[52] This is a cohort with a high disposable income, making them a prime investment audience, which opens up the opportunity of enabling them to protect and maximise the impact of their earnings. It's time that more financial service providers were alive to this idea.

CHAPTER 6

. . . .

Women and Sex

'You cannot decree women to be sexually free when they're not economically free.' **Shere Hite**

While we have discussed something of the social and economic revolution happening for women, it's worth looking at how attitudes towards women's sexuality have changed, and are still evolving. In a very well-discussed phenomenon: the pill decoupled the link between sex and procreation, an essential part of women's sexual liberation. But it seems that as a culture in some ways we're still getting our heads around the idea of women as sexual beings, particularly when we consider older women: for the film world read 'women over the age of 25'.

It's not just the pill that has promoted behavioural change. Rising divorce rates among the over-fifties have led to a thriving boomer dating scene, not to mention a spike in STIs. A 2017 study by the *Lancet* identified that one in six new cases of HIV infection was among the over-fifties.[1] Online or mobile-enabled 'dating' has deformalised relationships, and online porn has dramatically changed sexual practices, particularly for the teen audience, with a call for sex education in schools to play catch up: a 2017 British study by FPA sexual health charity found that 78 per cent of parents felt that schools should be teaching children about subjects related to porn.[2] Putting the impact of popular culture to one side, governmental policies have also created a ripple effect on our sexual behaviour; the unintended consequence of China's one-child policy has seen a fundamental shift in attitudes towards premarital sex. According to recent research conducted by sexologist Li Yinhe, approximately 71 per cent of respondents engaged in premarital sex as compared to a scant 15 per cent in 1989.[3] It's only relatively recently that premarital sex was legalised in China (1997), so these attitudes represent quite a rapid evolution of modern morality.

Equally important is the ongoing revolution in terms of women's relationship with sex, and their sense of empowerment or even entitlement. The idea that sex is no longer linked to children means not only that women have the right to enjoy sex, it's not merely a means to a fertile end, and significantly women can engage in and enjoy sex well past their fertile years: they don't have to retreat into 'early retirement'.

ATTITUDES TOWARDS SEX AND SEXUALITY

We probed the topic of sex and sexuality within our Women's Index survey, and the results revealed a few surprises. Firstly, we looked at the idea of sexual empowerment: globally 57 per cent of women say they feel sexually empowered, but this rose to 61 per cent in Asia Pacific, with Western world countries among the lowest at only 53 per cent in the UK and 54 per cent in the US. So much for the 'progressive Western world'. With the exception of Japan, where only 36 per cent of women felt sexually empowered, most countries in Asia Pacific ranked either equal or significantly above the West: in Taiwan 92 per cent of women felt sexually empowered, Hong Kong 83 per cent and Vietnam 77 per cent. Perhaps linked to this idea was the fact that women in Asia were much more likely to feel that they could use their attractiveness or femininity as a means of power and influence: 57 per cent of women expressed this sentiment in the region compared to only 48 per cent of women in the rest of the world, illustrating the phenomenon of 'soft power' prevalent among Asian women. When we delved into the idea of femininity among women in Asia Pacific, as mentioned they were much more comfortable reconciling more polar personality traits such as 'ruthlessness', 'fearlessness' and 'aggression' with softer more traditionally feminine traits, for example, 'patience' and 'gracefulness'.

For all this so-called 'soft power' and sexual empowerment, however, Asian women were significantly less likely to subscribe to the idea of premarital sex, with 53 per cent of women in Asia perceiving 'no sex before marriage' as an outdated idea, compared to 65 per cent of women in the rest of the world. Perhaps unsurprisingly, women in China were the most conservative with only 45 per cent feeling that sex outside of marriage was permissible. So, despite studies showing that premarital sex was prevalent in China, it's not publicly embraced or acknowledged.

In part, these conservative cultural attitudes contribute to the lower birth rates across Asia, meaning that unmarried women are much more likely to live alone rather than cohabit, and as a result many younger career-focused women in Asia are eschewing marriage and children, leading to a plunging birth rate. It's important to note, however, that this conservatism towards sex outside of marriage was much more prevalent among the older generation in Asia Pacific. When we compared millennials, attitudes were much more consistent with women in the rest of the world, so while 59 per cent of Asia's millennials and 63 per cent of millennials outside of Asia felt 'no sex before marriage' was an outdated concept, this plummeted to 48 per cent among Asian baby-boomers. Meanwhile, two-thirds of baby-boomers in the rest of the world supported premarital sex, meaning that, outside Asia, baby-boomers were the most progressive when it comes to sex before marriage, and more open-minded than millennials. Given that this is the generation who lived through the sexual revolution in the 1960s, maybe we shouldn't be so surprised.

Intriguingly, though, we observed that, while in Asia Pacific millennials were more liberal than older generations, in the rest of the world, and particularly the UK, this dynamic was reversed: namely millennials had the most conservative attitudes of all the generations towards premarital sex, and were significantly less likely to admit to a 'one-night stand' versus older Generation X women. This is perhaps indicative of a generation growing up among economic and social turbulence and more likely to embrace more 'old-fashioned' values, retreating to the safety of tradition. This also seems to chime with a new study that points to the teen audience becoming less sexually active versus a decade ago, with the US Center for Disease Control & Prevention reporting a near 20 per cent decline in teen sex.[4]

EMPOWERMENT VERSUS FULFILMENT

For all the sexual empowerment in Asia Pacific, women in the region were less likely to consider sexual fulfilment as important: 55 per cent of women in Asia felt this was important compared to 68 per cent outside of Asia. In Asia Pacific, the importance of sexual fulfilment declined sharply with age: 63 per cent of millennials felt it was important, declining to 56 per cent among Generation X and then 46 per cent among baby-boomers.

In the rest of the world, sexual fulfilment was just as important to millennial and Generation X women, with 74 per cent in agreement, declining to 56 per cent among baby-boomers. This illustrates the fact that, in the West certainly, older women are starting to embrace and prioritise their own sexual needs. Those countries where sexual fulfilment was most important (with 80 per cent of women or above in agreement) and most consistent across the generations were 'Latin' cultures, for example Brazil, and Mediterranean countries such as Italy and Lebanon. Indeed, women in Brazil, Lebanon and, curiously, Russia, were significantly more likely to claim to have had more than ten sexual partners. Almost universally it was Generation X members across all countries that were significantly more likely to have had more than ten sexual partners, far above millennials or baby-boomers. Brazil was almost the only country where more liberal attitudes or behaviours towards the number of sexual partners were consistent across generations.

At the same time, while baby-boomers in Asia Pacific may not personally prioritise their own sexual needs, there is universal agreement globally that sexual fulfilment is 'not just for the young', with 75 per cent of women in Asia Pacific and 78 per cent of women in the rest of the world subscribing to this idea, and the belief consistent across all age groups in all geographies. So, reassuringly women around the world almost universally believe that sex isn't just for the young: it's an enduring and important part of women's lives.

SEX AND THE OLDER WOMAN

Although still unusual, we are now starting to witness women presented as sexual beings well into their seventies and beyond. A great example here is *Grace and Frankie*, the hit Netflix series starring Jane Fonda and Lilly Tomlin, with one notable episode featuring their foray into entrepreneurship: making vibrators for older women, a moment that hit the headlines and seeded the idea in the public consciousness that perhaps older women were not done with sex just yet.

In fact, 2015 marked the US Food and Drug Administration (FDA) approval of Flibanserin, the female equivalent of Viagra aimed squarely at pre-menopausal women suffering with low libido. The journey towards approval was plagued with difficulties, including concerns surrounding side effects, but women's advocate bodies such as 'Even the Score' have lobbied vigorously for female sexual dysfunction to receive the same prioritisation as male dysfunction, when on average more US women than men suffer from sexual dysfunction, affecting up to 43 per cent of women.[5] There remains marked disparity in the prioritisation and treatment, so while the FDA has 26 drugs approved for male dysfunction, until recently the figure for women was zero. So, if you subscribe to the belief that sex is a fundamental human right, as endorsed by the World Health Organization (WHO), then you will understand the efforts that have to be made to redress the balance in research and treatment, even if drugs aren't always the answer.

A 2013 worldwide study by the WHO decried the paucity of research as regards women: 'Although the data are sparse, the importance of sexual health among older women is becoming increasingly evident.'[6] Equally, a ruling by the European Court of Human Rights in 2017 overturned the judgement that 'older women have less interest in sex', and awarded compensation to a 50-year-old woman who, following negligent surgery in Portugal, was unable to engage in sex. This set an important precedent that older women are entitled to both engage in and enjoy sex.

The quest for sexual equality, however, has been plagued by setbacks, and from some surprising quarters. For example, some commentators point the finger to the supposed feminist advocates behind 'female Viagra' as simply Big Pharma-sponsored lobbyists, and are quick to suggest that the pharmaceutical industry is cynically looking to repeat the success of Viagra. Personally, I find that comments like 'feminism is all the Viagra I will ever need'[7] miss the point here, because undoubtedly women approaching menopause do experience a perceptible decline in libido, and patting them on the head and telling them to busy themselves with their grandchildren is as helpful as the empty panacea of 'you go girl' feminism: empowerment alone is not a universal cure. If we're telling women that sexual fulfilment is their inalienable right no matter their age, then we have to offer the appropriate 'treatment' and support if this isn't happening for them: so, sorry, but sometimes 'the drugs do work'.

Increasingly women are expecting to remain sexually active throughout life, and a US research study revealed that 60 per cent of women over 60 years and in relationships continued to be sexually active, and sexual satisfaction experienced among 60- and 70-year-old women was similar to those women in their thirties and forties.[8] Interestingly, researcher Dr Holly Thomas discovered that those women sexually active in their sixties and beyond were not necessarily in committed relationships, with 13 per cent active but without a 'steady romantic partner', busting the myth of the 'golden couple'.

In wider popular culture, however, the 60-plus woman is often represented as sexually inert, and there is a rich cinematic tradition of representing women in this demographic as 'saintly mothers and asexual mothers'.[9] While US cinema is starting to embrace the idea of later-life sexuality (*Hope Springs, Something's Gotta Give*), the UK and Ireland lag behind, as concluded by a recent research study: 'midlife sexuality is absent in the vast majority of films produced in Britain and Ireland'.[10]

In *Something's Gotta Give* (2003), we had the familiar pairing of an older man, as played by Jack Nicholson, with a younger woman, but we also saw the more unfamiliar idea of a younger man (Keanu Reeves) sexually infatuated with an older woman (Diane Keaton): she becomes the sexual magnet. In earlier Hollywood, there seems to have been more of an acceptance of a female-to-male age gap. In *All about Eve* (1950), for example, Bette Davis's character Margo Channing is paired with a partner eight years her junior, and is positively encouraged in the match, and in *The Graduate*, Anne Bancroft oozes sex appeal as the 40-something Mrs Robinson, irresistible to 21-year-old Ben. In contemporary popular culture this older sexual magnet has earned publicity if not notoriety as 'The Cougar'.

PLIGHT OF THE COUGAR

If we believe the headlines then there is a whole cohort of fifty-something single women dating up a storm with younger men. These financially independent women are confident, sexually liberated, educated and not in a hurry to settle down, as perhaps epitomised in cartoonish form as 'Samantha' in *Sex and the City*. And it's their independence, experience and confidence that renders them particularly appealing to men.

The reality? Not so much. It is becoming increasingly socially acceptable for women to date younger men – Sam Taylor-Johnson, Jennifer Lopez, Demi Moore, Brigitte Macron and Madonna are notable trailblazers – but these are iconic and some would say ageless women, with huge personal power and influence. Who wouldn't want to be part of their social orbit? For ordinary mortals the experience can be quite different, and men even of the same age may not perceive them as a potential mate because many men seek younger women: cast your eye over men's dating preferences on online dating platforms to see this dynamic repeatedly confirmed.

Firstly, let's examine the term 'Cougar', which for some women is derisory and negative, not exactly celebratory of the midlife woman. At the same time, there are women seeking to reclaim the Cougar as a more positive empowered label, even spawning the emergence of Cougar dating sites (Cougarlife.com, Toyboydates.com).

Is the notion of Cougars so new anyway? A trawl through the 1800 Census data by Ancestry.co.uk revealed that there were twice as many couples with an age gap of ten years or more, and frequently women were the older partner. One has to bear in mind, however, that war and disease resulted in a generation of older available women, for whom marriage presented their only means to financial security, so pragmatism to a degree could underline the statistics. Still, it's slightly unsettling that modern society is now somewhat less tolerant of 'inter-generational' relationships where women are the older partner, and the Cougar woman faces a challenge when it comes to the dating behaviour of many men.

Numerous studies point to the fact that heterosexual men are consistently attracted to women in their twenties, and while women are more open-minded about the age of a potential partner, the same cannot be said for men.[11] The reason for this is assumed to be in part linked to women's fertility. I feel it only fair to point out, however, that men do this in blissful ignorance of the fact that their fertility, namely the quality and viability of their sperm, declines with age, leading researchers to suggest that women in their forties keen to get pregnant should likewise seek men in their twenties. In what has been charmingly dubbed 'The Cougar Phenomenon', scientists concluded that women in their forties will find it much harder to conceive with a partner of their own age,[12] with some postulating that this may well lead to an increase in Cougar dating behaviour. For men, female biology or fertility would appear to exert a marked influence on behaviour. An analysis of over 10 million online dating conversations by Dale Markowitz, a researcher at Okcupid, revealed that 61 per cent of 'successful' interactions occurred between men and women where the women were at least five years younger than the male partner.[13]

To my mind the reasons underlining men's proclivity for younger mates is far more complex, and reflects the idea of the partner as social or sexual status ('the trophy wife'), years of social conditioning, power and control (for example, the traditional model of male as primary breadwinner), and the fear of ageing. In short: the usual stuff. While I do not wish to sit in judgement, having spent my own time on dating websites, but this phenomenon is something of a frustration in the sense of how pervasive it is. Equally frustrating is the degree to which this behaviour is considered 'normal' or justifiable among men is frustrating, while women earn the special 'Cougar' label. Witness the online messaging behaviour of men, who focus their attention towards women even younger than their stated 'minimum' age preference: in some cases, this behaviour has spawned the 'age shaming' of men who are seeking ridiculously young women,[14] yet in societal terms this barely raises an eyebrow. The facts are this: men are much more 'predatory' among younger women than women among younger men, they are the true 'Cougars', but culturally it's less acceptable behaviour in women.

A further dynamic for midlife women on the dating scene to contend with – if we believe the headlines – is the new dating etiquette for older women. According to a recent article in the *Telegraph*, while men are willing to 'invest' in younger women, they expect older partners to 'go dutch' on dates. Chivalry, it would appear, has a sell-by date. To complete the picture, London psychiatrist Jane Morrow reports of her older female clients: 'they feel that not only are men taking advantage financially, but in this competitive environment, with younger women a continuous threat, they worry they can't afford to maintain that groomed and perfect look that is their one advantage.'[15] So far, so depressing, but things are changing. It's not all doom and gloom for the older woman.

Over in Japan, a culture previously obsessed with youth and beauty, and the cult of '*kawaii*' or cuteness, until recently only young women had a decent shot at the dating scene, but that is changing with the emergence of the 'Beauty Witches' or '*Bimajyo*'.

MEET THE BEAUTY WITCH

In Asia there is a new female tribe: she's in her forties to fifties but appears much younger … no, make that 'startlingly young'. Apparently, in Japan they call these women *Bimajyo* – Beauty Witch. It is said that the *Bimajyo* has to be an intellectual mature woman who looks younger than her age, continuously strives for improving her beauty and fashion sense, and always has a curiosity to learn things. The term was first coined by *Bisuto* magazine in 2009 in an attempt to democratise beauty and redefine beauty ideals beyond the obsession with youth.

While little is known yet about the size of the demographic, what we do know is that she's an extreme consumer of beauty and wellbeing products and an influencer for her peers. The Beauty Witch phenomenon, while relatively new, is hard to ignore. There is even a *Bimajyo* beauty contest in Japan, which is sponsored by a popular Japanese woman's magazine, and in 2013 winner Mayumi Nishimura was whittled down from over 2,500 entrants.

The Beauty Witch strives to maintain her youthfulness via a holistic programme of diet, fitness, supplements and beauty products. In keeping with the Japanese beauty consumer's love of ritual and routine, typically she may spend up to five hours a day on her beauty regime, consuming huge quantities of products, for example twenty bottles of facial toner per month.[16] With little time to focus on anyone but herself, I'd call her a true hedonist. Collagen, consume orally, is a key ingredient in her beauty repertoire. For years, collagen has been widely used in various types of cosmetic surgery, as a healing aid for burn patients, for reconstructing bones and ligaments, and in a number of dental and orthopaedic procedures.

Of course, all of this doesn't necessarily mean that drinking collagen will result in better skin, thicker hair, stronger teeth and healthier bones, and the scientific consensus on the benefits of liquid supplements remains undecided. This hasn't stopped Japanese health and beauty companies from packaging the stuff and selling it in bulk to the consumer, netting millions of dollars of profit each year.

In Tokyo, you can buy bottles containing 10,000mg of collagen dissolved in a vitamin-and-mineral packed peach-flavoured solution for approximately $2 (230 yen). And remarkably, you don't even have to go to a specialty shop to buy the product. In Japan, as a traditional culture, women's societal currency is still largely based on her appearance: more attractive women tend to get better jobs, better earnings and further in their careers, therefore the fear of ageing and the loss of attractiveness is understandable, and in some cases drives extreme behaviours in the pursuit of youth. Yet there is an upside to the Beauty Witch phenomenon, which is the decoupling of extreme youth and beauty, in a sense democratising beauty and allure as belonging to any age and ultimately female sexuality as a lifelong concept.

A COUGAR FUTURE?

In reality, there are signs of a gender rebalancing, certainly when it comes to the issue or acceptability of an age gap in relationships. In the research conducted by Okcupid, Markowitz noticed an interesting dynamic: where messages were initiated by women to younger men the outcomes were more successful versus if she had approached an older man. To be successful in making the first move, a forty-something woman was twice as likely to elicit a reply if she messaged a man in his twenties versus a man in his fifties, at around a 60 per cent reply rate. Psychologists have concluded, as older women tend to have greater financial independence and earning power, that makes for a relationship of equivalence rather than the more traditional male financial dominance, and a study in 2008 into age-gap relationships concluded that those pairings where the woman was ten years older were often happier and more committed.[17]

DOES AN AGE GAP EVEN OUT THE POWER BALANCE?

From our own data, we saw in the Women's Index study that almost half of women around the world were happy dating a partner younger than themselves, with trends consistent across geographies: so, this was a universal phenomenon. At the same time, around one in four women said they would actively prefer a partner younger than themselves, and this was slightly more prevalent among Generation X women. Interestingly we saw a consistent trend between those countries where women were most likely to feel sexually empowered and yet less likely to prefer a younger partner; this pattern was replicated across nearly all 19 countries in our study with the marked exception of Japan. But let me put it another way, in those countries where women felt the least sexually empowered, they were more likely to actively prefer a younger partner, leading us to hypothesise that perhaps a relationship with a younger man is a good way to even out the power dynamic.

THE NEW DATING CULTURE

Having discussed sexuality for midlife women, it's worth considering what's happening at the other end of the age spectrum. Things have changed since I was a twentysomething singleton, but 'change' doesn't really quite characterise the new app-enabled dating scene. Think what a stir *The Rules* created when published in 1995.[18] The idea of waiting for him to call and not accepting a date less than 48 hours in advance – this was dating in the 'slow lane', and in that sense dating apps have changed everything. *The Rules* feels positively arcane when set against the almost transactional speed-dating of the Tinder generation. A few statistics to consider: since its launch in 2012, Tinder has amassed

50 million users worldwide, 79 per cent of whom are millennials; 1.6 billion daily 'swipes' result in 26 million matches, every day.[19] While it's reputed that one-third of marriages in the US begin online, there is also a curious impermanence to the 'relationships' offered through apps like Tinder.

We now live in the era of the hook up, where a date can be ordered like pizza, and in some respects the 'swipe if you like' rule has evened the playing field a little in terms of the dating power balance because girls get to choose or reject the boys too; 63 per cent of women dating online said that they felt empowered and able to be more selective about a potential partner.[20] Let's not pretend, though, that Tinder relies on personality questionnaires and psychographics: it's a visual medium, where your picture says everything about you; it's survival of the 'fittest' using the contemporary meaning of 'fit'. And it's horribly addictive. A survey by Match.com revealed that one in six singles reported feeling 'addicted' to the process, and this was significantly more prevalent among millennials.[21] Arguably this, combined with the pornification of culture, exerts the dual pressure of holding up impossible ideals of beauty and sexual prowess for the teenage to millennial generation. What one can observe is the increasingly fluid nature of young relationships or, more appropriately, 'encounters', in which 'love' is much less enshrined. Thanks to the visual communication afforded through smartphones and dating apps, a dater almost becomes their own brand using self-promotion through the medium of the 'selfie' and Instagram as a means of attracting followers and admirers.

I'm not the first person to write about this, but an interesting phenomenon we are witnessing is the idea of sexuality as power among young women, who at one time would be expected to be the docile recipients of male attention and are now much more actively and powerfully engaged in the dating game. And, indeed, the nature or rules of the game itself have changed. In reference to the end of the 'life script', perhaps this is best exemplified by what I term the 'Modern Courtesan'.

THE MODERN COURTESAN

From WAGs (wives and girlfriends of footballers) to sugar-daddy dating, young women are entering into 'arrangements' that essentially trade their social and sometimes sexual services for financial benefits: essentially they are the 'Modern Courtesan'. And don't make the mistake of assuming these women are brainless – some 40 per cent of the women using one UK sugar-daddy dating service are said to be studying at Cambridge or Oxford. What's significant is that while the courtesan of old was compelled into the lifestyle as her only means of support, today's courtesan is making an active and she would say empowered choice. Like it or not, to her this is postmodern feminism.

So, what is a Modern Courtesan? Broadly speaking she could be described as a young woman who willingly and knowingly exchanges her social or sexual engagement for financial reward. Such arrangements may have a contractual agreement or they may be more informal, e.g. WAGs, but by entering into such an arrangement her only paid employment is that of 'courtesan'. In our study, we defined her as a single millennial with a belief that she can use her femininity as a means of power and influence, and a transient attitude towards relationships: for her love isn't the be-all and end-all, and she doesn't expect a relationship to last forever. Across all countries Modern Courtesans accounted for roughly 10 per cent of our sample, rising to 14 per cent across Asia and peaking at 24 per cent in Lebanon and Egypt – granted, however, that we used a looser definition than the particular behaviours I describe here. The point remains that women are prepared to use their femininity and attractiveness as a means of power and assertion: sexuality feels much less passive today.

The phenomenon has spawned dating websites specifically tasked with facilitating these arrangements, perhaps the most notorious of which is SugarDaddy.com, and seems to be most prevalent in the UK and the US, yet boasts over 10 million active members worldwide. However, a quick Google search reveals sugar-daddy dating sites in Australia and across Europe.

To some feminists the idea of the Modern Courtesan counters every instinct and smacks of disempowerment, handing over the financial reins and therefore power to her sugar daddy. However, the Modern Courtesan herself takes a somewhat different view: she sees herself as entirely empowered, it is she who has control over whom she dates and for how long. If she decides to terminate the arrangement – then that is her decision. In this sense the Modern Courtesan would argue that she is making an active and informed choice, to quote one such woman, 'I am happy being me. I am happy living this life, choosing this path, deciding things for myself, having the independence to live and enjoy everything. You can call it selfish, or maybe I have reached the level where it's hard to turn back anymore. It's very hard indeed.'[22] According to another Modern Courtesan in a *GQ* article, 'I don't want to deal with the dramas and the effort that you have to go through with having a normal relationship. This is very drama-free.'[23]

SeekingArrangement.com founder Brandon Wade has a slightly different perspective. He feels his site's popularity is born out of the impact of gender equality, that the advent of empowered independent women has left men wanting for a role. According to Wade, quoted in the same *GQ* article, 'Gentlemen are a dying breed, especially in America. I think there's this feeling that women have gone through a lot to fight for feminist rights, and now they are, indeed, equals. But they've lost something along the way ... This is what draws a lot of women to the site, and I think being taken care of by a stronger man is – deep down – what a lot of women really long for.'

So, what drives an otherwise emancipated and educated young women to enter into such an arrangement? The Modern Courtesans would claim they are empowered and making an active choice, free from coercion. A frequent justification centres on the sense of entitlement – 'Why shouldn't I be rewarded or benefit from my looks, in the same way that others benefit from their natural intellectual talents?' Others view it as a pragmatic choice to fund university tuition fees – harmless 'fun' before real-life kicks in, perhaps reflective of the modern attitudes towards relationships, namely their more transient and informal make-up. In the UK, the sugar-daddy dating site Seekingarrangement.com reported that 35 per cent of its 50,000 members were university students, therefore suggesting that Courtesans have aspirations beyond their current 'arrangement', which is very much temporary.

A key feature of the Modern Courtesan is that, whereas historically women pursued such an arrangement with the long-term desire of marriage and security, she values her independence, and perceives it as either a lifestyle choice or, as suggested, a temporary life stage. An uncomfortable irony is that historically many poorer women denied access to work by the prevailing societal rules were compelled into courtesanship (or worse) to earn a living – choice was not an option. Today's empowered and educated courtesans are free to work but choose not to.

What unites women of this particular tribe is their assertion that this is postmodern feminism: they are simply getting on in the world by virtue of their natural 'talents' and beauty, empowerment on their own terms. For them their role as courtesans is a repositioning of female emancipation and empowerment for the modern (consumer) age.

Dr Brooke Magnanti aka Belle de Jour, the 'infamous' blogger and former escort, reignited the debate with her opinions about whether it's a woman's right and choice to sell sex or a role she is forced into based on poverty and misfortune. Part of her argument centres on the idea that feminism comes in all shapes and forms and needs to be redefined in the modern age. She opined: 'Up until November 2009 [when she outed herself as 'Belle du Jour'], I would have said I was a feminist. Then I found out the hard way that feminism in this country is like the Ivy League: it's mostly filled with the sort of people you spent your school years avoiding.'[24] Key detractors, Germaine Greer the most outspoken, would argue that this takes feminism back a hundred years and objectifies and exploits women. Similarly, commentator Rachel Tan remarked on the 'WAG' phenomenon: 'The relationship between a WAG and her partner seems too often comprised of a mutual exploitation, where the woman capitalises on her partner's successes and pays the price by turning a blind eye to his indiscretions, by long periods of loneliness and constant pressure to remain a certain shape. Yet there is something distinctly unsatisfactory about this particular brand of female empowerment.'[25]

To build on the darker side of the Modern Courtesan, we should examine South Africa where it's reported that up to 24 per cent of schoolgirls are HIV positive, as compared to 4 per cent of boys the same age. The epidemic is attributed to sugar daddies exploiting young girls, according to Minister of Health Aaron Motsoaledi. The minister also highlighted the soaring rates of teen pregnancies and abortions.

If reports are to be believed, it would appear that the modern-day South African 'Professor Higgins' is leaving a corrosive legacy for young South African women seeking to elevate themselves out of poverty, and courtesanship may not be the empowering, informed choice for all women. And these courtesans mirror the history of the courtesan, are women with little choice compelled into the role as her only means of financial security. So courtesanship as an assertion of postmodern feminism is the preserve of the affluent and educated classes only. In this respect, i.e. power and self-determination being the preserve of the wealthy, very little has changed.

While we consider the relationship and sexual power dynamic, another way in which women are exerting their influence is the advent of 'the female gaze' in the portrayal of female sexuality.

THE FEMALE GAZE

While more women are breaking into the film industry, both in front of and behind the camera, the same is true for women in the sex tech and porn industry. Whereas before, porn was constructed with the primary aim of pleasing men, as the core audience, the industry has at last recognised that women like sex too, and it's estimated that women make up one in three of the viewing audience. While Candida Royalle had to earn her 'stripes' in front of the camera before moving behind it in the 1980s as reputedly the first female porn director, there are many more women these days behind the camera, with a new genre of 'feminist porn' emerging. Feminist porn has been described in some quarters as a form of 'erotic activism' seeking to reimagine gender norms, power constructs and sexuality; at its most elemental it seeks to give equal emphasis to female pleasure. What differentiates the female gaze within the porn industry is obviously a more empowering narrative, but also more relatable and diverse casting, not the hyperreal surgically enhanced male fantasy, with all its toxic ripple effects on the young and impressionable.

Women are also moving into the sex-tech industry, albeit encumbered by the issue of largely male and therefore prudish venture capital investor panels to contend with, and all the implied barriers to funding. Companies such as Unbound Box, House of Plume and Happy Playtime, all created by female founders, have one crucial ingredient: the prioritisation of female satisfaction, and in a world where women make up at least half of all sex-toy purchasers, then 'servicing' this audience presents a lucrative opportunity that has previously been largely ignored.[26] When Janet Lieberman, an MIT graduate, set up her own sex-toy company (as you do), Dame Products, she was startled by the lack of research into female sexuality, or even basic anatomical research. Similarly, OMGYes, an online platform founded by Lydia Daniller and devoted to female sexual pleasure, has filled the gap (no pun intended) by commissioning its own research in collaboration with academic bodies, their purpose being to demystify, destigmatise and educate around the female orgasm.

Undoubtedly these platforms will collectively help to establish female sexuality in the public consciousness. Allow me to suggest, however, that it's a little sad that the work of private investors is filling the gulf that should be addressed by academic and medical research bodies, for if we knew more about female sexuality, anatomy and sexual dysfunction, women collectively might feel more sexually empowered. When we look at our Women's Index data, only 19 per cent of women globally agree 'strongly' that they are sexually empowered, with between one in three and one in four women feeling unsure of their sexuality to some degree, and only one in three women feel they have control over their body.[27] Despite decades of progress, therefore, when it comes to women and sex, we have some way to go before we achieve true equality and control, but given that the global female sex-toy market is expected to experience growth of up to 11 per cent by 2021, this will persuade more companies to invest.[28]

FEMALE PLEASURE AND HEDONISM

A common element uniting the Cougar, Modern Courtesans and the theme of the female gaze is the idea of female empowerment or, more specifically, female pleasure and focus on the self, as opposed to what is culturally expected from women – a suppression of one's own needs in favour of those around us. Women are rarely given licence to prioritise or please themselves and get very little permission even from an early age to be 'selfish' or self-regarding: it's part of our nurturing to consider others first. In popular culture we rarely if ever see a woman enjoying leisure time, unless of course she's selling a chocolate bar, in which case it's a few guilty moments of pleasure hidden away, lounging in a bathtub scoffing Belgian chocolate: the implicit message – she is naughty for being selfish. When was the last time you watched a film and saw two women sitting on a couch, feet up with a bottle of beer: this never happens.

For us, therefore, it felt important to highlight the existence of what we call the 'hedonist' tribes, firstly to demonstrate their existence, the idea that women are and can be self-regarding, but also to use their existence to drive new models of female representation in culture. It's time we saw women pleasing themselves, having leisure time and prioritising their own needs.

THE HEDONISTS

We defined hedonist tribes as those women who prioritised the self, and unlike alphas career advancement was not their core vision of success: pleasure, adventure, and social and sexual fulfilment were their primary motivations. As further evidence of women's new role in society, hedonists were not a small minority in our sample. In fact, they numbered some 43 per cent of our sample globally: the second-largest 'master tribe' behind the 'alphas'.

While we have touched on Cougars, Beauty Witches and Modern Courtesans as key hedonist tribes, the 'Explorers' and 'Pleasure Seekers' were the other significant hedonist tribes.

For Pleasure Seekers, the clue is in the name: they prioritise taking care of themselves, and their social and sexual fulfilment. Success to them is defined as following their dreams, having fun and a stress-free life. Explorers, meanwhile, are motivated by broadening their horizons and seeing the world – perhaps reflecting the degree to which technology and social media have made us feel like global citizens. Success to the Explorer is defined as being active, travelling the world, taking risks and challenging herself: think of her as a female Indiana Jones, and we rarely see those in popular culture. Together the Explorers and Pleasure Seekers accounted for a quarter of our sample and were particularly prevalent in India: confounding some of the cultural stereotypes.

In fact, looking at India specifically, Pleasure Seekers accounted for 14 per cent of our sample and Explorers 23 per cent; demographically they present as an educated millennial audience, and reflect the new generation of Indian women who are self-determined and prepared to challenge traditional expectations of femininity.

HEDONISM MEETS ACTIVISM

To see that India is changing, one only has to witness for example the growth of women in motorcycling and motorcycle clubs, which although a global phenomenon is nonetheless significant in India with the emergence of, for example, the Bikerni all-women motorcycle club. According to the Bikerni's website, the club champions equality, breaking records and making history, which sounds a lot like the 'Explorer' mentality. But there's something more significant at the heart of the Bikerni's philosophy: they are explorers, yes, but also activists, and their rallies and even their presence is a symbol of women's independence and desire to feel safe on the streets. For all women's progress in India, this is a country where women contend with, on the one hand, a 'benign patriarchy' in the form of laws designed to protect women, but in reality curtail freedoms, and, on the other hand, a very real threat to personal safety. In a *Times of India* survey, 96 per cent of women in Delhi didn't feel safe after sunset, and 70 per cent of students on Delhi University's female campus don't feel safe after dark – even with the police around: which suggests much about institutionalised sexism and a culture in which, for all their education and empowerment, women face significant challenges.[29]

Despite the challenges, Indian women are also starting to assert their sexual freedom. The Pleasure Seeker tribe is a case in point, and from our Women's Index survey, one in four Indian women claimed to have had a 'one-night stand',[30] and since launching in India, Tinder has reported a 400 per cent increase in users with women outnumbering men. Equally, hotels like StayUncle are popping up, enabling young couples to navigate the strict cultural taboos, namely premarital sex: although there is no law prohibiting premarital sex, unmarried couples are frequently refused rooms, and even attacked by self-appointed 'moral police' in public. Since its launch, StayUncle is now present across 20 cities offering 'rooms not judgement'. StayUncle delivers a service to 'hedonism', offering rooms by the hour, yet at the same time, like Bikerni, a quiet activism, through their blog StayUncle which educates on safe sex and equally female sexuality, debunking the myth that women don't or shouldn't enjoy the act as much as men.

WHAT THIS MEANS:
KEY TAKEAWAYS FOR BRANDS

Perhaps the most significant conclusion to draw here is that for women the pursuit of pleasure, of gratifying the self sexually or otherwise, is no longer 'off limits'. We have an equal right to be satisfied and to be selfish, and popular culture needs to catch up with this idea. Hedonism for women, it seems, is still relatively unchartered territory, certainly in the film world. Generally within the movie narrative, on the rare occasions that we do see a self-serving woman she will ultimately earn her comeuppance for her 'selfishness' because she subverts our comfortable social norms. The existence and abundance of hedonist tribes through our research, however, challenges the passive and wholly altruistic ideal of femininity, and I offer a future to the reader where women can be and are in pursuit of their own agenda, be that world exploration, pushing boundaries, taking risks and or having fun. Promoting this narrative through our communication will also serve to normalise it, and make it much more acceptable for women to prioritise the self, which is yet another way to further female empowerment.

Pleasure Seekers and Explorers: an untapped opportunity

In recognition of women's focus on the self, it's worth noting that the Pleasure Seekers and Explorers represent a prime and relatively underexploited opportunity for luxury brands, automotive market and travel companies – tuning into their desire for new experiences, broadening their horizons and pleasure in all shapes and forms. Both tribes are heavily millennial and are highly digitally enabled – particularly the Explorers – and one could say that the experience of the transaction should be as enjoyable as the purchase itself. Explorers, for example, present an interesting cohort for the sportier or off-road end of the automotive market, given their desire to assert their independence, seek adventure and take risks: yet consider how often this audience is assumed to be almost exclusively male. What these tribes demonstrate is that thrill-seeking and hedonism in all its forms are no longer the male preserve, and it's time that brands recognised this new and sizeable audience.

Sex and sexuality: not just for the young

The phenomenon of the 'Cougar' goes to emphasise the point that women are sexual beings and can be sexually assertive throughout life. A few of the more enlightened lingerie brands, for example Lonely lingerie in Australia, recognise that maybe women over the age of 40 aren't resigned to big knickers and beige corselettes as their undergarments of choice; recently Lonely featured women in their fifties resplendent in their creations, while Triumph lingerie have engaged Julianne Moore, aged 57, as a key campaign model.

Yet brands like Lonely and Triumph are still the exception to the rule. Society still struggles with the idea of an older woman as a sexual being, and yet here is a great opportunity for brands to move at the speed of culture and tune into this audience. The world of condoms and sex tech, for example, sex toys, still relies heavily on a narrative that puts men in charge, prioritises male satisfaction and equally focuses on youth. If the statistics are to be believed, then in reality it's the older generations and not millennials (despite Tinder) or teens for that matter who are getting it on in greater numbers and represent a huge (and one assumes enthusiastic) audience.[31]

If she's still conscious, she's fashion conscious

In the dynamic beauty world, cosmetic brands like L'Oréal deserve kudos for discussing the language of 'beauty' among women in their seventies and beyond, casting Jane Fonda, Diane Keaton and Helen Mirren as role models for not just the baby-boomers but women of any age, serving to democratise the notion of beauty and redefine it as an ageless concept. In Japan, meanwhile, women in their forties and beyond aspiring to the Beauty Witch ideals are potential 'super consumers' of beauty, presenting a highly lucrative and discerning audience. The language of ageing is starting to evolve, too, and the concept of beauty and older age being compatible has moved from cultural banishment through to acceptance, or more precisely 'ageing well'. After all, not everyone aspires to the overly Botoxed frozen 'rabbit in headlights' expression.

Yet, strangely, retail fashion still has some catching up to do, in designing or even accepting the existence of women over 40 with more than a passing interest in fashion. Iris Apfel is an idiosyncratic fashion icon in her tenth decade, but visible women like Iris are few and far between, and perhaps it shouldn't be as remarkable as it is when a woman over 40 steps down the fashion runway. It's not that women in their forties, fifties and beyond need 'special garments', easy-open or elastic waistbands for example, or for that matter that they make necessarily safer fashion choices wanting to retire into the background, yet their invisibility within the fashion pages is telling.

Through imagery, advertising and equally the instore service offering, enlightened retailers should recognise this audience as visible and also in possession of a sizeable disposable income. In the UK the over-fifties possess 69 per cent of all household wealth.[32] Beauty and fashion retailers need to stop writing off women as settled mothers after the age of 35, and dare I say magazines should get their head around the idea that a wealthy woman in her forties, fifties and beyond does not relate to a 13-year-old model wearing couture: wake up. fashionland. These are the women with the disposable income, but pre-pubescent is not a look they want to or can aim for. Thanks to student debt and housing price inflation, millennials, certainly in the West, are not the ones with the money. In China the reverse is true, but certainly in the UK and to a lesser degree the US, baby-boomers and boomers have the most spending power.

Towards empowered sexuality and the female gaze

In the same way that women are evolving, it would be reasonable to suggest that feminism and the idea of empowerment is evolving, too. Or at the very least we need to acknowledge that the concept of emancipation is continually being redefined and reinterpreted, otherwise we end up with just another set of rules by which to define female behaviour. The traditional 'life script' of 'find boyfriend, get married, have children' feels arcane, particularly to the millennial generation and with the arrival of Tinder. The relaxing of 'moral codes' towards sexual behaviour has achieved a profound shift in attitudes: clearly there are many facets to modern womanhood and the definition of feminism, and within that female sexuality. A key take is that it's no longer safe to assume that all young women aspire to marriage or even a long-term partner, so forcing these stereotypes upon her even implicitly within the advertising narrative may prove alienating and patronising.

What we can conclude is that there exists a cohort of self-determined and individualistic young women seeking not to conform to the conventions of traditional life and even morality. She interprets her femininity and sexuality as a means of power and assertiveness. What's significant about this cultural dynamic for marketers is the reframing of beauty as a passive means of attracting a husband towards a more active and empowered means of self-determination and expression. She may want a man, but she may not – and if she does it will be on her own terms.

What we can observe in the Modern Courtesan tribe and even among the Pleasure Seekers is that women are asserting their beauty and sexuality as a means of power and influence: beauty is no longer passive or submissive. It feels a missed opportunity that so many lingerie retailers, jewellery brands or other 'adornment' brands still frame the product as 'human gift-wrapping' with women as passive objects of male desire or even of male gifting when they could be presenting a much more powerful narrative or vision of femininity and female sexuality. Our research within the lingerie market revealed that women are significantly more likely to buy and wear lingerie for their own gratification, and wanted to see this reflected in communication. They also wanted to see greater diversity in terms of the age, ethnicity and size of models featured.

Good Hair Day (GHD), which specialises in hair straighteners, provides a great example of a brand aligned to this idea of female sexuality as power. Not for them the happy shiny altruistic notion of beauty: no, for GHD female beauty unlocks a dark powerful force. Their 'Modern Fairytales' campaign, where Snow White may reject the Prince to seek a better model, subverted the traditional narrative, putting the heroine in charge.

A further example of 'beauty as power' is the idea of 'the revenge body', the post break-up hot bod, publicised on Instagram (of course), with the prime intent of making your ex realise what a fool he or she has been. And notice it's revenge 'body': it used to be the case that you 'washed that man right out of your hair', but how empowering is that? In those days we had the post break-up haircut, but a new fringe is hardly going to scythe fear into your ex however forcefully you swish it. The revenge body is physical, visceral feminine power: it's not half-starved and winsome, it's firm, toned and hot, a weapon to be aimed. It may be born of pain, but it's used to inflict pain: that is interesting to me.

In a milder sense, Bobbi Brown's 'Pretty Powerful' campaign is born of the concept that beauty and femininity can be powerful, something of which to be proud. It discusses beauty not in the realms of hooking a mate (which used to be the way it worked) but in the sense of confidence and pride, yes pride. Again, it's not revolutionary, Estée Lauder espoused the idea that 'confidence breeds beauty', together with the idea that a woman could conquer the world with the right lipstick (ah, if that were true), but she has a point. Perhaps Ms Lauder was onto something because research does demonstrate that women with more 'feminine' facial features are perceived by both men and women as better, more competent leaders.[33] What I think we are witnessing is the recognition in femininity of innate power, that the two are indivisible, and one doesn't contradict or undermine the other. You can be a feminist and wear heels – I am in danger of being flippant here but, as women, we shouldn't shy away from beauty or think it will hold us back. There's a message within this that our beauty as women, our femininity, our sexuality, is a powerful gift and we shouldn't hide it, we should be proud of it and we should remind ourselves of this daily. This, to me, is part of female power.

CHAPTER 7

Religion Rewritten

'I regard irreligious people as pioneers. If there had been no priesthood the world would have advanced ten thousand times better than it has now.' **Anandibai Joshi**

Ah, Eve, naughty naughty Eve. You see, she ruined the party for everyone. Had it not been for her, women would not be spending a lifetime atoning for her sins. I'm being facetious, and to be clear, I don't speak as an atheist, I am a confirmed member of the Church of England, my husband is Jewish by birth, and I have enormous respect for religious practice. With one exception, and let me give you an indication as to what that is: first man on the moon, 1969; first female Church of England bishop, 2015. How is this possible or even conceivable when man and woman were allegedly created equal? The problem that I have, the thing that I find so hard to understand, is that will all the prevailing equal rights acts and legislation to prevent sexual discrimination, religion seems to have a special pass to ignore the idea. The Church of England and Catholic Church are essentially employers, so how is it justifiable to exclude women or curtail their advancement? Imagine the uproar if a FTSE 100 company instituted a policy that simply said no women could advance to C-Suite positions. Now, one might say with some justification that implicitly or tacitly some advancement within religious bodies is happening, and there would be truth to the assertion, but the point is that religion is somehow exempt. I'm not sure that's the message we want to give to society, and the last time I checked my ovaries had nothing to do with my ability to commune with the Divine One.

One has to assume that women are as equally spiritual as men, if not more, as suggested by data from Pew Research, and certainly, if we look back into history even as far back as Druid times, women played an important role in the foundation of religious practice. This is true the world over. It's said that Boudicca was descended from a Druid mother, who was also a '*bandrú*' or priestess.

An inconvenient truth that the Vatican may wish to ignore is the largely 'hidden history' of women in ministry in the medieval West, and references to women's ordination exists in ancient papal and theological texts, yet for all women's involvement how can it be that women were latterly excluded from positions of power within organised religion?

It's theorised that it was a reformation of the ordination process in eleventh and twelfth centuries that successfully barred women from ordination but also sought to airbrush them from history. Under new ordination rites, those ordained would not only have power within their community but 'wherever they chose to exercise it', so again we have the idea that once a profession grows in power and status, women are edged out, and we see the repetitive theme of women's absence or in this case removal from history.[1]

RELIGION AND INEQUALITY: A MATCH MADE IN HEAVEN?

Equally some social commentators and academics draw a link between women's subjugation within religion and corresponding disempowerment in society, in the sense that one lends tacit legitimacy to the other. There is also growing evidence that suggests religion thrives in economically unequal societies.[2] While the research supports a not unexpected link between those at the poorest end of society seeking comfort in religion, it also suggests that in economically polarised societies the most affluent become more religious in an attempt to justify and legitimise their 'elevated' position in society, suggesting that they are in fact 'the chosen ones'. This theory sheds a little light on Donald Trump's courtship of the religious right, perhaps, and it's worth pointing out that in the GINI Index of income inequality, the US ranks fortieth in the league of unequal societies, while the UK ranks at 111 next to Canada 112.[3] The US sits between Peru and Cameroon for income inequality. Research also demonstrates that American states with the highest income inequality are the most religious, and the reverse is also true, the more economically equal, the less religious.[4] So an argument exists that religion is in some cases 'used' to generate acceptance with our lot, to quell resistance and act as a pacifier, in the sense that a greater will is at work that we cannot or should not question.

ATHEISM VERSUS SEXISM

The link between religion and inequality means one can understand the existence of activist organisations such as Femen, atheist in philosophy, and seeking to publicly challenge religion's grip on cultural values and more specifically the rights of women. Femen's mission is to destroy patriarchy in all shapes or forms, and its members set their sights on the Church as one of the fundamental 'instruments' of women's subjugation. It's worth pointing out, however, that atheism doesn't preclude sexism, and there have been reports that sexism is 'rampant' in atheist communities, with many atheist conventions fielding all-male panels and actively excluding women, using a warped interpretation of Darwinian gender theory to suggest male superiority. The gender issue was highlighted when Richard Dawkins tweeted a video poking scorn on feminists, and Sam Harris, highly visible in the atheist movement, suggested, 'The atheist variable just has this – it doesn't obviously have this nurturing, coherence-building extra estrogen vibe that you would want by default if you wanted to attract as many women as men.'[5] It's funny because for a movement said to be built upon rationality and facts, some atheists are obviously ignorant to the fact that simple biological differences do not adequately explain atheism, nor are they proven to do so: to quote two eminent sociologists, Marta Trzebiatowska and Steve Bruce, 'nothing in the biological make-up of men and women ... explains the gendered difference in religiosity'.[6] Although data are scarce, across eight countries analysed by the Pew Research Center men were more likely to be atheist versus women: 59 per cent versus 41 per cent, yet it was more complex social and cultural factors hypothesised to underline the trend, for example, men's pressure on women to be religious as a means to control female sexuality.[7]

There are signs of change, however, both within the Church and without. According to Giselle Vincett's research, women are deserting traditional Christianity at a faster rate than men, and more women than men are seeking alternative spirituality, yet at the same time there is a movement of women who are seeking to drive reform within their own religious communities.[8]

RELIGION AND SPIRITUALITY: IMPORTANT BUT NOT AS IMPORTANT AS FRIENDSHIP

We asked women about their spiritual side within the Women's Index survey: more than two-thirds of women globally said that religion or spirituality was important to them, but this was outweighed by the importance of friendship and family, with nearly 90 per cent of women perceiving this as a greater priority. Yet only 18 per cent of women across Asia and 28 per cent of women outside of Asia described themselves as spiritual.

When we compared attitudes across generations, something quite surprising emerged from the data, the fact that millennials, particularly those outside of Asia, described themselves as more religious than the older generations, which put a bit of a dent in the stereotype of the pious little old lady. Equally millennials across Asia and the rest of the world were slightly more likely to say they practised their religion regularly, and subscribe to the belief that religion brought their family together.

To be a little provocative, when we looked at the role of technology in bringing family and friends together, tech trumped religion hands down. While 15 per cent of women globally saw the role of religion as social glue, more than 80 per cent of women felt that technology had brought them closer to their loved ones: this was a sentiment that held true across generations.[9] Equally, the idea that technology trumped religion in bringing people closer together was a belief firmly held across more traditionally religious cultures, for example, India, Saudi Arabia and the US, which in itself felt quite revelatory.

We also probed around the idea of religion and disempowerment: while religion was cited as a limit to the fulfilment of one's potential as a woman by only 4 per cent of the global sample, this ratcheted up to 11 per cent in India and Saudi Arabia, and 26 per cent in Lebanon. It was social conventions that were perceived as the more limiting, cited by 16 per cent of our global sample, and between 25 and 40 per cent of women across India and the Middle East.

So, what we observed in some part at least was an interesting dynamic in the role and social importance of religion and cultural norms. At the same time, there's also a cohort of women who are forging their own spiritual paths not necessarily aligned to traditional doctrines.

THE MODERN SPIRITUALISTS

There's a movement of women who are nurturing and defining their spiritual needs in their own terms not aligned with traditional religious bodies. We call them the 'Modern Spiritualists'. Within our Women's Index data, Modern Spiritualists accounted for around 9 per cent of our sample, and were particularly prevalent in the Philippines (37 per cent), South Africa (16 per cent) and the USA (13 per cent). In the UK, Modern Spiritualists constituted only 4 per cent of our sample. It seems we are not particularly spiritual in the UK; we were also significantly less likely versus the global average to say we practised religion regularly, reflecting what is a highly secular society.

In relation to the Modern Spiritualists, Timothy Shriver reported from the California Women's Conference:

> most of the women I spoke with don't feel empowered by religion, but they aren't letting that stop them. They're creating a new spirituality from within the shell of the old, discarding the parts that exclude and divide and replacing them with prayers, rituals, and readings drawn from every imaginable source ... I'm not exactly sure what to call this evolving spirituality of women, but I am sure it's real.[10]

This is something of a global trend. For example, *Happinez* is the second biggest-selling magazine in the Netherlands with a 300,000 print run – significant when you consider the average *Vogue* UK print run hovers around 50,000; and female luminaries such as Oprah tread a very public spiritual journey, and act as champions for women in their quest.[11]

In trying to account for this movement, consider that today's woman, increasingly empowered and potentially in a position of high responsibility, may find her personal or professional empowerment hard to reconcile with a traditional Church that doesn't ordain women or allow them access beyond the lower tiers, and in its more traditional teachings seeks to instruct women how to live and what to do. It seems that in many cases equality stops at the church door.

So, disenfranchised by the formal religions, where does she express her innate spirituality? From what we are witnessing, women are turning to each other to provide spiritual support and guidance, drawing on 'New Age' philosophies and a more holistic perspective – by implication, more inclusive. In fact, books and films such as *Eat, Pray, Love* and *The Secret* are just the tip of the iceberg, and educated affluent New Yorkers are adding 'spiritual guru' alongside therapist, masseuse and manicurist to the list in their little black books.

This new spirituality movement originated in the 1970s as part of second wave of feminism, in recognition that 'God' was a male concept, and embraced a kind of 'neo-paganism' incorporating witches and goddesses. Central to the philosophy was the idea that spirituality and religiosity didn't preclude women's equality, and so combined worship with activism. In the Goddess movement, the earth is perceived as the body of the Goddess, changing and evolving through the seasons. One connects with the body of the Goddess through her own body.[12] In the UK, Glastonbury is home to many proponents of the Goddess movement, as a centre of 'alternative' spirituality. Meanwhile, the witchcraft movement embraces the idea of women's innate power incorporating Wiccan and shamanic rituals.

What makes the feminist spirituality movement distinct from traditional organised religions is that it lacks a formal hierarchy or leadership structure, and is therefore by implication inclusive and egalitarian; it also lacks the concept of heaven and hell and therefore the instrument of fear as a means of controlling behaviour.

In the contemporary spiritual movement, Gabrielle Bernstein is just one of the new breed of personal or spiritual guides springing up in New York. To quote the *New York Times*, 'now there is a new role model for New York's former Carrie Bradshaws – young women who are vegetarian, well versed in self-help and New Age spirituality, and who are finding a way to make a living preaching to eager audiences, mostly female'.[13] One only has to witness the rise in spiritual retreat holidays, mindfulness classes and 'personal growth' retreats to see that this is now 'a thing', with the '10 best spiritual holidays' listings in *Vogue* cementing this into mainstream culture.

Thomas Amelio, president of the New York Open Centre, which has specialised in self-transformational coaching for the past 25 years, has witnessed the trend, particularly prevalent among young women in their early twenties, of people signing up for the courses in meditation, shamanism and healing, 'They are looking for something that is functional and practical that makes life easier to deal with.'[14]

For this audience, there's no shortage of self-help books, blogs and self-appointed spiritual gurus, often with eccentric but highly marketable monikers such as 'the Charlie's Angels of Wellness', 'Spiritual Cowgirls' and 'Spiritual Superheroines'. 'Downtown Dharma' is one such blog written by Ilana Arazie, who was fed up with being just a single girl around town wanted to pursue a more holistic existence.

The 'Sister Fund' is a women's foundation that 'supports and gives voice to the marginalized, especially women working for healing in the world from a faith-based perspective', started by Meggan Watterson, a former teacher of world religion at a private Manhattan college.

The advent of the Modern Spiritualists means that there's a cohort of more questioning, spiritually curious and awakened women out there, unafraid to reject traditional religion to pursue enlightenment and self-discovery in other ways.

And these women come from all walks of life – to dismiss them as the hessian-clad minority is a mistake. Many of these Modern Spiritualists are high-earning, high-profile women: think Oprah as the poster girl for this tribe.

EATING YOUR WAY TO ENLIGHTENMENT: FOOD IS THE NEW RELIGION

The quest towards spiritual enlightenment over the past decade has taken some surprising twists and turns, and in the shape of the 'clean-eating' movement, food has taken on a new spiritual and moral significance. To be fair, food has long been intertwined with religion through forbidden foods, cultural culinary practice and food as a form of worship. Some of it is based on quasi-scientific concerns; in a hot climate, for example, it probably doesn't make sense to mix meat with milk, the ideal bacterial culture. In other cases, it's often informed through sketchier evidence and more philosophically rooted beliefs. In her seminal book, *Purity and Danger*, anthropologist Mary Douglas observed that the distinction of and rationale for clean and unclean are less robustly based on known evidence, and much more keenly based on moral and behavioural ideals, and in particularly the maintenance of boundaries.[15] Mary's theories are particularly resonant in some respects as, although there is now more cynicism around the whole 'clean-eating' movement, we live in an era, certainly within the developed world, where some foods are 'good' and some are 'bad'; worse still, perfectly healthy (for many) foods have been demonised, for example gluten and dairy.

Even the language around food has acquired a semi-religious significance: the juice 'cleanse' or 'purge', the 'wellness diet', 'super foods', 'miracle foods' and so on. As a scientist, I find the logic surrounding

181

many of the claims fuzzy, and laboured moralising over diet particularly unjustifiable. Much of this whole industry is aimed at women, and as a cynic I would suggest this is just another means by which our behaviour is controlled, regulated and judged. In its more extreme forms the link between 'clean eating', demonising foods and weight loss or body image presents a dark underbelly to the whole movement. This is just the diet industry repackaged in a more 'digestible' (pardon the pun) or contemporary form, so I question the motivation and the unrealistic ideals, and suggest that spiritual enlightenment and chocolate are not mutually exclusive.

THE RELIGIOUS REFORMERS

In the quest for enlightenment, not all women feel the desire to leave their 'traditional' religion and are seeking to forge change from within. In Buddhism, men and women are treated as equals but within the religious orders there is a significant difference in the way that Buddhist nuns (*bhikkhuni*) are treated compared to Buddhist monks (*bhikkhu*), and in many Asian countries they are expected to be subservient to the monks, and are regarded junior to even those of one day's ordination.[16] From the thirteenth century until very recently, there were no female monks in Thailand, and a religious order in 1928 prohibited ordination, possibly influenced by the idea that the Buddha initially forbade the ordination of women, warning that in doing so his teachings would only endure for half as long. There are signs of gradual change: Chatsumarn Kabilsingh, a Thai scholar, retired from her post as a professor to become a *bhikkhuni*. Her journey has taken a circuitous route, studying in Taiwan with ordination in Sri Lanka, changing her name to the Venerable Dhammananda and returning to Thailand. While initially met with opposition, she now runs the first all-female temple in Thailand, Songdhammakalyani, and some 150 *bhikkhuni* now practice across Thailand. In the process Chatsumarn has also gained acceptance and even the embrace by the locals.

The status of women as *bhikkhuni* also serves to elevate women's status within the community, which is particularly important in countries such as Thailand, where women's disempowerment and poverty leads to startling rates of child prostitution and HIV transmission rates. Whereas young boys can become temporary monks in order to receive an education this has historically been denied to girls, leaving them trapped in a cycle of poverty.[17]

It feels that Thai Buddhist leaders may have to revise their attitudes on ordaining women, as it seems somewhat contradictory for an organisation happy to receive substantial financial support in donations from women such as sex workers, while being unwilling to let them into the religious orders: female exploitation is OK but empowerment is not OK.[18]

Chatsumarn's decision to pursue religious orders is part of an observable phenomenon of women entering into ministry later in life. So, while many women desert traditional religion, there is a growing cohort embracing it in their midlife.

Within the world of Islam, there are women creating their own religious communities, challenging the often patriarchal leadership, for example the Mariam mosque in Denmark is the first female-run mosque of its kind in the country, with two female imams and a female voice calling the community to prayers. While the mosque was set up with the intent of affording women greater participation in prayers, the women at the heart of the initiative were also committed to a more progressive interpretation of the Qur'an. Although relatively new to Europe, female-run mosques are not necessarily something 'new', and in China they have existed for centuries. Meanwhile, over in the US, the

Women's Mosque of America based in Los Angeles is run by women for women.

Looking towards Judaism, women have been accepted as rabbis for some time among the Reform community. Regina Jonas of East Berlin was the first recorded female rabbi in 1935, and was tragically murdered at Auschwitz in 1942. Even conservative Jews are embracing the idea of women rabbis, and with Israeli 'Ortho-feminists' and the 'Women of the Wall' challenging traditional doctrine, there is momentum for change and acceptance of women's equal right of worship within the 'traditional' organised religions.

THE MIDLIFE MINISTERS

In the quest for spiritual enlightenment there are women who are inspired later in life to pursue their own journey. Even back in the 1970s, the dramatic rise in the number of women entering seminaries in the US was observed, with an increase of 118.9 per cent between 1972 and 1977.[19] Of course, this was from a much smaller base than for male priests, but the spike was significant. Today, while the boomer generation is the fastest growing demographic entering theological school, we observe that in 2011 there were 40 per cent more women in American theological schools versus 1991, representing a 'significant proportion' of students within North American theological schools.[20] Among the many different reasons for the pursuit of religious calling at this juncture in life were, for example, feeling frustrated with career progression, but more deeply there was a desire to participate in something more meaningful and purposeful, which perhaps coincides with a woman having moved beyond her 'childrearing' years.[21] Nevertheless, midlife can also be a time of transition for many, and one's awareness of mortality can also force a reappraisal, and a desire for a higher purpose.

OVERCOMING INSTITUTIONAL BARRIERS

The desire for a higher purpose and to pursue a special calling, in the case of women, often implies more drastic measures to navigate institutional barriers, and possibly a higher level of commitment not to let these barriers prove a deterrent. One such example is 'The Danube Seven'. The Danube Seven refers to a group of seven women ordained as Catholic priests on the Danube River in 2002, so chosen as it constituted 'international waters' and was therefore free from any specialised jurisdiction. While many women in the Catholic Church in the US support the ordination of women, the Vatican has other ideas, and the women were summarily excommunicated along with the independent Catholic bishop, Rómulo Antonio Braschi. Yet another example of religion contradicting its own teachings, in respect of 'we are all created equal under God'. Perhaps a small asterisk denoting 'except for women' should have been noted.

THE RISE OF THE RELIGIOUS RIGHT AND THE TRADITIONALISTS

For all the women leading the charge for modernisation, and more liberal attitudes within their own religious communities, one cannot ignore the rise of the religious right, both in the East and West. One only has to look to the US as a case in point, and women are by no means absent from these movements. Phyllis Schlafly is perhaps the most iconic example of a woman in the 'anti-feminist' conservative right movement, although arguably her power, influence and self-determination – both as a scholar and prominent member of the Republican Party (she ran for Congress in 1952 as a working mother) – owed much to the feminist movement she claimed to oppose. In Schlafly's worldview, in opposing the Equal Rights Act amendment, she was fighting for the rights of housewives, 'pro-women', but preaching an entirely different doctrine. The Equal Rights Amendment proposed that all US citizens were treated equal under the constitution, regardless of gender, but thanks to Schlafly's ardent campaigning, the amendment was defeated. In the era of Trumpism and Christian conservatism, there are plenty more Phyllis Schlaflies to follow in her footsteps. In the 2016 US election, 76 per cent of evangelical Christian women aged 35 or under voted for Donald Trump, significantly more than their male peers, and they represent a cohort of women who aspire to traditional conservative values.[22]

THE TRADITIONALISTS

Within our Women's Index research, we found a significant proportion of women who aspired to a more traditional lifestyle, the 'Nurturers' for example, for whom success was defined as raising happy, healthy children, or the 'Spouse Focused' tribe for whom marriage and keeping their other halves happy is the centre of their world. Together, the Nurturers and Spouse Focused tribes numbered only 22 per cent in Asia Pacific yet 37 per cent of our sample outside of Asia, which tells you much about the rise of the 'alpha' tribes in Asia. Perhaps most surprising was the prevalence of 'Traditionalists' in the US and UK, making up 46 per cent of the sample, while in India they numbered 26 per cent and in Saudi Arabia only 17 per cent: so much for liberated Western values. In fact, I'm not going to suggest dismissively that Traditionalists simply haven't drunk the 'feminist Kool-Aid' since, if feminism represents a woman's right to choose, then women have every right to choose home and family as their calling. As with all things, the idea of choice is the crucial part of the equation. In fact, the data suggested a strong overlap between Late Starter mothers and Nurturers, suggesting that women who have children later in life maybe prioritise home and family more once they do reach that particular chapter, perhaps because they may have higher earnings to fall back on or because conceiving in the first place was more challenging. Whatever the case, it's interesting to see that the Traditionalists still exist in significant numbers, but equally they are prevalent in geographies or cultures we may not have expected, confounding some of our own cultural stereotypes along the way.

WOMEN AND RELIGION: THE FUTURE

Excluding 50 per cent of the population from its ministry flies in the face of the principle that religion is all-inclusive. Women as ministers, leaders and theologians bring a unique understanding, and particular style of leadership, most notably 'shared involvement' and 'mutual pilgrimage'.[23] Women have the potential to reach members of the community, who may otherwise feel excluded or judged, through the application of particular female insight, insight that is very obviously excluded in an all-male society. For example, female priests can counsel women on often difficult or taboo subjects, such as sexual abuse, prostitution or violence, which they would feel uncomfortable discussing with a male priest. In this way, they are able to reach out to the most vulnerable within society. Equally women within the religious institutions can help to modernise and they bring 'feminist' principles in striving for equal representation. To quote Emma Tomalin, lecturer at Leeds University Department of Theology, 'Whilst it is unlikely that the feminist transformation of religious traditions alone is capable of mitigating women's oppression ... it presents a potentially fruitful, yet largely overlooked dimension of women's empowerment.'[24]

The presence of women in religious institutions is a modernising force by implication as they would challenge the reliance on traditional Scripture versus religious knowledge, and in doing so offer a more contemporised interpretation of Scripture.[25] It's too simplistic and condescending to suggest that feminism is incompatible with religion, and this falls into the trap of creating the idea that there is one model of feminism. While on the one hand we can renounce religion as oppressive, this denies women the potential to fulfil their spiritual lives in the manner of their choosing. The problem with feminism as a secular concept, perhaps more prevalent in the Western World, is that it ignores the often profound religious belief among many poor women around the world.[26] Equally, Western feminism has not necessarily sought to absolve all religious belief. The suffragette movement was not atheist by nature, and the principle of equality reflected for the most part their religious principles. What women bring to religion is inclusion, enlightenment and a sense of shared purpose, and their exclusion is, I believe, a huge loss to organised religion.

WHAT THIS MEANS: KEY TAKEAWAYS FOR BRANDS

As women, we are socialised to think outwards, to consider those around us and community. Therefore, it's little surprise that women in significant numbers are seeking to build and foster a greater sense of community and enlightenment through traditional religious practice and other means. Our data suggested that, in fact, the younger millennials were slightly more religious versus older women, and equally our data across cultures serves to contradict some of the ingrained cultural stereotypes we may all possess, so the first lesson here would be to see beyond our own prejudices.

The brand relationship: less transaction, more transformation

The emergence of the mindfulness movement, increase in spiritual retreats and women's nascent spirituality illustrate that there are opportunities for brands to engage beyond a mere transactional relationship. Obviously, we have to be realistic and selective in approach: few women will be seeking life coaching or spiritual enlightenment from their instant coffee or mouthwash brand. But my point is that it's often said that women don't just buy brands, they join them, so it's worth considering how to foster a stronger connection through tuning into deeper emotional or spiritual needs.

Some commentators even suggest that brands are borrowing from organised religions and certainly the emergence of the Brand Purpose movement, CSR (corporate social responsibility) programmes and creating brand communities appear to mirror religious structures.[27] The cynical mind might question if this is just contemporary marketing seeking to acquire more effective means of generating brand loyalists or 'followers', but if it means that brand organisations themselves adopt the principles of mindfulness and consider their existential value in the world, perhaps we'll see a little less corrosive consumerism in the world.

In terms of putting this into practice, a financial service provider may wish to explore the potential of ethical investment products; gyms could do more in the way of satisfying a holistic approach to wellbeing; and travel companies and even hotels are missing opportunities in 'added value' services that stretch beyond the standard 'spa' offering but create an authentic spiritual experience. Remember, we live in an 'experience economy' allegedly, and if *Vogue* is reporting on spiritual retreats this is no longer the preserve of the hessian-clad minority.

Religion, spirituality and consumerism can coexist

It's a pretty sweeping assumption to make that the pious or religious don't indulge in consumerism, and our studies of women in the Middle East or Muslim communities within South-east Asia reveal on the one hand an emerging young middle class, highly interested in fashion and technology yet equally observant of their religious beliefs. Rather than consumerism fighting with religious observance, consumerism can actively embrace it, and we see the global emergence of halal cosmetics and modest fashion, with 2017 marking the launch of Nike's first sports hijab.

This is not merely a passing trend. The halal cosmetics market is expected to achieve sales of £52 billion by 2025, indicating that modest women still wear make-up.[28] Meanwhile, mainstream manufacturers like Unilever have launched specialised hijab haircare, for example Sunsilk Hijab Recharge shampoo, which promises to revive hair removing excess oils and promoting touch activated fragrance release. Despite the paucity of market research, the modest or Islamic fashion industry is said to be growing rapidly, with early estimates in 2010 suggesting the Islamic fashion industry globally to be worth $2.9 billion and little sign of the growth slowing down.[29] In the UK, 2017 marked the launch of London's first modest fashion week, and upscale online retailers such as Net-a-Porter boast a dedicated modest fashion filter, while Marks & Spencer was moved to stock the controversial burkini. In future, we are likely to see yet more blending and blurring of Eastern and Western values within the fashion industry: 'mainstream' brands now include hijab designs in their collections, Muslim models are signed to international modelling agencies, and Kanye West was savvy or inclusive (depending on your worldview) to include hijabi model Halima Aden in his fashion collection. I think it's safe to conclude that the Islamic influence on the consumer goods industry looks set to continue and if anything accelerate in line with the growth of a young, increasingly affluent audience across the world.

Equally, one of the factors that differentiates the new female spirituality movement from traditional religions is the expression of spirituality through the use of 'tools', for example, crystals, tarot, jewellery and the employment of specific herbs or essential oils for incantations. We witness the blurring of this mystical movement within the fashion and beauty industry, through jewellery promising healing properties utilising specific stones, or beauty products promising wellness and spiritual healing or calming properties. And who doesn't need this when we live in such a turbulent, hectic world?

Technology and community

Perhaps the finding that stood out most for us in our research was the idea that technology trumps religion in bringing friends and family or communities together. Arguably, access to technology and the internet has afforded people enlightenment through knowledge, and therefore the inequality of access to technology and internet access globally for women is an issue that requires urgent attention. To illustrate the global digital gender gap that exists, while an estimated 47 per cent of the world is online,[30] there are 250 million fewer women online, and the global internet user gap has crept up to 12 per cent in 2016 from 11 per cent in 2013,[31] representing a move in the wrong direction. Unsurprising therefore that women in our survey universally felt that technology for the most part was designed by men for men, and access remains a major issue in women's empowerment.[32] If brands now exist in a 'digital world' or, to put it another way, if digital is as ubiquitous as electricity, then the more forward-thinking brands should consider how they can help include more women in this digital world. Equally, the preponderance of meditation and mindfulness apps, and online meditation communities and guides, demonstrates the way in which technology and spirituality can coexist.

The plurality of religion and feminism

A further finding of our research, and set against the backdrop of an increasingly diverse and individualistic spiritual landscape, is the diversity and individuality of the *feminist* landscape, and in reality this is a consistent theme within this book. There is, and neither should there be, no one model of feminism, no scripture on what is. 'Good feminism' does not come in only one variety. Many brands have fallen short in understanding this principle, and reaped the justified criticism.

The existence in large numbers of more 'Traditionalist' tribes, women for whom career is less important than home and family, does not represent a failure of feminism or women who simply haven't 'got with the programme' because there is no 'programme'. In actuality, the illustration of the diversity of women's interests should represent the success of women's empowerment: empowerment to follow whichever path suits.

Therefore, brands should tread a very cautious line in attempting to prescribe a feminist narrative, to dictate what empowerment does and doesn't mean, because from what we have observed this is a very diverse and personal concept.

CHAPTER 8

....

The Cultural Icons

'There are only three ages for women in Hollywood – babe, District Attorney, and Driving Miss Daisy.*'* **Goldie Hawn**

In this chapter, I want to tell the story of women's contribution to popular and artistic culture, because whether you are aware of it or not, women have played significant roles in shaping what we perceive as popular culture, through their work in film, literature, advertising, journalism and art, even if their contributions have been largely marginalised. Take the comedy world: how often have you heard the idea that 'women just aren't funny'? This idea pervades culture and means that within the comedy world women get roughly a third of the visibility of men, since on any average live comedy night, out of three acts only one will be female, if you're lucky. All-female comedy nights are reserved for 'special occasions', for that read 'hen nights'. Yet this ignores the rich history of women in comedy, from Phyllis Diller, Lucille Ball and Moms Mabley in the 1950s, to Mary Tyler Moore in the 1960s and the fearless Joan Rivers, who in 1986 became one of the first women to host her own talk show. Yet somehow, perhaps because many reviewers and studio executives are male, women's contributions to comedy have been forgotten, like they have in so many other industries.

It is hugely surprising to me, given women's early endeavours in the film industry and the wealth of female talent in the advertising industry, that these worlds have become so male-dominated over the years. Perhaps now is the tipping point and the gender balance will be reset. Certainly in Hollywood in the post-Weinstein era, a force of reckoning is sweeping through the industry and may serve to promote a much more diverse and meritocratic approach.

WOMEN WANT THEIR VOICES HEARD

Within our Women's Index data, we explored the issue of cultural representation and empowerment, and the results painted a consistent picture of both frustration and exclusion in every corner of the globe; 80 per cent of all women surveyed said they wanted women to have a louder voice when it comes to cultural influence, and 49 per cent felt there were too many men in the arts sector.[1] What's also significant is the fact that the numbers held true across all age groups, so it's not as if the situation has shown any sign of improvement for younger women: millennial through to baby-boomer, we all felt excluded.

The sense of exclusion was pretty comprehensive and carried across sectors of the arts, so 49 per cent of women felt there weren't enough female artists, or if they did exist we certainly didn't hear about them. Just over half of women surveyed felt there weren't enough female leads onscreen, yet over 70 per cent of women were interested in seeing more women in leading roles (a clear opportunity for studios), and just over 60 per cent of women felt there weren't enough older women onscreen, with similar numbers feeling there wasn't enough racial diversity of women onscreen. Tellingly, when women were represented onscreen, 80 per cent of all women in our survey felt all too frequently we were portrayed as sex objects. Again, these attitudes held true across generations, indicating the slow progress we are making: women feel universally excluded, regardless of age or geography. So far so depressing – we are only half the population after all! Yet if only we knew how important and influential women had been in the inception of the film world.

THE FEMALE STORYTELLERS

In reality there is a rich history of women in the cinema, not just in front of the camera, but behind the camera. I want to tell the story of the female storytellers, and why Hollywood really belongs to women: step aside Mr Weinstein.

When I went to school, the careers advice was pretty simple: for the smarter girls, it was a toss-up between doctor or lawyer as a profession; for the less-gifted girls education was more a means of marking time before you married a pig farmer. Engineering? In these shoes? Advertising? I don't think anyone even knew what that meant, but at least in terms of careers advice, we kept it simple. Study science or study English, learn to cook (we were not after all, barbarians). The end. Which is why I was surprised when I learned that in the 1920 edition of *Careers for Women* potential vocations included advertising, architecture, business and, wait for it, 'motion pictures'.[2] To say I was surprised, envious even, was something of an understatement, but on further investigation a more startling story emerged, and I'd like to tell you something of that story.

In pre-1930s America, essentially the silent-movie era, cinematography's inception women were highly influential within the film industry and heavily involved both behind the camera and as actors in front of the lens. Women worked as editors, set designers, scriptwriters and directors, facing little opposition in what was seen as a 'creative' industry, for that read 'feminine'. At the same time, women formed the bulk of cinemagoers, with estimates suggesting that between 75 and 83 per cent of the audience was female.[3]

During this era, women were the pioneers of film-making, and credit for the first fictional motion picture belongs to little-known Alice Guy-Blanché, secretary at the Gaumont et Cie photography company. Gaumont produced a new camera capable of filming moving images, and while working at Gaumont, Alice started to immerse herself in the field of moving images, envisioning a potential beyond purely factual demonstration films. Bored with the limited scope of film-making, Alice produced the first narrative or 'fictional' film in 1896 with *La Fée au Choux* (*The Cabbage Fairy*), a tale of a woman growing babies on a cabbage patch: how's that for creativity. She would later run her own studio, writing, producing and directing films – and perhaps should be regarded as the Mother of Modern Cinema, as it was fiction feature films that would prove to be the studio money-makers.[4] In fact, Gaumont, itself influenced in no small part by Alice's vision for film as a means of storytelling, would go on to invest in the cinema industry and produce Alfred Hitchcock's early works.

So, while the credit for the first moving picture images undoubtedly belongs to others, Alice Guy-Blanché was a significant figure in realising their full potential. What is startling is the lack of credit that Alice would receive,[5] a frustration that haunted her later years, and in fact if you consult 'A brief history of Gaumont' in *Variety*, Alice is strangely absent from the story.[6] This absenteeism of women in film is a recurrent theme to which we'll return. Once again, it is an example of history literally being 'his' story in the airbrushing out of women's contributions.

By the 1920s women's influence in cinema had gained pace; at least 30 current film directors were women;[7] Lois Weber was Universal Studio's highest paid director in 1916;[8] and many scriptwriters were women, responsible for scripting about a third of American silent movies. Screenwriter Frances Marion was the highest paid screenwriter of that era, and would go on to win the Best Screenplay Academy Award in 1930.[9]

It's galling that women's influence in the cinema industry has been so assiduously 'forgotten', and that one of the dynamics that holds women back from securing directorial work is the fact that they are deemed 'high risk' or 'unproven', yet the reverse is true: women have made a significant contribution to cinema from its earliest inception.

The influence of female screenwriters was significant, and reached beyond pure commercial success to have a 'strong social impact ... an essential role in modernising society'.[10] Concentrating on more than just feather-light romantic comedies, writer and director Lois Weber covered contemporary subjects such as abortion and birth control, marriage and marital issues, capital punishment and drug addiction, challenging the idea that while women are competent at churning out 'chick flicks', they can't be trusted with more serious subject matter.[11]

And if we're going to discuss film-making we can't overlook the luminaries of their era, Ida Lupino and Dorothy Arzner. Lupino was a renowned actress who went on to direct and produce numerous ground-breaking movies working as an independent filmmaker with her production company, the Filmakers [sic], again tackling subjects often ignored by the studios, such as bigamy. Her film *Outrage* (1950), for instance, depicted the social impact of rape and the societal factors that tacitly permit rape not only to occur but to go unpunished.[12] As a piece of work, and more profoundly as a commentary on the lot of women, *Outrage* still resonates today, particularly in the #MeToo era. Lupino would also become the first female director to work within film noir, co-writing and directing *The Hitch-Hiker* (1953), which ranks among the best films noir of the era, and is credited with inspiring Martin Scorsese, who went on to write her obituary, 'Behind the camera, a feminist', for the *New York Times* magazine.

Dorothy Arzner, meanwhile, was no less a film-maker, working her way from script writer to editor to then becoming a director, and succeeded in making 16 movies while working within the studio system, a record as yet unsurpassed in Hollywood.[13]

We couldn't discuss women's early involvement in cinema without recalling Leni Riefenstahl, the Nazi propagandist, but nonetheless pioneer of extraordinary cinematic techniques such as the 'rhythmic visual montage' still in use today.[14]

WOMEN EXIT STAGE LEFT: THE UNSEATING OF WOMEN

Perhaps indicative of the prevailing winds of change was the 1934 reprint of *Careers for Women*, which while 'enlarged and expanded' had surreptitiously removed references to film as a suitable career option, for all women's early success and pioneering within cinema.[15] So began the systemic 'purging' of women from positions of influence within the very industry they had helped to create. If you are wondering what prompted such a transition, there is no one factor but a number of social dynamics that colluded in effect to force women out.

Women's involvement in the movies, prior to the big studio era, was pre-union and relied on informal networks of women collaborating: 'Women created a strong network of female colleagues ... an abundance of female writers were tied in friendship to many of the female stars of early Hollywood.'[16] As the film industry expanded it attracted an organised labour movement and unionisation, and the unions of the era were very much about protecting 'jobs for the boys', and in that respect perhaps little has changed. Aligned to this was the labour legislation that served to protect jobs for men during the Great Depression: 26 states had laws prohibiting the employment of married women, and women would often be forced to conceal their marital status in the hope of protecting their career.[17] The creation of the big studio machine placed a new commercial imperative on the work of the studios, and film production now was very much part of a big corporate machine, requiring large capital investment particularly once 'talkies' arrived and the crew and production requirements mushroomed. In essence, 'studios were run by men, and men hired men'.[18]

Large-scale movie production led to screenwriting teams and 'writers' buildings – think of them as the writing 'battery farm' – with extended working hours, which served to exclude many women who previously worked at home or who combined writing with family responsibilities.[19] Remember, this was the era where childcare was the sole responsibility of women. And so the new ways of working served to push women out to the sidelines. Unable to compete or simply excluded, their voices would progressively become lost in the annals of time.

Fast forward to today, and sadly little has changed. Women behind the camera still represent a pitiful minority of active film-making talent: in 2013–14, just 26 per cent of behind-the-camera roles were taken by women, and 6 per cent of big studio films were directed by women.[20] Female directors exist, but they just don't get the work. What is also remarkable is the length of time that even an Oscar-winning director, as a woman, may have to wait before she directs again, looked over in favour of more 'reliable' – yet often unproven – male directorial talent. Despite writing and directing *Monster* (2003), featuring an Oscar-winning performance by Charlize Theron, Patty Jenkins would wait more than a decade before securing her next major feature (*Wonder Woman*, 2017). This is a common story for women.

Certainly within the bigger studio system women have been essentially 'shut out', a situation perhaps perpetuated by the rampant success since the late 1980s and 1990s of the action movie genre and the received wisdom that 'women can't direct action films'. According to film commentator Susan Wloszczyna: 'In the nearly-four decades since Christopher Reeve took flight, superhero films have grown into Hollywood's most popular and profitable genre. Sadly, these films continue to be directed by males and marketed to boys of all ages.'[21] And women's representation in front of the camera hasn't fared much better, with women making up only 15 per cent of protagonists among the top 100 US films.[22]

THE CASE FOR CHANGE

There are, however, winds of change starting to blow through Hollywood, based on the box-office earnings potential of female-led features. While actresses may not make as much as their male rivals – a discrepancy highlighted recently by Jennifer Lawrence – they are high box-office earners, and this isn't just a blip. In fact, a recent study trawling over the last ten years of big box-office earners reveals that female-led films cumulatively out-earned male-led films,[23] perhaps unsurprising given that women make up 52 per cent of the cinemagoing audience.[24] The scale of the earnings disparity is impressive: over the past decade women-led films earned a cumulative $45 million more than those about men. No doubt influenced by this, and the success of female-led franchises such as *The Hunger Games*, studios are waking up to the idea of mainstream films led by women if for no other reason than the financial imperative, so we have a female *Ghostbusters* reboot, a female *Ocean's Eight* and a female-led narrative dominating the *Star Wars* reboot. Even Disney has reimagined its fairy-tale heroine as independent and empowered, with *Frozen*'s Queen Elsa in very little need of a saviour prince and *Maleficent* telling the troubled back story of the Wicked Witch. So things are changing – although not fast enough – because Hollywood follows the money, and women may once again start to dominate the film industry. Anyone thinking this is a purely 'creative industry' should wake up to the fact that this is a highly commercial industry as evidenced by increasingly unsubtle product placements.

We also have the influence of billionaire female backers, such as Megan Ellison, enabling female film-makers (Katherine Brooks/*Waking Madison*, Kathryn Bigelow/*The Hurt Locker*). Independent film producers such as Ellison, Gigi Pritzker and Molly Smith are creating films that are starting to move us away from a reliance on the all-male action genre.

Meanwhile, in TV things are changing a little faster, perhaps thanks to the increasingly fragmented TV production market with Netflix and Amazon now producing their own content. Equally, this could be because more modest production budgets make it easier for women to get a leg up. The *Supergirl* series (CBS) has been a hit with its premiere attracting a significant audience for the season (13 million viewers), while Netflix has released its own superhero genre with a characteristic indie twist in the shape of *Jessica Jones*, a super-strength, super-troubled private investigator.[25] Meanwhile, Shonda Rhimes, Mindy Kaling, Julie Plec and Lena Dunham have all had hit shows while demonstrating women's power in creating diverse and engaging narratives that play well to the new 'binge-watching' TV audience. Most recently, on the back of the success of *Big Little Lies*, Reese Witherspoon has set up her own production company, Hello Sunshine, in a move dedicated to creating more female-centric content, observing that women want 'quality content … not mommy blogs and 14 ways to cook a turkey'. In the highly fragmented and competitive TV landscape, women like Reese and Shonda, creating ratings powerhouses through female narratives, may ultimately pave the way for greater female representation and a much more meritocratic industry.

One couldn't discuss the moving image and its influence upon popular culture, however, without examining women's contribution to the advertising industry.

MAD MEN AND MAD WOMEN: THE WOMEN OF THE ADVERTISING WORLD

When one considers that women buy up to two-thirds of all consumer products worldwide, it's surprising that we don't hear more about women's contribution within the advertising industry beyond that of our role as consumers or 'housewives'. In *Mad Men* Peggy Olson, the struggling copywriter, was presented as something of an anomaly, a woman struggling in a man's world. Today the situation persists: only 11 per cent of creative directors are female,[26] and when you cast your eye through any advertising journal, 90 per cent of interviews with the great 'advertising luminaries' are guaranteed to be male. Their stories will celebrate the 'golden age' of advertising, with fantastic anecdotes in which women will either be absent or perhaps cast as the secretary. As a woman in this industry, it's hard not to be discouraged or to feel like an imposter – but the idea that advertising should be male-dominated, that men were instrumental in shaping the industry and created the best work, is just an idea: like an advertising concept, it is not necessarily burdened by facts. Much like the belief that only men created Hollywood and only men pioneered all fields of science, and almost everything else you can think of, the idea that 50 per cent of the population had no hand in shaping the world of advertising is laughable. So, let's consider some of the facts about women's contribution to the advertising industry.

THE EARLY FEMALE PIONEERS

Working at J. Walter Thompson, I'm very much aware of women's contribution to shaping one of the oldest advertising agencies in the world. Helen Lansdowne Resor was one of the first female copywriters, hired by J. Walter Thompson in 1908, and by the 1920s she was leading her own female editorial department as part of her pioneering approach to the industry. Before the creation of the editorial department, products were sold on purely rational benefits (which may sound familiar to those of us working in the industry), but Helen developed a more emotional psychological approach to the art of selling. Reasoning that women were better at communicating to women, she staffed the department with female writers, many of whom were immersed in the suffragette movement. Her approach challenged some of the early wisdom of the era and sidestepped many of the restrictive cultural conventions, for Helen's audience to her mind aspired to be a modern 'working woman'. In relaunching Woodbury soap, for example, Helen knew that 'sex sells' and, flouting conventions, created advertising that touched on the idea of women's sexual power: sales of the soap smashed forecasts and the campaign was a success. Helen was also an ardent supporter of women, and is known within the agency for her mentoring of young female copywriters, which is why we have honoured her contribution with the Helen Lansdowne Scholarship for young female creative talent.

But Helen wasn't alone. The first female-owned advertising agency launched in 1880 in New York, presided over by Mathilde C. Weil together with her partners Meta Volkman and Mary Compton. The agency thrived on its profitable medicines accounts and Mathilde ran the agency until her death in 1903, bequeathing her office to Mary Morrow Craig who ran the agency despite her husband's opposition.

Phyllis Kenner Robinson, often credited as 'The First Lady of Madison Avenue', was the first female copy chief hired by Doyle Dane Bernbach, in 1949, and pioneered a new approach to copywriting, with a playful use of idiom and often sparing use of words. By 1956, Phyllis was promoted to vice president and presided over a creative department that was 50 per cent female; few, if any, creative departments can make that claim today. Phyllis was behind some of the most iconic print campaigns of our time, including the memorable VW ads of the 1960s. She was also instrumental in paving the way for the 'creative team', namely the pairing of copywriter and art director, now very much established within the advertising world.

In 1971, Barbara Proctor founded the Proctor & Gardner advertising agency, based in Chicago, and was the first African-American woman to run her own agency. She built it into the second largest African-American advertising agency in America. Barbara formerly worked at the Post-Keyes-Gardner agency, scoring 21 awards in just three years.[27] She used her obvious talents not just to further her commercial interests but as a keen supporter of the women's and civil rights movement. She has exerted a powerful influence, acting as a mentor, and has also steadfastly refused accounts or campaigns she felt were discriminatory or damaging, reasoning, 'We mold opinions ... therefore we have a responsibility to those people whose opinions we influence.'[28]

As an industry luminary and accomplished businesswoman, Mary Wells Lawrence stands out as one of the highest earning female executives of her time. An alumna of Doyle Dane Bernbach, she ran her own agency Wells Rich Greene for over 20 years from 1966. Her more audacious initiatives include rebranding the Braniff airline, which included painting the planes and dressing the cabin crew in Pucci, boasting the slogan 'The end of the plain plane'. By 1968 the agency was in the top 15 rankings, with billings of nearly $60 million thanks to award-winning work attracting many blue-chip clients, for example, P&G, General Mills and TWA. Wells Rich Greene was responsible for some of the most iconic campaigns of the era, including the 'I heart NY' campaign that restored a sense of pride in the formerly ailing metropolis, creating an internationally recognisable branding property that still endures today. Mary Wells Lawrence was also the youngest copywriter, male or female, to be inducted into the Copywriters' Hall of Fame, and she is described as 'the force behind one of the most creative shops in the history of advertising'.

So much for women's invisibility in the industry, I'm not going to pretend there wasn't inherent gender (and racial) discrimination within the industry at the time, but anecdotally it appears that women had a greater presence, certainly within the creative department in the case of products marketed to women. To quote a *Time* magazine article dated 1967: 'When Foote, Cone & Belding won the Clairol account in 1955, the agency assigned it to Shirley Polykoff, a Brooklyn-born mother of two who can write better advertising copy than most men in the game.'[29] Shirley created the campaign still recalled today: 'Does she or doesn't she?', an idea that dramatically transformed sales for the brand.

This idea is supported by Lola Cherson, who worked in PR during the Mad Men era: 'Advertising and PR were two fields in which there were women who were at the top ... Polykoff, she was famous. There were women copywriters. I won't say all over town, but at every major agency, there were women.'[30]

The fact is that many of the approaches we use today – the copywriter/art director pairing, the more emotional approach to selling, the power of simple yet beautiful copy – we owe to female pioneers of the industry, who have helped shaped popular culture through advertising over decades. But where did it all go wrong, how did advertising forget about women?

ONCE AGAIN WOMEN ARE SIDELINED

There's very little research on the subject, but piecing together the evidence, and based on observing what happened across similar industries, my theory is this. From its inception advertising had been deemed a creative industry, making it a little easier for women to gain access. An advertising recruitment handbook dated 1963 and produced by J. Walter Thompson was designed specifically to recruit female graduates into the industry, and boasted, 'Advertising is a particularly promising field for women because so much advertising is directed to women and so many products are purchased by women. At J. Walter Thompson, women work in all departments and in all phases of advertising.'[31]

In the 1960s advertising relied on big personalities, ideas and creative thinkers, which again favoured diverse departments. In fact, Doyle Dane Bernbach famously recruited 'outsiders', boosting racial and gender diversity. Equally, agency executives as early as Helen Lansdowne Resor concluded that if women were buying most of the products, it made sense to have women creating the campaigns, and re-reading interviews from the era and even the 'JWT Advertising Handbook', there is proof positive that women specialised in female brands, using their female insight (the irony).

But then things started to change. In the late 1970s and 1980s, advertising became more of a 'profession' and more of a 'science' with the birth of the 'planning department' and latterly econometric modelling. The planning department, formerly 'market research', devised advertising strategy and commissioned research. It was pioneered by luminaries such as Stephen King and Stanley Pollitt, and largely male-dominated. Out went the idea that a woman could 'think up' insight for a product targeting women, and in came advertising pre-testing, sophisticated research techniques and segmentation studies. It's my belief that as the planning department grew in scale and influence, the industry became more masculinised. The planning department exerted much more power within the agency and this closing of the male ranks served to exclude women: why do you need women copywriters for female insight when you have the planning department?

Don't get me wrong, I have a great respect for planning departments and advertising strategy as a craft (note, I say 'a craft' and not 'a science'), and I speak as a planner, but I have been lectured one too many times on female insight – even in the field of women's intimate health – by industry men who presume to know better based on scrutinising their 'research'. And let me say this, certainly when it comes to understanding what makes a woman tick, particularly in the field of intimate health, having a vagina *really* helps.

Early on in my advertising career I remember being excluded from a client pitch presentation, despite having written the entire strategy. The reason given: 'I lacked gravitas', which is code for I was a young woman. In the event an all-male team, unfamiliar with the strategy, presented the pitch: we didn't win. This is my analogy for what happened on a grander scale for women across the industry: we lacked the necessary 'gravitas'. Yes, you can blame it on antisocial working hours and the career breaks – in short, the usual excuses or justifications –but then millions of women in low-paid part-time jobs work antisocial hours and combine work with childcare, so for me these reasons don't stack up. What I believe excluded women is that something much more systemic was at work: an unconscious or even conscious bias served to exclude women. Advertising became a serious *business* obsessed with the 'science' of advertising, the 'laws', the 'theory' and less of a creative industry, less about intuitive insight, and less about relationships and personalities.

This is something I would like to change. As a scientist, I believe in principles not laws; I believe that advertising is a creative discipline, it is not a science – humans are not rational beings. We can taking from the best of science, but I believe that continuous curiosity, creative problem-solving and intuitive insight all have a role to play, and women should definitely have a huge role within an industry that essentially for the most part targets women.

WOMEN AND ADVERTISING – THE VITAL STATISTICS

In 2017 as part of our partnership with the Geena Davis Institute on Gender in Media, inspired by its work analysing the representation of gender in film – or should I say lack of representation? – we decided to give advertising the same scrutiny. From our own study, 85 per cent of women interviewed told us that when it comes to depicting women, the film and advertising industries were woefully out of touch, and it was clear that as an industry we are not keeping pace with the real world. But we wanted the facts, to diagnose the scale of the issue and the hard evidence because data is a powerful tool: you can't argue with the numbers. What the analysis would reveal was that as an industry we were being hugely complacent. The standout creative work around female empowerment had led to the perception that we were much more progressive in the representation of women, whereas in reality the standout work was not part of an industry-wide movement, it was more accurately 'standalone' work. Nobody expected the data to be quite as bad as it was.

We co-funded a study using the highly innovative and sophisticated software that the Geena Davis Institute launched last year. The Gender Inclusion Quotient (GD-IQ) software analyses audio and video media content; funded by Google.org and incorporating Google's machine learning technology, and the University of Southern California's audio-visual processing technologies, GD-IQ is the only software tool in existence with the ability to measure screen and speaking time through the use of automation. This revolutionary tool was co-developed by the Geena Davis Institute and led by Dr Shrikanth (Shri) Narayanan and his team of researchers at the University of Southern California's Signal Analysis and Interpretation Laboratory (SAIL), with additional analysis from Dr Caroline Heldman.

To adapt it to advertising we needed to rethink the criteria, our hypothesis being that unlike the film world, in advertising women get lots of screen time but their characterisation may be stereotyped … sitting in the kitchen or standing at the window marvelling at how white the washing has become. Working with Institute and Dr Caroline Heldman, we pulled together the key indicators we felt would characterise 'stereotyped' advertising, but then we had to source the advertising itself.

The Cannes Lions International Festival of Creativity granted us access to their archive so we could look at the best that our industry has produced over the past ten years. This is an important point because Cannes represents the pinnacle of creativity, and although we didn't analyse the entire industry's body of work (and only looked at English language material in order to avoid translation issues), we studied the most creative advertising, and arguably therefore the most memorable and persuasive work. In effect, this study focused on the most visible and impactful advertising within culture, therefore making the results more important: these are the ideas shaping culture. When you consider that globally we spend $524 billion on advertising media, you start to appreciate the scale and power of the advertising industry to influence public consciousness.

The first key finding that really surprised us was that, contrary to our assumptions, women do not get lots of screen time. In fact, male characters account for 67 per cent of screen time and appear twice as often as women, and men total 70 per cent of speaking time, securing three times more dialogue. And these numbers changed very little over the decade's worth of ads in our study. But it got worse. We analysed the quality of dialogue, and we observed that even when women do get to speak, the dialogue contained fewer words and simpler words, perhaps like a Donald Trump tweet. This is important because it confers the implicit message about intelligence, since there is much evidence to suggest that intelligent people use a greater vocabulary and more varied vocabulary, so subconsciously we risk sending the message that women aren't very bright.[32]

We also looked at how women are portrayed and characterised, and in Adland it seems women do not work: only 8 per cent of women in ads had a job, compared to the real world where up to 70 per cent of women are gainfully employed. We don't have to entirely replicate the world through advertising, but surely we could get to be funny or smart or vaguely three-dimensional? The study said otherwise: men are twice as likely to provide the laughs and significantly more likely to be defined by intelligence as part of their character; we are given the impression that women are too busy weeping silently off set. Yet contrast this with the real facts: it's women who earn most bachelor, masters or doctoral degrees. In the UK, for example, the latest UCAS figures revealed that, among teenagers, females entering higher education outnumbered men by 22 per cent.[33]

What was very illuminating was the analysis of the dominant advertising protagonists – the major players in front of the camera: our study revealed that the most popular characters are male, aged 25–35 years and white, which funnily enough is a lot like the demographic of most creative departments. So, while we're not holding a mirror up to society with our work, we're executing the creative department equivalent of a selfie. Creatively as an industry we're writing about what we know or feel most comfortable with: ourselves (and, in advertising, you could argue, that means pretty much from a white, male perspective). If this is true, it doesn't take a genius to figure out that the easiest way to change representation onscreen, in front of the camera, is to change representation behind the camera. There is a very real issue, however, preventing women from getting onto the creative floor.

Working with Creative Equals, an organisation that seeks to improve female representation in creative departments, we created a gender filter to highlight Cannes awards won by female creatives so that we could start to track the progression of women in the industry and create an imperative for change: because the fact is that while women constitute 29 per cent of creative departments in London, only 12 per cent of creative directors are women.[34] Looking at the awards, the numbers were pretty stark: for 2016 in the Cannes Film Craft category, just 7 per cent of awards were won by women and in Creative Effectiveness the number rose to 23 per cent. These figures are nothing to celebrate because women are not a minority, we are half the world population.

ADVERTISING: THE GREAT PERSUADER

The fact is that advertising, like any medium that pushes out ideas and images into society, helps to create the landscape of culture: it teaches us what the world looks like and shapes our understanding of how the world works. Advertising is designed to be a repetitive 'frequency' as repetition is one of the key tenets of persuasion or, more cynically, 'brainwashing'. Psychological studies demonstrate that the more often a subject hears a statement, the more likely they are to believe it to be true.[35] The simple act of repetition persuades, even if the statement has no relationship with the truth.

The creative work that we are pushing out into culture risks teaching society, particularly young people, that women don't work, that they aren't powerful or smart and that they're mostly silent. We should care about that very much indeed. The unintended consequence of benign advertorial stories that sell soft drinks, cars, washing powder and chocolate is that at the same time they are informing our unconscious bias, infecting our subconscious minds with ideas of what a leader looks like, a president looks like, what powerful looks like – and it's not female.

Advertising informs the way we see the world, our belief systems and ultimately behaviours, and can create a cultural 'ripple effect', either good or bad. In the years following the release of the film *Jaws*, great white sharks were hunted almost to extinction – such was the perceived threat. The fact is that you are significantly more likely to die at the wheel of a car.[36] Similarly, from our own Women's Index study we witnessed that a strong female role model onscreen inspired nearly 60 per cent of women off screen to be either more ambitious or more assertive, and 67 per cent of women said that if they saw more women onscreen as leaders it would make it easier for them to become leaders in real life.[37]

So, if advertising industry changes the narrative we use, the images we deploy and the stories we tell around women, we can change the way the world works for women. When it comes to driving equal opportunity, the fact is that public policy takes years to effect, yet we can open doors and remove the glass ceiling just through the ideas and images we present to the world: surely this is a future we all want to have a hand in creating.

FROM BUYING DECISIONS TO LIFE DECISIONS: THE MOVING IMAGE MOULDS US

Through the Women's Index research, we probed around the influence of onscreen role models and the results were startling. Across all markets, nearly 70 per cent of women described role models as very influential in their lives, with 58 per cent saying that seeing a strong onscreen role model inspired them to be either more ambitious or more assertive. One in four women in Brazil said they were inspired to leave an abusive relationship purely through what they saw onscreen, which is all the more powerful when one considers that some one in three women in Brazil are impacted by domestic violence.[38] The findings suggested that the moving image, the medium we use to sell goods and services, was persuasive enough not only to impact on women's career decisions, but their life decisions. This convinced us that the work we do in pushing out images of women into culture could wield a powerfully persuasive force for change – and it was an irresistible opportunity.

While we have discussed women in the film world and advertising world, home of the moving image, perhaps we should also turn our attention briefly to the art world, in a sense home to the 'static image', because the art world presents us with another female frontier in terms of shaping the overall cultural commentary.

GUERRILLA GIRLS AND GAVELS: WOMEN OF THE ART WORLD

'Less than 5 per cent of the artists in the Modern Art Sections are women, but 85 per cent of the nudes are female.' The Guerrilla Girls

If the world of the moving image has excluded women, then the art world or static image has not exactly championed their work either. Consider that art made by women not only suffers from lower values in galleries and at auction, significant because artists survive by selling work, but also in terms of exhibition and curation. The paucity of women's art on display was highlighted by an audit conducted by UK Feminista in 2010 that revealed that 83 per cent of the artists displayed in Tate Modern, London, were men; even today only 35 per cent of Tate Modern's collection is by a female artist, and care to guess how much of the public art in central London is made by a female artist? That would be around 8 per cent.[39] That does not exactly scream 'equal representation'. The public exhibition of work serves to raise collective consciousness and awareness, and the obvious disparity between the space devoted to male artists versus female artists conspires to shield the world from the great body of work created by women, suggesting that we just aren't capable. It sets the wrong precedent. This in turn influences aspiring artists, or collectors, which influences market value and auction prices, and so the cycle continues.

The most 'expensive' work by a female artist is entitled *Jimson Weed/ White Flower No.1*, by Georgia O'Keeffe, attracting an auction price of

$44 million in November 2014. It's true that $44 million is a fantastical amount of money, but in the art world or 'art stock market' that's small change. Equally, the auction result is most definitely a blip on the art radar: the highest value female artworks previously attracted a quarter of this price and in the giddily expensive art world, no women feature in the top 100 most expensive artists.[40] The $44 million for the O'Keeffe pales by comparison to the price for Leonardo da Vinci's *Salvator Mundi*, sold in New York for $450 million.

Sadly, had it not been for the Guerrilla Girls bursting onto the art scene in the 1980s, we probably wouldn't even be having this discussion right now, complacent that thanks to the acclaim devoted to, say, Tracey Emin, female artists do just fine thank you. It took the Guerrilla Girls, a feminist artists' collective and self-styled 'conscience of the artworld', to punch through this complacency and focus public opinion on the shocking lack of female representation. This lack of representation is keenly felt, as 49 per cent of women globally in our Women's Index survey said they wished there were more female artists; the fact is that there are women in the arts, but we don't see them or hear enough about them.[41]

The Guerrilla Girls themselves work anonymously, wearing gorilla masks for public appearances and adopting the names of dead female artists, which has the dual benefit of protecting their identities (the art world, after all, is a small world) and raising awareness of the legacy of women's art. They work through posters, 'guerrilla' demonstrations and campaigns to point the finger at the scale of the gender imbalance, using humour to convey a serious message. The flash point for the group's inception was the 1984 MoMA (Museum of Modern Art, New York) exhibition, entitled *An international survey of painting and sculpture*, purporting to be the definitive collection of significant works. The show itself featured 169 artists, of which 13 were women,[42] and today still only around 7 per cent of works exhibited at MoMA are by female artists.[43]

particularly galling when one considers that MoMA was founded by three women: Abbie Rockefeller, Lillie P. Bliss and Mary Quinn Sullivan.

Exhibitions and major retrospectives in national galleries and institutions help to establish artists' careers and set the standard of who's worth collecting, and therefore tend to have direct influence on auction value. Despite many women working in the art industry as gallerists, many collectors (given the concentration of wealth) and critics are male, which serves to perpetuate the favouring of male artists. To quote the critic Brian Sewell, 'The art market is not sexist ... There has never been a first-rank woman artist. Only men are capable of aesthetic greatness.'[44] His views illustrate some of the barriers women have to contend with on an uphill struggle for recognition.

But to assert the idea that female artists don't create great work, despite being a jaundiced and stupidly subjective slight on women's work, ignores the huge canon of fantastic work both contemporary and classical.

In fact, as demonstrated by a new archaeological study, some of the earliest artwork was created by women: up to three-quarters of cave paintings were from a female hand, according to Dean Snow, archaeologist at Pennsylvania University.[45] Professor Snow analysed the relative lengths of men and women's fingers to arrive at his findings, musing that previous assumptions about male paintings reflected the fact "there has been a male bias in the literature for a long time now". That same male bias served to preclude women from the artworld establishment for quite some time. Take Plautilla Nelli, for example, an Italian nun who was entirely self-taught as an artist. Her work was previously excluded from texts detailing the early Renaissance art movement, yet her work is of considerable beauty and thankfully is now exhibited by the Uffizi Gallery in Florence as part of its mission to promote female work. Then there's Louise Élisabeth Vigée Le Brun, a French noblewoman who also happened to be the most successful and expensive portrait painter in eighteenth-century France, yet she registers little on the radar of renowned artists. Looking towards the Impressionist movement, it's often catalogued as an exclusively male domain, yet there were significant female artists within this movement, for example Berthe Morisot, Marie Bracquemond and Mary Cassatt. Meanwhile, while Wassily Kandinsky is often regarded as the founding father of abstract art, that title really belongs to Hilma af Klint, a female artist working out of Stockholm with a fascination for the occult, who created her first abstract work some five years before Kandinsky. Therefore, it's a false assertion to suggest that women have not led or participated in major movements within the artworld, or that there are no great female artists. It's also true that to some degree art institutions themselves manufacture the great artists through their patronage, exhibition and publicity, something denied to female artists, given that museum and gallery directors, critics and professional institutions were and still are largely male.

Yet there are artists who have deliberately or subtly challenged the 'establishment', creating work with a feminist subtext, sometimes explicit, sometimes more implicit. Barbara Kruger for example, whose characteristic pairing of photographic visuals with subversive text has rarely shied away from challenging messages, chooses to work on billboards as a medium; her art often resembles advertising hoardings and plays with consumerist ideals, identity and power. Her *Your body is a battleground* was made in support of the 1989 Washington pro-choice march in support of abortion, and featured the bold title text juxtaposed over a photograph of woman's face at once divided into photographic positive and negative, creating an eerie sense of light and dark, *Love hurts* meanwhile focused on domestic violence, while *Who does she think she is*, with a caption 'it's time for women to stop being politely angry', is a call to arms for women – both within and without the artworld.

We couldn't discuss female artists without touching on photographic artist, Cindy Sherman, whose work arguably carries a subversive feminist subtext. Sherman has spent her career exploring and deconstructing the portrayal of women in the media and public consciousness, using herself as the subject of her work. While her work is often humorous, it is at times dark and unflinching, and it grapples with some of the tensions and contradictions in the social stereotypes used to characterize women: 'she directly confronts the viewer's gaze, no less in the case of posed sex dolls, as though to suggest that an underlying penchant for deception is perhaps the only "value" that truly unites us'.[46] Rachel Whiteread, the first woman to win the Turner Prize, with her quietly subversive sculptures has created a hugely impressive canon of work, at times challenging, yet had the ignominy of – on the same evening as she won the Turner Prize – being presented with 'the worst artist of the year' award by the K Foundation, led by the former pop band the KLF. It seems almost inconceivable that this could happen to a male artist, and illustrates how hard it is for women to be taken seriously despite their huge contributions to the art world.

If art shapes our worldview, if it at once pleases yet challenges, if it promotes and pushes ideas, it feels particularly important to have an equal voice for women, to have a female perspective infecting the public consciousness, because women have just as much to say yet we are often denied the platform.

One independent organisation seeking to redress the balance is Artfinder, an online exhibition and sales platform. Artfinder has openly challenged the disparity in exhibition of male versus female artists, publishing its own reports, and so combining commercialism with activism. What's most interesting is that although Artfinder has gender-equal representation across the platform, female artists sell 40 per cent more artwork, and sell faster and at a higher price versus male artists. As Artfinder points out, this suggests that when the 'middlemen' or barriers are removed, women have equal if not more appeal and the playing field is levelled. Meanwhile, Maria Balshaw's appointment as the director of Tate in 2017 represents a force for change within the artworld, committed as she is to redressing the gender balance. The idea of gender balance within the artworld is important because, like so many other creative disciplines, it lends us a female perspective for creativity, and without this we only ever see art from the male point of view.

While we have discussed the world of the moving image and the artworld, it's worth looking towards real-world storytelling, namely journalism, an equally powerful influence on public opinion.

SHE MAKES THE NEWS: WOMEN IN JOURNALISM

I was keen to explore the world of journalism since it represents such an important part of culture and how we see the world. In the new era of 'fake news', we are alive to journalism's power in influencing our belief systems and perhaps world events.

Traditionally journalism has been a male-dominated field, due historically to the fact that journalism involved travelling alone, often to dangerous places in the world, and by implication a job unsuited to a woman. The preponderance of men in the field means that the reporting of events and news has often been framed through a male lens, a male narrative. A recent example of the journalistic male lens include the 2016 US election coverage and the gendered narrative towards Hillary Clinton, which focused far more on her age and 'grandmother' status and her husband Bill, effectively weakening her status compared to Donald Trump's all-powerful 'testosterone'. Another was, as mentioned. the Rio Olympic sports coverage, which was often dismissive of women's achievements or conflated them with their parental responsibilities, as demonstrated by a Cambridge University Corpus study which found that adjectives like 'aged', 'pregnant' and 'married' were most frequently used to describe female athletes compared to 'fastest', 'strong' and 'great' for their male peers.[47] And it gets worse, analysis of over 2.3 million articles across 950 media outlets by researchers at Bristol and Cardiff universities revealed that 'When women do show up in the news, it is often as "eye candy", thus reinforcing women's value as sources of visual pleasure rather than residing in the content of their views.'[48] This matters because to quote Julie Burton, president of the Women's Media Center, 'media tells us our roles in society – it tells us who we are and what we can be',[49] and to remove women's contribution from the news narrative reinforces the sense that women have a passive role in the world as part of the scenery. The under-representation of women in the news happens on a global scale: the Global Media Monitoring Project recorded that only 25 per cent of news stories relate to women.[50]

Women do make the news, however, both as the subject of the headline and as the author. For example, it was *Telegraph* journalist Clare Hollingworth who reported Germany's invasion of Poland, effectively breaking the story of the start of the Second World War: apparently this was not just news to *Telegraph* readers but also to the British government. Women were also instrumental in the breaking of the Watergate scandal and National Security Agency cover-up, and our contribution to investigative journalism and the quest for truth also stretches far back into history, for example, Ida Tarbell's 1904 exposé on US Standard Oil led to national outrage and succeeded in breaking up a business monopoly engaging in 'immoral and unethical' business practice.[51] In the 1950s, Ethel Payne, dubbed 'First Lady of the Black Press', was tenacious in her coverage of the civil rights movement in the US and thanks to her persistence succeeded in making the issue of national importance. Equally, journalist and war reporter Martha Gellhorn showed the world the human impact of armed conflict, reporting from the Second World War through to the Vietnam War, and her unflinching detail introduced a bold humanity without bravado.

We owe much to women's unique perspective and tenaciousness in their contribution to the world news narrative, and this demonstrates why we need the all-important 'female lens'.

WOMEN IN CULTURE: WHY IT MATTERS

If the lack of representation or at least presence of women in popular culture didn't bother you, then perhaps it should. Popular culture impacts on how we see the world, how we understand and interpret it – helping to influence conversation, social norms and values. Consider that storytelling centuries ago was used as a means of disseminating valuable information, but what if that information reinforces negative stereotypes and expectations, as it does today? If you're a young girl growing up and you never see a woman as a scientist, politician, or a hero, doesn't that serve to reinforce a limited worldview of what women are capable of? This is why, when Disney reframes a fairy-tale narrative to include a feminist subtext, it's an important moment in popular culture. Children, particularly when they're developing their sense of self, play out the roles they see through the stories they hear. Helping girls imagine a future where they are strong and independent, and important even, matters: 'filmmakers make more than movies, they make choices' was among the conclusions of the UN Women Gender Bias without Borders film study.[52]

In the same way, seeing art made by women, films made by women and films about women attaches visibility and significance to women. To quote Phumzile Mlambo-Ngcuka, under-secretary general and executive director of UN Women, '"it's just a movie" ... ignores the influence of film to shape and solidify social norms'.[53]

WOMEN'S ABSENCE IN THE SCHOOL CURRICULUM

A further factor that is serving to perpetuate the myth that women aren't creative or have little place in the artworld is women's absence from the school's curriculum, and this is also true for scientific subjects. For example, a reading list proposed by a UK exam board proposed only 8 female authors among a list of 45 authors for the English Literature curriculum;[54] in 2017, the #Balancethebooks initiative found that 69 per cent of UK GCSE English Literature texts were written by men, and this demonstrated an increase in men's dominance of literature since 2014.[55] Across science and maths, while Marie Curie does get a namecheck, Lise Meitner and Ada Lovelace are absent, and I recall seeing not one female scientist referenced in my Physics textbooks. This is not just a UK phenomenon as similar studies across Australia and the US have revealed the same problem: women are absent from educational curricula, and we wonder why girls develop such low expectations or are dissuaded from STEM subjects early on in their education. From our own research, 74 per cent of women said that growing up they wish they had seen more female role models as inspiration, and 82 per cent of women wanted to see more female achievement recorded in the history books, so it's not like the dearth of women in our curricula goes unnoticed.[56]

It's a sad fact that not only are women marginalised and under-represented through popular culture as the 'subject', they are also marginalised as the makers or storytellers within the same culture: women struggle not only for the work but for critical acclaim. It doesn't help, of course, that film critics and art critics are largely male: some 73 per cent of the top critics on film site Rotten Tomatoes are male, and 80 per cent of reviewers writing for the entertainment press are male. This matters because critical opinion shapes a film's release and distribution patterns, and male reviewers are significantly less likely to review a film featuring a female lead according to research conducted by the Center for the Study of Women in Television and Film.[57]

Women also have the phenomenon of 'man-splaining' or unconscious bias to contend with, whereby the same work derided when produced by a woman is lauded when the very same ideas are represented by a man. Perhaps the most memorable example was 'The mansplaining of Taylor Swift'. The problem with Ryan Adams covering the entire song catalogue on Taylor's album *1989* was in the sudden critical acclaim it received, acclaim reserved for Ryan, not the artist who wrote the songs in the first place. Critics' comments highlight the condescending attitude, because apparently we have Ryan to thank for 'giving her a masterclass in lyrical interpretation', revealing the low expectations reserved for women in the artistic realms.[58]

There are signs of change. In film, while women struggle to get behind the camera, a number of high-profile female-led movies are now in production, and in theory the track record of female-led movies' box-office earnings should make it easier to attract finance to subsequent 'women's' projects. We could be at something of a tipping point, but it's a shame that female stars' earnings have yet to achieve parity. In TV, the pace of change has accelerated, thanks in no small part to the success of female-led shows and powerful female 'show runners'. At the same time, the recent scandals and the #MeToo movement have at once created awareness of the scale and impact of sexual discrimination and harassment, but also – it is my hope – mobilised greater intolerance. This could represent something of a watershed moment, opening doors for women based on their abilities, finally.

WHAT THIS MEANS:
KEY TAKEAWAYS FOR BRANDS

It's easy to think that the work we do in the communications industry is 'only advertising', we're just selling stuff, it's pretty innocuous or transient in impact and therefore should be immune to criticism or any attempts to foster a move for gender diversity. When one notable executive creative director declared recently that he was, 'Bored of diversity being prioritised over talent',[59] he perhaps articulated a latent view within the industry that this whole 'gender and race thing' was a distraction at best, and at worst meant that creative work was being compromised as a result. When you're a white middle-class male at the top of the industry you can afford to be bored with diversity. This ignores the fact that for an industry that thrives on the originality of its ideas, having a diverse workforce leads to a diversity of ideas, yet having a creative department that looks and behaves and thinks in the same way will undoubtedly lead to 'group think', something to which Doyle Dane Bernbach was alive even as far back in the 1960s. But that is to consider ideas for the benefit of the brand or the agency, whereas with our work on the JWT Women's Index we considered the impact of ideas upon the audience.

The importance of a female narrative

As evidenced here, so much of the way in which we see the world and interpret it is shaped through a male lens and a male narrative, thanks to men's historic dominance within the media landscape. This serves to deny women representation, a voice and an all-important perspective. The fact is that we may experience the world differently – nature and nurture shape how we respond to our environment – and our stories and experiences deserve to be told. A female narrative shapes how we interpret and frame female achievement, for example, or how we interpret world events, how we respond to culture and see culture, and this perspective is enormously important in the context of brands seeking to understand their place and role in the world. Without a female narrative, a true and authentic female perspective, can you really ever arrive at female insight?

The impact of the moving image: why it's not 'just advertising'

As part of our study we asked women how they felt about the onscreen representation of women: 80 per cent of women globally felt that too often women were portrayed as sexual objects in film or on TV, and this held true across all generations.[60] Just over half of women said that found it difficult to relate to female characters onscreen, and as we've touched on earlier, 85 per cent of women globally said that when it comes to understanding women the film world and advertising world need to catch up with the real world. These are particularly important statistics for advertisers since a major part of an ad campaign's success or failure is its ability to engage the audience, and by that I mean interrupt their consciousness and attract attention: this is in part how we measure campaign effectiveness. Equally, more than one-third of women claimed to have stopped watching a film, TV programme or advert that they felt was stereotyping them, and a resounding 85 per cent of women felt that media and culture were blind to how much they stereotype women, indicating that they feel the industry as a whole has a huge blindspot.

Through the data we also observed a strong case for getting more women into your business, since nearly two-thirds of women said they preferred products designed by women since they better understand their needs, which once again underlines the importance of having women in your creative teams as was so easily understood in the 1960s.

But the most persuasive data for me, and the argument for change, was the sense of just how influential onscreen representations of women could be. So, as highlighted earlier, some 58 per cent of women said that seeing a strong onscreen female role model had inspired them to be either more ambitious or more assertive, rising to 68 per cent in Asia Pacific. We also saw overwhelmingly that women felt seeing more women onscreen as corporate leaders, scientists or politicians would make it easier for women to realise these roles in real life.[61] This should send a very clear message on the importance of onscreen female representation: through the simplest of casting decisions we can change perceptions and perhaps open more doors for women. While this is good for society, it's also positive for brands, as reinforced by a 2017 Facebook IQ study, which found that a brand promoting gender equality generates a buying preference not just among women but men, and generates greater loyalty.[62] The analysis also revealed that social media sentiment was significantly more positive towards brands creating content that promoted gender equality. So, these findings suggest a clear connection between positive or progressive representations of gender and advertising effectiveness but also brand loyalty and preference: show me a brand that wouldn't want these metrics. For anyone bored with the diversity argument, I think these findings should prove pretty persuasive.

CONCLUSIONS

· ·

A Time for Women

'It took me quite a long time to develop a voice, and now that I have it, I am not going to be silent.' **Madeleine Albright**

THERE HAS NEVER BEEN A BETTER TIME TO BE A WOMAN

There was a moment when approaching this chapter I was tempted simply to write: 'women are great: the end', and if I'm honest that does tend to be my mantra. It's true that within our research we witness huge optimism among women the world over, and 76 per cent of women globally within the Women's Index felt it had never been a better time to be a woman, a sentiment shared across generations. Within the data we observed a sense that things were changing for women so 71 per cent of the sample felt that feminism was on the rise, and 62 per cent of women claimed to be proud to be a feminist.

Encountering the 'fourth wave' of feminism, the women's marches, the #MeToo movement and subsequent 'naming and shaming' of those engaged in sexual harassment within the entertainment industry but spreading into sport, fashion, politics and even the business world, it's hard not to feel encouraged that perhaps we are entering into a new era – one of meritocracy where a woman can finally take an equal share of opportunities or, at the very least, discrimination will be much less acceptable.

That said, the picture wasn't universally positive. As witnessed throughout the research, Japan was an outlier, thanks to its more traditional culture, which has been slower in embracing the idea of female progress, so it was little surprise that only 43 per cent of Japanese women felt there had 'never been a better time' to be a woman. That contrasted markedly with Saudi Arabia and Egypt, where 61 per cent of women were optimistic about women's lot, and in Lebanon, with 70 per cent of women sharing this sentiment. This counters, perhaps, many of our prejudices within the Western world about femininity and empowerment in the Middle East. But there's no point in glossing over the fact that despite women's optimism there are still considerable barriers to our progress: one-third of women felt their opinion was less valued at home purely because they were a woman, 40 per cent of women claimed to experience sexism in the workplace 'on a regular basis', and nearly half felt they were held back professionally due to their gender: plenty to still inspire anger.[1]

For all the obstacles, we also observed an innate understanding of our own power as women even if the world needs to play catch up, with 76 per cent of women globally in agreement that femininity was a strength not a weakness. Yet nearly all women (92 per cent) felt that femininity today represented something very different versus 50 years ago, and that we needed to redefine this as a concept. What proved intriguing was that when we asked women to articulate what contemporary femininity meant, while on the one hand there was a global consistency in definition, the qualities selected by women were not those of pretty passivity but those of leadership, of alpha characteristics.

WOMEN AND SUCCESS: WHAT DOES IT MEAN?

Building on the idea that femininity is an alpha characteristic and not a soft, fuzzy, pink-hued concept, we observed among women of all ages, among mothers and the childfree, huge personal ambition, with half of women citing starting their own business as important in life, and three-quarters saying that their work was very much linked to their sense of identity. When we looked at women's definition of success, however, this was a more holistic concept, embracing on the one hand financial independence indicative of a rational pragmatism, but combining this with health and happiness as the top three values defining success across our core nine global markets. When we broadened this to include the top five values of success, what felt significant was that marriage didn't make the cut in all but two markets: China and Russia. This isn't surprising: given that Russia is the divorce capital of the world with one in three marriages failing in the first three years,[2] a high value is placed on keeping one's marriage together, but equally in China the cultural pressure to be married as a measure of success is one felt keenly by women. Perhaps more depressingly, personal happiness did not make it into the top five values of success in China.

Yet it was interesting that within countries where one would expect more 'traditional' attitudes towards what success for women looked like, for example, India and Saudi Arabia, marriage was absent, and a more self-focused definition prevailed. For example, in Saudi Arabia, following one's dreams and passions was the second most popular definition of success among women.

The findings demonstrate that for the most part women's vision of success is not tied to marriage and finding a partner, an idea with which popular culture and journalists alike still struggle. We should also note that financial autonomy is a high priority: 67 per cent of all women cited this as very important and 92 per cent as important, with three-quarters of women citing having a career as important, indicating that we neither expect nor desire to be a 'kept woman'. The data paints a more contemporary definition of womanhood, yet 'raising happy healthy children' features prominently and reflects the importance of our role as nurturers, although I should point out that this was skewed heavily by women who had children – when we re-analysed the data for childfree women, 'raising happy healthy children' dropped down in importance and was prioritised by only 9 per cent of women in the survey.

BARRIERS TO SUCCESS

We asked women whether they expected to be successful in life. Although a resounding 68 per cent of women did expect to achieve their goals, we probed around potential barriers to fulfilling one's potential. Although 44 per cent of women cited themselves as a barrier to their own achievements, with 27 per cent attributing this to their insecurities, the barrier of family, parent and spouse received 25 per cent of the vote, indicating that a woman's immediate family can thwart her progress. We should also point out that nearly one in ten women perceived their looks or attractiveness as a barrier to fulfilling their potential, underlining the significance of appearance for women as personal equity. In fact, nearly one-third of women cited being attractive as 'very important' in life, perhaps representing a degree of pragmatism as to what the world is really like for women, even today.

FEMALE PROGRESS

Although it took many months to interpret the numbers, to cut and recut the figures to extract as many insights as possible, the story within the Women's Index data and what the numbers present is a picture of women as a strong, fearless and empowered force for change, intent on progress and self-determination. Although there were cultural nuances and countries like Japan and Russia were outliers, on the whole the findings were very consistent across geographies, across generations, and among those women who had children and those who did not. Women were telling us that marriage and children do not necessarily feature as the centre of their universe, that instead financial independence, following our dreams and passions, and the pursuit of happiness are what drives them.

It was also very clear through the data that women wanted much greater recognition for who they were, beyond society's limited expectations or outdated ideals, and to see their achievements and significance within the world reflected back to them. In short, they wanted to feel visible and included in the cultural narrative: there is very clear evidence that up to this point they felt that they had been excluded or airbrushed out, and they wanted to have a louder voice in culture.

FEMALE CAPITAL

A concept that I was very keen to explore and seed within the book was the idea of what I call Female Capital, namely the value that women bring to the world: as women. Within our research a resounding 94 per cent of women said that we need to recognise the value that women bring to the world, indicating that we are not there yet in this regard.[3] My theory is that, if we understood the value that women bring to the world across every field, then the inarguable logic of quantitative evidence would pave the way for female progress and would open doors previously shut to women. In researching the book, I discovered the quite startling body of evidence as to women's value, our Female Capital, across a wide variety of sectors, and I have tried to capture this. It's my hope also that through the concept of the 'New Female Tribes' I have also made clear the diversity of Female Capital, seeding the idea that as women we are not homogeneous, we do not conform to a binary definition of either mother or singleton. While admittedly I have explored the changing nature of motherhood as an essential part of the female 'condition', I have also perhaps persuaded you that while motherhood is a very diverse concept, it bears little or no relation to a woman's professional or creative capabilities: it in no way diminishes her Female Capital.

I should also point out again, perhaps defensively, that the concept of the Tribes is not an attempt to create a new set of female stereotypes, but a desire to introduce a more diverse and meaningful language with which to describe women, in the knowledge that in today's media landscape, language has powerful equity and the idea of tribes often act as a shortcut to understanding. Consider, for example, the way in which the term 'metrosexual' ignited public discussion but also introduced to the world a tribe of men intent on rejecting some of the traditionalist macho ideals; the term 'metrosexual' became not only socially acceptable but also a badge of pride for men, who might previously have been labelled 'effeminate'. In the same way, and having spoken to many women on the issue, there was a keen desire to break free from the 'busy working mum' label, with its inherent meaninglessness, and take pride in embracing monikers such as 'alpha female' or 'social pioneer'. I should say again here that most of the women to whom I speak embody several tribes: they are not confined to one box.

What is surprising to me, and has been a constant source of revelation, is not so much the enormous amount of data providing evidence of women's capabilities, our effectiveness as managers, our performance in the armed forces, our creativity and innovation, and our entrepreneurial flair, but the fact that it is not more widely known. My hope is that this evidence, the extensive and diverse data points, will provide a persuasive argument to give women the status they deserve in society, finally.

WHY HAS THE DATA BEEN HIDDEN?

While it proved immensely rewarding to discover the 'hidden history' of female achievement, to realise that women were just as pivotal in our global enlightenment, our understanding of how the world works, and pioneering the essential theories of science, maths, medicine, astronomy and computing through to the artistic fields, what then occurred to me was the crucial question: why weren't our contributions to the world, prevalent as they were, more widely known? This is a pretty fundamental and urgent question, since one of the key factors that serves to hold women back in almost every field is the lack of precedent. Without precedent, there is no proof, no reassurance or evidence of competence, and this goes to 'explain' why so frequently women are perceived as high risk, unproven and therefore incompetent: no precedent, no opportunity. The more I researched, however, the more I realised with a sickening consistency how systematically women's contributions had been at best minimised and at worst completely airbrushed from history.

THE MARGINALISATION OF FEMALE PROGRESS

My research revealed two key dynamics that went to explain how women's achievements had been marginalised. Firstly, there's the airbrushing from the history books and textbooks; since many historians and textbook writers were male, over the years the collective narrative has favoured male achievement: simple but true. At times, a more systemic sexism was at play. For example, women were not admitted to many professional bodies and their scientific discoveries would be attributed to their husbands or male colleagues.

School curricula perpetuate this phenomenon so from an early age we are instilling in both genders that women have played little or no role in the furthering of human progress.

The second dynamic I observed, and one which was repeated almost to a defined template, was the active 'purging' or sidelining of women within professions, This was evident time and time again in the computing industry, advertising, film and even religion. The moment a field of industry or employment became established, became significantly commercial or monetised, it was masculinised through its transformation into a 'profession': according to the male-as-breadwinner ideal, men work in professions, women don't. In the computing industry, for example, the industry morphed, with the assistance of language and recruitment criteria, from a 'clerical' practice, think women, to a professional one, ergo male. In Hollywood, the studio system and commercialisation transformed it from an artistic or creative endeavour into an industry, with unions protecting jobs for the boys, and the money men or financial backers lending to their own kind, i.e. men. The advertising industry evolved from a creative practice to become a science, and women disappeared from creative departments.

At its most simplistic, what I observed amounted to the idea that as soon as any endeavour proved successful or profitable, men moved in and women were meanwhile edged out: again, and again, and again. It's hard not to feel a little angry on behalf of all these women, whose hard work in pioneering these industries was benignly forgotten or at worst systematically and deliberately swept aside.

In order to overcome this phenomenon and to redress the injustice, it is imperative that we rediscover and promote women's contribution to society, that we share and publicise the achievements of pioneering women and we lobby for greater recognition in school curricula, history books, public records and popular culture. In doing so, we will create the much-needed precedent, the proof of women's capabilities and the female role models we need in society to generate greater awareness of women's aptitudes and our innate Female Capital. We need female role models because, as the saying goes, 'if she can see it, she can be it', but perhaps more importantly, if those in the positions of power understand Female Capital, we will become the 'safe bet', the smart hire, the capable, and the proven pair of hands: we will remove doubt as to our potential. Therefore, in future it will become easier for us to elect a female president, we will see and hear more about female artists, it will become easier to invest in female start-ups, easier to support women in education and smarter to hire women to executive boards.

THE IMPORTANCE OF FEMALE ROLE MODELS

One of the easiest ways to create awareness for Female Capital, and to create female precedents where there are seemingly none, is to promote women into positions of high visibility through hiring decisions, but also through the cultural narrative, for example, making sure female achievement gets the same press coverage, ensuring that women in positions of power garner the visibility and respect they deserve. It is crystal-clear through our data, across all geographies and all generations, that there is a significant lack of female role models now, and there has been through generations.

Role models are the shortcut to establishing female precedent: they evidence Female Capital, they inspire and lead, and they open doors. So, for example, 67 per cent of women said if we saw more women onscreen as corporate leaders it would be easier for them to realise this in real life; they said the same for scientists and political leaders.

The simple truth is that men live with a cultural surround sound that teaches them and reinforces the idea that they can do anything they want to, be anything they want to, they can reach for the sky: for women no such parallel exists. In the language of praise we use for our sons, telling them that they are brave and powerful and clever, compared to the language of praise we use for our daughters, telling them they are pretty, we conspire with the cultural imagery from films and TV that serves to sexualise women. Even from a very young age, we teach women that our only equity or currency in the world is our attractiveness. As evidenced within our data, 82 per cent of women said that the sexualised representation of women and girls teaches us that if we're not pretty then we don't matter.[4]

And dare I say that advertising informs that 'cultural surround sound'; as highlighted in our study of the past ten years of Cannes advertising submissions, the overriding representation of women was either in the kitchen or the bedroom, and primarily as a sexual object.[5] Therefore, as an industry with such persuasive power we have permission if not a responsibility to change it, and I truly believe that advertising and role models can change the way the world works for women. That is one of the key reasons why we sought a partnership with the Geena Davis Institute on Gender in Media, an organisation that have assiduously campaigned for greater gender parity within the world of TV and film.

ROLE MODEL RIPPLE EFFECT

OK, so it's a pretty flippant assertion that role models can in some way change the world, and you may pour scorn on the idea that advertising could play a part, but let me explain. As part of our Women's Index research, while we probed around the concept of real-world role models, we also – and, remember, we are an advertising agency – felt it important to delve into the influence of the moving image, be it film, television or advertising. So we asked women about their experience of onscreen female role models, and we included reference to film, TV and advertising within our line of questioning. From our first question we saw that 90 per cent of women across all countries felt that showing female role models onscreen was important. Then we asked about their influence in life: 61 per cent of women said that onscreen role models (and by that we mean TV, film or advertising) have been influential in their life, rising to 70 per cent in Asia Pacific.

We then probed more specifically on the real-life behaviours these onscreen role models had inspired, and we saw significant influence across a wide variety of behaviours. What I have attempted to do is to join the dots, projecting (using real data) the world or cultural impact generated from that onscreen stimulus as a kind of 'role model ripple effect', and framing it in commercial terms: Role Model ROI (return on investment), a kind of onscreen or 'reel world' to off-screen 'real world' payback. Here are some examples to illustrate this:

Example 1: Education

Reel-world influence: from the Women's Index data, 11 per cent of our sample said that an onscreen role model had inspired them to go to school and further their education.

Real-world impact: data suggests that every additional year of schooling can increase a woman's earnings by 10 per cent, and across a female population each additional year of schooling can lift annual GDP by 0.37 per cent.[6]

Example 2: Sport

Reel-world influence: 16 per cent of women in our survey claimed to have taken up a new sport inspired by an onscreen female role model.

Real-world impact: data suggests that sports participation makes women 40 per cent more employable,[7] and for every marginal dollar a woman earns she will invest 90 per cent back into her community.

Example 3: Leadership

Reel-world influence: 15 per cent of women in our survey said that an onscreen female role model had inspired them to seek a leadership position

Real-world impact: companies with women on management boards generate on average a 15 per cent increase in profitability compared to those with none,[8] yet around 5 per cent of S&P 500 companies have women as CEOs.[9]

Example 4: Discrimination

Reel-world influence: 21 per cent of women in our survey said that an onscreen role model had inspired them to stay determined in the face of gender discrimination.

Real-world impact: 44 per cent of women in our survey said they had been held back professionally because they were a woman, yet if women achieved their full potential and had gender parity in the labour market, $28 trillion could be added to the global GDP by 2025.[10]

It's this last example that for me illustrates the potential global societal impact of the imagery we see onscreen, and yes, the answer to women achieving their full potential in the labour market isn't just down to women's determination because we also need men in a position of power to believe in women's potential. One can only assume and wish, unless the audience were guilty of entrenched immutable belief systems, that there would be a cultural ripple effect across both genders: given that men are more likely to be in a position of power, we assume can that onscreen female role models would impact on *everyone's* belief systems.

It's my hope, therefore, that even the most cynically minded could perceive the value of changing and evolving women's onscreen representation. Putting altruism to one side, as I have been at pains to underline, there are commercial benefits in tapping the latent potential of women as consumers and wealth generators, entrepreneurs and employees.

SO WHAT DO WE DO NOW?

If you're reading this as a person employed within the marketing or advertising community, then I hope I've said enough to convince you to take even a cursory look at the way in which you're currently speaking to and engaging women as an audience. There are numerous examples of advertising and product design that persist in stereotyping women, and fail to really tune into their needs, and as any marketer will tell you, this is commercial death. The insights provided within this book are by no means exhaustive, and part of the work we do within Female Tribes Consulting is to dive deep into the research across specific tribes to apply the thinking across specific categories, but I have attempted to provide initial thoughts as to the commercial application of the thinking. What is fundamental as a principle is that if you are targeting women based on blunt demographics, namely their age and the presence of children, you're doing it wrong and you will not have authentic or 'actionable' insight: this is where the problems start.

Well-designed products and truly inspirational or transformational brands and services stem from great insight. I passionately believe that in using powerful insight to design and configure business through a female lens we can truly change the way the world works for women. A financial product that doesn't force a women to postpone children in favour of meeting mortgage payments for ... a lingerie brand that recognises the innate sexuality in women across all ages and sizes ... a car safety system that protects women from whiplash to the same level as men ... these types of products could create a seismic shift in women's experience of the world.

Putting brand value to one side, it's my mission also to remove some of the institutional barriers to women's progression, so I would hope that serving up the body of evidence as to women's value in organisations as leaders, innovators, entrepreneurs, managers and creators may prove persuasive and inspire change.

BE YOUR OWN ACTIVIST

If you're a woman reading this, in terms of your own self-interest and the furthering of your *own* career, I trust that some of the data outlined here will prove useful and help you to have the arguments ready to convince others of your Female Capital. If you're returning to work from maternity leave, embrace the idea that motherhood has served only to sharpen your acuity and make you even more productive – don't accept the 'baby brain' myth. If you're a female entrepreneur seeking investment, push forward and reinforce arguments relating to your business's potential for growth – don't accept the vision that frames your business in terms of potential for loss. If you're working or considering a career in the world of science and technology, embrace the idea of the many female pioneers before you, and assert your legitimacy to be in the lab – don't accept the rebranding of science as a male profession and don't suffer the imposter syndrome. If you're pushing for promotion to the board, go armed with the data on your effectiveness in management and the belief that you will bring new ideas, efficiency and productivity through your unique insight.

In short, it's my hope that every woman will ultimately know and embrace her own Female Capital; that we will continue to feel that there has never been a better time to be a woman; that we will know our own power and influence through understanding just how many women before us have shaped the world; that we can continue driving and shaping the world in future because, after all, femininity is a strength not a weakness.

TOWARDS A BETTER FUTURE

Women are evolving, and elevating their economic and political status. If we want to understand modern womanhood, we need to accept that we can no longer define women in just one role and assume we know and understand her, top-to-toe. Should motherhood be her greatest achievement, or the only achievement we recognise? We need to embrace a more nuanced understanding of women and, crucially, we should accept that while she may sometimes be a mother or a carer, she is many more things besides. By exploring this idea we can start to embrace the idea of Female Capital: the value that women bring to the world as women.

What keeps me motivated and part of the stimulus for this book is the idea that the simple act of being born a woman substantially reduces the chance of a person fulfilling their full potential. That scares me, it enrages me, and it's made me determined in whatever small way I can to do something to help correct that. To quote the controversial philosopher Slavoj Žižek, 'true thinking starts when you ask the difficult questions', and the question I ask myself is why should girls grow up not fulfilling their true potential?

APPENDIX

. . . .

The Female Tribes

TRIBE DEFINITIONS

It's important to note that, since this is not an attempt to slot women into one box or definition, women can encompass many tribes and we witnessed strong overlaps between particular tribes. We would assume, however, that there are likely to be one or two dominant types of tribe in particular that characterise an individual woman based on her primary motivations, i.e. the most important drivers to her attitudes and behaviour.

Alphas – their focus is the self and they prioritise career and achievement

Alpha Female: ambitious and career-driven, she wants to get to the top of her career and says that her sense of self is linked to her work.

Asian Alpha: the Asian Alpha is distinct from the Western Alpha as she is subject to specific cultural factors, for example, the intense pressure she may face to be married in China in order to be perceived as 'successful'. She is also more willing to postpone motherhood to focus on her career.

African Alpha: the rise in education combined with a fierce work ethic has spawned a generation of powerful and successful young African female entrepreneurs – from initiators of tech start-ups to fashion designers. She still grapples with cultural factors such as patriarchal society and entrenched stereotypes.

African Political Class: Africa is now home to an active, vocal and energised female political class intent on progress. Our proprietary research revealed that a woman in South Africa is significantly more likely to feel that she should display the qualities of leadership and ambition.

Latina Matriarch: ambitious, educated and politically active. She doesn't want solo success, however, and Brazilian alphas, for example, are much more likely to want to bring their community with them. She recognises the importance of helping younger women succeed in their careers and mentoring women in the workplace.

'Not Mom'/Child Free: there's a growing tribe of women who are not 'childless' but happily childfree. She doesn't feel the need to procreate in order to feel complete. Equally we observe that more women are postponing starting a family, so essentially childfree for longer.

Mumbai Millennial: university-educated and hugely ambitious, the Mumbai Millennial is defined by her career, but she wants to work in a career that interests her. She is significantly less likely vs Asian Alphas to consider that she is a barrier to her own success: she sees her family and her spouse as potential barriers, yet she is the most confident of all our Alphas that she will be successful.

GI Jane: the realities of war have propelled women to the front line, seeing them participate in active combat. In the US women make up 15 per cent of the armed forces and, in a landmark decision, were allowed into combat roles in the US Army at the end of 2013.

Hedonists – their focus is the 'self' and they prioritise self-development, pleasure and fulfilment

Pleasure Seekers: the Pleasure Seeker prioritises taking care of herself, 'me time' and her sexual and social fulfilment. Success to her means following her dreams and passions, having fun and a stress-free life.

Explorers: she reflects, perhaps, the degree to which technology has been so influential in making women feel like global citizens; success is aligned to being active, travelling the world, and taking risks and challenging herself. Worldwide travel and broadening her horizons are 'very important'.

Cougars: with the rise in divorce among the boomer generation in both the UK and US, increasingly women in their fifties are single and dating. We seem to be uncomfortable, though, with the idea of older women as sexual beings.

Modern Courtesan: millennial, single and pre-children. She believes she can use her looks as a means of power and influence. To her, relationships may be transient: love isn't the be-all and end-all.

Beauty Witch: in Asia there is a new female: she's in her forties to fifties but appears much younger … no, make that 'startlingly young'. In Japan she is called '*Bimajyo*' – Beauty Witch.

Altruists – their focus is others, being possessed of a strong desire to improve their community around them and make the world a better place

Social Pioneer: from philanthropy to community volunteering, women have a long legacy of working to improve their communities and the world around them. The Social Pioneer is motivated by a strong desire to make her community or the world at large a better place.

Teen Activist: one of the interesting contradictions of the Teen Activist is how level-headed and mature she is, and likely to conform, yet equally she has a desire to change the world around her. Growing up in a hostile world has given her a desire to change it and, armed with idealism and social media connectivity, she is making her voice heard.

Modern Spiritualist: she is part of a new movement of women who are nurturing and defining their spiritual needs in their own terms, and not aligned with traditional religious bodies.

Culture Shaper: a woman in the creative arts, she prioritises a female narrative through her work, which could be in art, media, film or advertising, and believes the world is enriched through experiencing creativity through the female lens.

Traditionalists – their focus is towards others, and home and family is the centre of their universe

Nurturers: home is where the heart is – she is a homemaker, and family is the centre of her world. She has children and defines her success as 'raising happy healthy children' or having a good relationship with her family. She is least likely to prioritise career over motherhood.

Spouse Focused: marriage is everything – it defines her success and her happiness. In fact, the importance of her spouse is prioritised whatever her age. She is particularly prevalent in the US.

Tiger Mother: characterised as a strict disciplinarian who devotes herself to raising her children to achieve high standards of education, overseeing every aspect of their development. In doing so she prioritises the educational needs of her child over her own needs.

NOTES

Chapter 1: Women and the New Rules of Engagement

1. 'Special K Inner Strength Study', J. Walter Thompson, 2014.
2. '2016 domestic grosses', *Box Office Mojo*, 2017, http://www.boxofficemojo.com/yearly/chart/?yr=2016.
3. Clara Guibourg, 'Oscars 2018: female-led Oscar films "more profitable"', *BBC News*, 1 March 2018, http://www.bbc.co.uk/news/entertainment-arts-43146026.
4. Kevin O'Keefe, *Mic*, May 2016. https://mic.com/articles/127095/here-s-exactly-how-much-movies-about-women-make-at-the-box-office-versus-movies-about-men#.V5fVU8tPr
5. 'Births in England and Wales: 2016', Office for National Statistics, 19 July 2017, https://www.ons.gov.uk/peoplepopulationandcommunity/birthsdeathsandmarriages/live-births/bulletins/birthsummarytablesenglandandwales/2016.
6. US Census, 2010.
7. TheNotMom.com.
8. Singapore Department of Statistics, *Statistics on Marriage and Divorce: Reference Year 2016*, Singapore Department of Statistics, Singapore, 2016, http://www.singstat.gov.sg/docs/default-source/default-document-library/publications/publications_and_papers/marriages_and_divorces/smd2016.pdf.
9. J. Walter Thompson Women's Index, 2016.
10. Michael J. Rosenfeld, 'Who Wants the Breakup? Gender and Breakup un Heterosexual Couples', in D. F. Alwin *et al.* (eds), *Social Networks and the Life Course*, Springer, 2018, https://web.stanford.edu/~mrosenfe/Rosenfeld_gender_of_breakup.pdf.
11. 'Mind the gaps', Deloitte Millennial Survey, 2015.
12. J. Walter Thompson Women's Index, 2015.
13. Women Entrepreneurs 2014: Bridging the Gender Gap in Venture Capital, Babson College, 2014, http://www.babson.edu/News-Events/babson-news/Pages/140930-venture-capital-funding-women-entrepreneurs-study.aspx
14. Dana Kanze, Laura Huang, Mark A. Conley, E. Tory Higgins, 'We ask men to win & women not to lose: Closing the gender gap in start up funding', *Academy of Management Journal*, 27 April 2017.
15. Women Unbound: Unleashing Female Entrepreneurial Potential, PwC in collaboration with the Crowdfunding Center, 2017.
16. 'Washington post poll: reaction to women's marches January 25–29 2017', *Washington Post*, 1 February 2017.
17. J. Walter Thompson Women's Index, 2015.
18. Jessica Taft, *Rebel Girls: Youth Activism and Social Change Across the Americas*, NYU Press, 2010.
19. 'WHO multi-country study on women's health and domestic violence against women', World Health Organization, 2005, http://www.who.int/gender/violence/who_multi-country_study/fact_sheets/Brazil2.pdf.

20. J. Walter Thompson Women's Index, 2015.
21. 'Special K Inner Strength Study: UK, US, India, Brazil', J. Walter Thompson, 2014.
22. Nash Jenkins, 'Watch kids tell Jimmy Kimmel why women can't be president', *Time*, 6 November 2015, http://time.com/4102597/jimmy-kimmel-hillary-clinton-women-president.
23. 'A study in leadership: Women do it better than men', Zenger Folkman Management Study, 2012, http://zengerfolkman.com/women-vs-men-report.
24. 'Reading the face of a leader', University of Cambridge, 10 May 2016, http://www.cam.ac.uk/research/news/reading-the-face-of-a-leader.
25. Rebecca Smith, 'Commentators and press need to stop being sexist in Rio – and PR can help', *PR Week*, 11 August 2016, http://www.prweek.com/article/1405218/commentators-media-need-stop-sexist-rio-pr-help.
26. Sarah Grieves, 'Aesthetics, Athletics and Olympians' report, Cambridge University Press, 2016.
27. John Inverdale, Radio 5 Live, 5 July 2013.
28. https://twitter.com/chicagotribune/status/762401317050605568\.
29. Karen Crouse, 'His latest innovation: the world's best swimmer', *New York Times*, 6 August 2016, http://www.nytimes.com/2016/08/07/sports/olympics/katie-ledecky-swimming-coach-rio-2016.html?_r=0.
30. J. Walter Thompson Women's Index, 2015.
31. 'Hitting the bullseye: reel girl archers inspire real girl archers', Geena Davis Institute on Gender in Media, 2016, https://seejane.org/wp-content/uploads/hitting-the-bullseye-reel-girl-archers-inspire-real-girl-archers-full.pdf.
32. J. Walter Thompson Women's Index, 2015/16.
33. J. Walter Thompson Women's Index, 2016.
34. Festival Insights research, 2013; see Saffron Alexander, 'Picture a typical Glastonbury goer. Now tell us their age', *Telegraph*, 24 June 2015, https://www.telegraph.co.uk/goodlife/11681483/Picture-a-typical-Glastonbury-goer.-Now-tell-us-their-age.html.

Chapter 2: The Dow Jane Effect and the Female Economy

1. Bruce Handy, 'Women-centric films out-gross male-centric films on average: twist!', *Vanity Fair*, 15 March 2014, http://www.vanityfair.com/culture/2014/03/women-films-out-gross-male-films.
2. Marcus Noland, Tyler Moran and Barbara Kotschwar, 'Is gender diversity profitable?', working paper, Peterson Institute for International Economics, February 2016, https://piie.com/publications/working-papers/gender-diversity-profitable-evidence-global-survey.
3. 'Women in Alternative Investments', Rothstein Kass, 2013, http://gender.stanford.edu/news/2013/women-run-hedge-funds.
4. Stephen Foley, 'Put women at the top and lift hedge funds higher', *Financial Times*, 17 September 2015, https://www.ft.com/content/d923da76-5d1d-11e5-9846-de406c-cb37f2.
5. *The Bottom Line Report: Women on Corporate Boards and Profitability*, Catalyst, 15 January 2004, http://www.catalyst.org/system/files/The_Bottom_Line_Connecting_Corporate_Performance_and_Gender_Diversity.pdf.
6. *Growing Under the Radar: An Exploration of the Achievements of Million-Dollar Women-Owned Firms*, American Express OPEN, January 2013, http://www.womenable.com/content/userfiles/Growing_Under_the_Radar_Jan2013.pdf.

7. J. Walter Thompson Women's Index, 2015/16.

8. J. Walter Thompson Women's Index, 2015/16.

9. Simi Kuriakose, 'Men are wary of alpha women', *Times of India*, 22 October 2012.

10. 'Women in the labour market: 2013', Office for National Statistics, 25 September 2013, https://www.ons.gov.uk/employmentandlabourmarket/peopleinwork/employmentan-demployeetypes/articles/womeninthelabourmarket/2013-09-25.

11. Carmen Nobel, 'Children benefit from having a working mom', Harvard Business School, 15 May 2015, https://www.hbs.edu/news/articles/Pages/mcginn-work-ing-mom.aspx.

12. Mark Hugo Lopez and Ana Gonzalez-Barrera, 'Women's college enrolment gains leaves men behind', Pew Research, 6 March 2014. http://www.pewresearch.org/fact-tank/2014/03/06/womens-college-enrollment-gains-leave-men-behind.

13. 'Rise in rate of 18 year-olds applying for UK higher education', UCAS, 5 February 2018, https://www.ucas.com/corporate/news-and-key-documents/news/rise-rate-18-year-olds-applying-uk-higher-education.

14. 'Women increasingly outpacing men's higher education participation in many world markets', ICEF Monitor, 22 October 2014, http://monitor.icef.com/2014/10/wom-en-increasingly-outpacing-mens-higher-education-participation-many-world-markets.

15. Ehsan Masood, 'Islam and science, an Islamist revolution', *Nature*, 1 November 2006; UNESCO.

16. Andy Coghlan, 'Iran is top of the world in science growth,' *New Scientist*, 24 March 2011, https://www.newscientist.com/article/dn20291-iran-is-top-of-the-world-in-science-growth/

17. Natasha Ridge, 'Why women graduates outnumber men in the UAE', *Gulf News*, 14 April 2011, http://gulfnews.com/gn-focus/why-women-graduates-outnumber-men-in-the-uae-1.790849.

18. Kathleen McGinn and Katherine Milkman, 'Looking up and looking out', *Organization Science*, July/August 2013.

19. J. Walter Thompson Women's Index, 2015/16

20. Gender Equality in Education, Employment and Entrepreneurship: Final Report to the MCM, OECD, 2012, http://www.oecd.org/social/family/50423364.pdf.

21. 'ender pay gap: new transparency rules show female managers earn £12k less than male colleagues', CMI, 25 September 2017, http://www.managers.org.uk/about-us/media-centre/cmi-press-releases/gender-pay-gap-new-transparency-rules-show-female-managers-earn-less.

22. Global Gender Pay Gap Report, World Economic Forum, 2017.

23. Paul Tudor Jones, University of Virginia Symposium, April 2013; see Julia La Roche, 'Paul Tudor Jones: Babies are the biggest killer of women's trading success', *Business Insider*, 23 May 2013, http://www.businessinsider.com/tudor-jones-babies-killer-to-trad-ing-2013-5?IR=T.

24. Dustin M. Logan *et al.*, 'How do memory and attention change with pregnancy and childbirth', *Journal of Clinical and Experimental Neuropsychology*, vol. 36, no. 5, 12 May 2014, http://www.tandfonline.com/doi/abs/10.1080/13803395.2014.912614#.VSUCOf-nF_HW.

25. Amelia Hill, 'Having babies can sharpen women's minds', *Observer*, 8 February 2009, https://www.theguardian.com/science/2009/feb/08/pregnancy-maternity-sharp-en-womens-brains.

26. J. Walter Thompson Women's Index, 2015/16.

27. 'Becoming a father can "rewire" a man's brains', *IFL Science!*, undated, http://www.iflscience.com/brain/becoming-father-can-rewire-mans-brain.

28. *The Motherhood Pay Penalty*, TUC, March 2016, https://www.tuc.org.uk/sites/default/files/MotherhoodPayPenalty.pdf.

29. *General Social Survey 2017*, US Council on Contemporary Families, 2017.

30. Elaine Allen, Amanda Elam, Nan Langowitz and Monica Dean, *2007 Report on Women and Entrepreneurship*, Global Entrepreneurship Monitor, 2008, http://sites.telfer.uottawa.ca/womensenterprise/files/2014/06/GEM-2003_Eng.pdf.

31. J. Walter Thompson Women's Index, 2015/16.

32. Therese Huston, 'We are way harder on female leaders who make bad calls', *Harvard Business Review*, 21 April 2016.

33. J. M. Coates and J. Herbert, 'Endogenous steroids and financial risk taking', *PNAS*, 22 April 2008.

34. *Women in Alternative Investments: A Marathon Not a Sprint*, Rothstein Kass Institute, 2013.

35. Stephen Foley, 'Put more women at the top and lift hedge funds higher', *Financial Times*, 17 September 2015.

36. James Crabtree, 'Indian banks lead the world on gender equality', *Financial Times*, 2 January 2014.

37. Geeta Sachdeva, 'Glass ceiling converted to glass transparency, *Journal of Business Management & Social Sciences Research*, April 2014.

38. Ruth David and George Smith Alexander, 'Top women at India banks prove ICICI gender neutral', *Bloomberg Markets*, 22 June 2011.

39. Vishal Dutta, 'Only 26% Indian women have banking relations', *Times of India*, 19 June 2014, https://economictimes.indiatimes.com/industry/banking/finance/banking/only-26-indian-women-have-banking-relations-usha-ananthasubramanian-cmd-bharatiya-mahila-bank/articleshow/36835596.cms.

40. 'Advantage Women Savings Account', ICICI Bank, undated, https://www.icicibank.com/Personal-Banking/account-deposit/advantage-woman-savings-account/index.page.

41. Katie Hope, 'The Thai women bucking the global trend', *BBC News*, 12 July 2016, http://www.bbc.co.uk/news/business-36761788.

42. Aimee Hansen, 'Spotlight on Asia: gender diversity is both catching up and leading', The Glass Hammer, 11 August 2016, http://theglasshammer.com/2016/08/11/spotlight-asia-gender-diversity-catching-leading.

43. Hu Haiyan, 'Cooking up success', *China Daily*, 2 November 2012.

44. J. Walter Thompson Women's Index, 2015/16.

45. 'Girl power up', *Economist*, 27 June 2012, https://www.economist.com/blogs/analects/2012/06/place-young-women.

46. Tania Branigan, 'Women in North Korea', *Guardian*, 11 December 2012.

47. Leslie T. Chang, *Factory Girls*, Spiegel & Grau, 2008.

48. 'Girl power: factory women', *Economist*, 11 May 2013.

49. J. Walter Thompson Women's Index, 2015/16.

50. *Supporting our Vision 2020 D&I Roadmap*, Ernst & Young, 2015, http://www.ey.com/Publication/vwLUAssets/EY-EMEIA-Diversity-and-Inclusivenes-Review-FY14/$-FILE/EY-EMEIA-Diversity-and-Inclusivenes-Review-FY14.pdf.

51. The markets studied were China, Hong Kong, India, Indonesia, Malaysia and Singapore.

52. Barbara Hannah Grufferman, 'What Diane von Furstenberg says about starting over', *Jerusalem Post*, 24 November 2010.

53. *2017 Kauffmann Index of Startup Activity: National Trends*, Ewing Marion Kauffman Foundation, 2017.

54. 'Monster Study: multi-generational worker attitudes', Millennial Branding, February 2017, http://millennialbranding.com/case-studies/monster-study.

55. Daniel Martin and Tom Kelly, 'Rise of the "silver separations"', *Daily Mail*, 18 November 2011.

56. 'Empowering girls and women', Clinton Global Initiative, 2009, http://www.un.org/en/ecosoc/phlntrpy/notes/clinton.pdf.

57. '2017 US Trust Findings on Wealth and Worth', US Trust, 2017, https://ustrustaem.fs.ml.com/content/dam/ust/articles/pdf/Detailed_Findings_Deck_Final.pdf.

58. Holly Sargent, Senior Director, Women's Studies, Harvard University, in 'Barclays Wealth Insight: A Question of Gender', Barclays Wealth and Economist Intelligence Unit, 2008.

59. 'Women and Wealth', US Trust, Bank of America.

60. *World Development Report: Gender Equality and Development*, World Bank, 2012.

61. Nicholas Lemann, 'The hand on the lever', *New Yorker*, 21 July 2014.

62. Jonathan Woetzel *et al.*, *The Power of Parity: How Advancing Women's Equality Can Add $12 Trillion to Global Growth*, McKinsey Global Institute, 2015, https://www.mckinsey.com/global-themes/employment-and-growth/how-advancing-womens-equality-can-add-12-trillion-to-global-growth.

63. Dipan Bose, Maria Segui-Gomez and Jeff R. Crandall, 'Vulnerability of female drivers involved in motor vehicle crashes: an analysis of US population at risk', *American Journal of Public Health*, vol. 101, no, 12, December 2011, https://www.ncbi.nlm.nih.gov/pmc/articles/PMC3222446.

64. Chalmers University of Technology, 'Female crash test dummy can reduce injuries', Phys.org, 20 August 2012, https://phys.org/news/2012-08-female-dummy-injuries.html.

65. 'Women-led businesses are driving force of the UK economy', Founders4schools, 5 March 2017, https://www.founders4schools.org.uk/about/press/release/2017-03-05-women-led-businesses-are-driving-force.

66. Women's Business Council, 2017.

67. 'Women unbound: Unleashing female entrepreneurial potential', PwC in collaboration with the Crowdfunding Center, 2017.

Chapter 3: The Leading Ladies – Women and Leadership

1. Will Yakowicz, 'Christine Lagarde: women lead better in crisis', *Inc.*, 23 October 2013.

2. Katherine Phillips, Susan K. Perkins and Nicholas A. Pearce, 'Ethnic Diversity, Gender, and National Leaders', *Journal of International Affairs*, vol. 67, no. 1, 2013.

3. J. Walter Thompson Women's Index, 2016.

4. Ruth Sealy, Elena Doldor and Susan Vinnicombe, *Women On Boards: Taking Stock Of Where We Are*, Cranfield University School of Management, 2016, http://30percentclub.wardourdigital.co.uk/assets/uploads/UK/Third_Party_Reports/Female_FTSE_Board_Report_2016.pdf

5. Aaron H. Dhir, 'What Norway can teach us about getting more women into boardrooms', *Atlantic*, 4 May 2015, http://www.theatlantic.com/business/archive/2015/05/what-norway-can-teach-the-us-about-getting-more-women-into-boardrooms/392195.

6. Karen Rubin, 'Research: investing in women-led Fortune 1000 companies', Quantopian, 11 February 2015, https://www.quantopian.com/posts/research-investing-in-women-led-fortune-1000-companies.

7. 'Women do it better than men: Leadership Effectiveness Study', Zenger Folkman, 2012, http://zengerfolkman.com/media/articles/ZFCo.WP.WomenBetterThanMen.033012.pdf.

8.   C. A. Moss Racusin *et al.*, 'Science faculty's subtle gender biases favor male students', *PNAS*, vol. 109, no. 41, 9 October 2012.

9.   Isabelle Fraser, 'Women earn more than men in their 20s – until the pay gap hits at age 30', *Daily Telegraph*, 28 August 2015, http://www.telegraph.co.uk/women/womens-business/11832042/Women-earn-more-than-men-in-their-20s-until-the-pay-gap-hits-at-age-30.html.

10. Abdoulie Janneh, United Nations Economic Commission for Africa, April 2012, http://www.un.org/esa/population/cpd/cpd2012/Agenda%20item%204/UN%20 system%20statements/ECA_Item4.pdf.

11. Bartholomäus Grill, 'Africa's future is female', *Spiegel Online*, 5 December 2013.

12. Rekha Mehra and Mary Hill Rojas, *Women, Food Security and Agriculture in a Global Marketplace*, International Center of Research on Women, 2008, https://www.icrw.org/wp-content/uploads/2016/10/A-Significant-Shift-Women-Food-Security-and-Agriculture-in-a-Global-Marketplace.pdf.

13. R. Chattopadhyay and E. Duflo, 'Women as policy makers: evidence from a randomized policy experiment in India', *Econometrica*, vol. 72, no. 5, 2004. See: http://www.unwomen.org/en/what-we-do/leadership-and-political-participation/facts-and-figures#notes.

14. Phumzile Mlambo-Ngcuka, 'Turning words into action, involving women for lasting peace', *Huffington Post*, 12 October 2015.

15. Donna Goodman, 'The struggle for women's equality in Latin America', *Dissident Voice*, 13 March 2009.

16. Leslie Schwindt-Bayer, 'Women's Representation in Latin American Legislatures: Current Challenges and New Directions', World Policy Centre, 2013, http://www.scielo.edu.uy/pdf/rucp/v23nspe/v23nspe02.pdf

17. Speech to the United Nations General Assembly, 21 September 2011.

18. Sophia Huyer and Nancy Halfkin, 'Brazilian women lead in science, technology and innovation, study shows', Elsevier Foundation, 26 March 2013, https://www.elsevier.com/connect/brazilian-women-lead-in-science-technology-and-innovation-study-shows.

19. João Pedro Azevedo and Louise Cord, 'Latin American Women Driving Region's Prosperity', World Bank, 12 September 2012, http://blogs.worldbank.org/latinamerica/latin-american-women-driving-region-s-prosperity.

20. *The Effect of Women's Economic Power in Latin America and the Caribbean*, World Bank, August 2012, http://www.bancomundial.org/content/dam/Worldbank/document/PLBSummer12latest.pdf.

21. Azevedo and Cord, 'Latin American Women'.

22. Natalija Novta and Joyce Wong, 'Women at Work in Latin America and the Caribbean', IMF Working Papers, 14 February 2017, https://www.imf.org/en/Publications/WP/Issues/2017/02/14/Women-at-Work-in-Latin-America-and-the-Caribbean-44662.

23. *The Effect of Women's Economic Power in Latin America and Caribbean*, World Bank, 2012.

24. J. Walter Thompson Women's Index, 2015.

25. Hua Wang, 'Encouraging women entrepreneurs in Brazil', *Entrepreneurship Review*, 2010, http://miter.mit.edu/tudo-bem-encouraging-women-entrepreneurs-brazil.

26. Jackie Vanderbrug, 'The global rise of female entrepreneurs', *Harvard Business Review*, 4 September 2013.

27. David M. De Ferranti *et al.*, *Inequality in Latin America: Breaking with History?*, World Bank, 2004.

28. Tanja van der Lippe, Judith Treas and Lukas Norbutas, 'Unemployment and the division of housework in Europe', *Work, Employment and Society*, 12 March 2017.

29. Anu Bhagwati, 'Why the Military needs to recruit and promote more women', *Washington Post*, 24 May 2013.

30. The study used data from the 2005 US Department of Defense 'Survey of Health-Related Behaviors Among Active-Duty Military Personnel', focusing on healthcare personnel who had been deployed at least once to Operation Enduring Freedom (OEF) or Operation Iraqi Freedom (OIF).

31. Ibid; and Ellen L. Haring, 'What women bring to the fight', *Parameters*, vol. 43, no. 2, Summer 2013.

32. *Harvard Business Review*/Carnegie Mellon Tepper School of Business, cited in, Ellen L. Haring, 'What women bring to the fight', Parameters, Summer 2013, http://ssi.army-warcollege.edu/pubs/parameters/issues/summer_2013/3_haring_article.pdf

33. Peter Bergen, *Manhunt*, Crown, 2012.

34. Paul Lashmar, 'Spy Scandal', *Independent*, 11 September 1999.

35. 'Hoover Institution acquires Melita Norwood papers', Hoover Institution, 2 November 2009, https://www.hoover.org/press-releases/hoover-institution-acquires-melita-norwood-papers.

36. Kate McCann, 'British spy chief's mission to recruit female spooks', *Stuff*, 27 May 2016, http://www.stuff.co.nz/world/europe/80448909/British-spy-chiefs-mission-to-recruit-female-spooks.

37. Michal Shmulovich, 'What the Mossad's female agents do – and don't do – for the sake of Israel', *Times of Israel*, 15 September 2012.

38. Phumzile Mlambo-Ngcuka, 'Turning words into action, involving women for peace',, *Huffington Post*, 12 October 2015.

39. 'Infographic – women in peace processes', Conciliation Resources, 2015, http://www.c-r.org/news-and-views/multimedia/infographic-women-peace-processes

40. Mary Caprioli, 'Primed for violence: the role of gender inequality in predicting internal conflict', *International Studies Quarterly*, vol. 49, no. 2, 2005, https://www.amherst.edu/media/view/233359/original/Caprioli+2005.pdf.

41. McKinsey, February 2011 survey of 1,000 female professionals and 525 male professionals; see Joanna Barsh and Lareina Lee, 'Changing companies' minds about women', *McKinsey Quarterly*, September 2011, https://www.mckinsey.com/business-functions/organization/our-insights/changing-companies-minds-about-women.

42. Peter Harms, Seth Spain and Sean Hannah, 'Leadership development and the dark side of personality', University of Nebraska, *Management Department Faculty Publications*, no. 82, 2011.

43. Paul Cawkill, Alison Rogers, Sarah Knight and Laura Spear, *Women in Ground Close Combat Roles: The Experiences of other Nations and a Review of the Academic Literature*, Defence Science and Technology Laboratory, 2010, https://assets.publishing.service.gov.uk/government/uploads/system/uploads/attachment_data/file/27406/women_combat_experiences_literature.pdf.

Chapter 4: The Change Makers and Female Pioneers – Mothers of Invention

1. J. Walter Thompson Women's Index, 2015/16.

2. Michael Greshko, 'Famous Viking warrior was a woman, DNA reveals', *National Geographic*, 12 September 2017, http://news.nationalgeographic.com/2017/09/viking-warrior-woman-archaeology-spd.

3. 'Women spread civilisation during Stone Age in Britain, research suggests', *Thema News*, 5 September 2017, http://en.protothema.gr/women-spread-civilisation-during-stone-age-in-britain-research-suggests.

4. Richard Rhodes, *Hedy's Folly: The Life and Breakthrough Inventions of Hedy Lamarr, The Most Beautiful Woman in the World*, Doubleday, 2011.

5. Elaine Burke, 'The Computer Girls: 1967 Cosmo article highlights women in technology', *Silicon Republic*, 18 August 2015, https://www.siliconrepublic.com/people/women-in-technology-the-computer-girls-cosmopolitan.

6. Stephen Mihm, 'How women got crowded out of the computing revolution', *Bloomberg*, 19 August 2017, https://www.bloomberg.com/view/articles/2017-08-19/how-women-got-crowded-out-of-the-computing-revolution.

7. Tia Ghose, 'Study: female coders better than men, but perceived as worse', *Live Science*, 17 February 2016, http://www.livescience.com/53729-bias-against-female-coders.html.

8. J. Walter Thompson Women's Index, 2015.

9. Kate Conger, 'Exclusive: here's the full ten-page anti-diversity screed circulating internally at Google', *Gizmodo*, 5 August 2017, https://gizmodo.com/exclusive-heres-the-full-10-page-anti-diversity-screed-1797564320.

10. Christopher M. Schroeder, 'A Different Story from the Middle East: Entrepreneurs Building an Arab Tech Economy', *Technology Review*, 3 August 2017.

11. https://en.wikipedia.org/wiki/Matilda_effect.

12. Angela Saini, Inferior: *How Science Got Women Wrong – and the New Research that's Rewriting the Story*, Fourth Estate, 2017.

13. J. Walter Thompson Women's Index, 2015.

14. J. Walter Thompson Women's Index, 2015.

15. J. Walter Thompson Women's Index, 2015.

16. *Barclays Wealth Study*, 2009; see, Robert Frank, 'Rich women give more to charity than men', *Wall Street Journal*, 13 July 2009, https://blogs.wsj.com/wealth/2009/07/13/rich-women-give-more-to-charity-than-men.

17. Rebecca Jeffrey, 'Women are more charitable than men in nearly every causal area', *Civil Society*, 14 December 2010, https://www.civilsociety.co.uk/news/women-are-more-charitable-than-men-in-nearly-every-causal-area.html.

18. J. Walter Thompson Women's Index, 2015.

19. *The World's Women 2015: Trends and Statistics*, Department of Economic and Social Affairs, United Nations, 2015, https://unstats.un.org/unsd/gender/downloads/worldswomen2015_report.pdf.

20. Michelle Lodge, 'Dispelling myths about women and charitable giving', *Forbes*, 20 October 2014, http://fortune.com/2014/10/20/dispelling-myths-about-women-and-charitable-giving.

21. *Women 2000 and Beyond: Women, Gender Equality and Sport*, United Nations, December 2007.

22. M. Colton and S. Gore, 'Risk Resiliency and Resistance: Current Research on Adolescent Girls', manuscript, Foundation for Women, 1991.

23. Betsey Stevenson, 'Beyond the classroom: using Title IX to measure the return to high school sports', University of Pennsylvania Scholarly Commons Working Paper Series, 31 January 2010, https://repository.upenn.edu/cgi/viewcontent.cgi?article=1017&context=psc_working_papers.

24. *Her Story: The Female Revolution*, BBC World News and J. Walter Thompson, 2016.

25. Meaghen Brown, 'The longer we race, the stronger we get', *Outside Magazine*, 11 April 2017.

26. David Epstein, *The Sports Gene*, Yellow Jersey, 2014.

27. Meaghen Brown, 'The longer we race, the stronger we get', *Outside Magazine*, 11 April 2017.

28. Ahmad Shafi, 'Afghan female boxers strike a blow for girl power', *MPR News*, 28 May 2012.

29. Azadeh Moaveni, 'Parkour life: Iranian women get physical,' *Guardian*, 10, June 2013.

30. Sonar, J. Walter Thompson, 2016.

31. J. Walter Thompson Women's Index, 2016.

32. J. Walter Thompson Women's Index, 2016.

33. J. Walter Thompson Women's Index, 2016.

34. Marguerite Del Giudice, 'Why it's crucial to get more women into science', *National Geographic*, 8 November 2014, http://news.nationalgeographic.com/news/2014/11/141107-gender-studies-women-scientific-research-feminist.

35. Matthias Wullum Nielsen, Jens Peter Andersen, Londa Schiebinger and Jesper W. Schneider, 'One and a half million medical papers reveal a link between gender and authorship and attention to gender and sex analysis', *Nature Human Behaviour*, 2017, https://www.nature.com/articles/s41562-017-0235-x.epdf?referrer_access_token=d3D53GwGAM_r3hftq-q2P9RgN0jAjWel9jnR-3ZoTv0PEScLc7bbzmcIHMa5P4HLPNTjxcAdhd5gvBW4KmYsruuDpMIH-CIKg_DA2toNwsNW_saDxA5v2TAQq6PavTVogJ_-otbemVzJdK7v18UGFrgw-gV_lNprrjPupcuYtwgBxrGiza4ZcvsMXttaoYxIJ0q9bCCqG1LlXiWAlAM9g4E1T-6BADFCaVKH63GvsQEr-nj4vmqYAM5ceB4IK_0Y5_1FPPB-tcHHnt33QFya-ODr52A%3D%3D&tracking_referrer=www.newyorker.com.

36. Sarah Boseley, '"Listen to women": UK doctors issued with first guidance on endometriosis', *Guardian*, 6 September 2017, https://www.theguardian.com/society/2017/sep/06/listen-to-women-uk-doctors-issued-with-first-guidance-on-endometriosis; 'Endometriosis: diagnosis and management', NICE, September 2017, https://www.nice.org.uk/guidance/ng73/chapter/Recommendations.

37. *Making Sustainable Living Commonplace: Unilever Annual Report and Accounts 2017*, Unilever, 2017.

38. 'Brandz Top 100', Millward Brown, 2017, http://www.wpp.com/wpp/marketing/brandz/brandz-2017.

39. Yusuke Tsugawa, Anupam B. Jena, José F. Figuera *et al.*, 'Comparison of Hospital Mortality and Readmission Rates for Medicare Patients Treated by Male vs Female Physicians', *JMA Internal Medicine*, vol. 177, no. 2, December 2016.

40. Rachel Williams, 'Spyware and smartphones: how abusive men track their partners', *Guardian*, 25 January 2015, https://www.theguardian.com/lifeandstyle/2015/jan/25/spyware-smartphone-abusive-men-track-partners-domestic-violence.

41. UN Women National Committee United Kingdom, 2017, https://drawaline.org.uk.

42. 'This Girl Can', Sport England, December 2016, https://www.sportengland.org/our-work/women/this-girl-can.

43. 'Case study: Always Like a Girl', *Campaign*, 12 October 2015, https://www.campaignlive.co.uk/article/case-study-always-likeagirl/1366870.

44. 'Clothes for Humans. United Colors Of Benetton Launches a Brand New Creative Platform', *Benetton*, 27 July 2016, http://www.benettongroup.com/media-press/press-releases-and-statements/clothes-for-humans-united-colors-of-benetton-new-creative-platform.

Chapter 5: Motherhood Reimagined

1. Office for National Statistics.

2.	Gretchen Livingston, 'They're waiting longer, but US women today more likely to have children than a decade ago', Pew Research Center, 18 January 2018, http://www.pewsocialtrends.org/2018/01/18/theyre-waiting-longer-but-u-s-women-today-more-likely-to-have-children-than-a-decade-ago.
3.	Office for National Statistics.
4.	Margaret Sanger Award Presentation, Planned Parenthood Federation, 5 May 1966.
5.	J. L. Herr, 'Does it pay to delay?', University of California, Berkeley, November 2007, https://eml.berkeley.edu/~webfac/cbrown/e251_f07/Herr.pdf.
6.	C. Goldin and L. F. Katz, 'The power of the pill: oral contraceptives and women's career and marriage decisions', *Journal of Political Economy*, vol. 110, no. 4, 2002.
7.	E. T. Wilde, L. Batchelder and D. T. Ellwood, 'The mommy track divides: the impact of childbearing on wages of women of differing skill levels', *NBER Working Paper*, no. 16582, 2010.
8.	'Obese mums more likely to give birth to babies with birth defects', *PubMed Health*, 15 June 2017, https://www.ncbi.nlm.nih.gov/pubmedhealth/behindtheheadlines/news/2017-06-15-obese-mums-more-likely-to-give-birth-to-babies-with-birth-defects.
9.	J. Walter Thompson Women's Index, 2015/16.
10.	Office for National Statistics, 2013.
11.	J. Walter Thompson Women's Index, 2015/16.
12.	Sarah Knapton, 'Soaring house prices reduce number of babies born in England', *Daily Telegraph*, 12 April 2017, http://www.telegraph.co.uk/science/2017/04/12/soaring-house-prices-reduce-number-babies-born-england.
13.	J. Walter Thompson Women's Index, 2015/16.
14.	Christine Lagorio, 'Japan's women defy pressure to wed', *CBS News*, 22 November 2004, https://www.cbsnews.com/news/japans-women-defy-pressure-to-wed.
15.	J. Walter Thompson Women's Index, 2015/16.
16.	J. Walter Thompson Women's Index, 2015/16.
17.	Justin McCurry, 'Japan's "grass eaters" turn their backs on macho ways', *Observer*, 27 December 2009.
18.	'Balancing paid work, unpaid work and leisure', Organisation for Economic Co-operation and Development, 2014, http://www.oecd.org/gender/data/balancingpaidworkunpaidworkandleisure.htm
19.	'Myth-busting the black "marriage crisis"', *The Root*, 18 August 2011, https://www.theroot.com/myth-busting-the-black-marriage-crisis-1790865391.
20.	J. Walter Thompson Women's Index, 2015/16.
21.	*Women returners*, PwC, November 2016, https://www.pwc.co.uk/services/economics-policy/insights/women-returners.html.
22.	J. Walter Thompson Women's Index, 2016.
23.	Emma Wallis, 'Pregnant at 53: childbirth at any age?', *Deutsche Welle*, 11 February 2012, http://www.dw.com/en/pregnant-at-53-childbirth-at-any-age/a-16345633.
24.	A. Goisis, M. Myrskylä and D. Schneider, 'The reversing association between advanced maternal age and child cognitive development: evidence from three UK birth cohorts', *International Journal of Epidemiology*, vol. 46, no. 3, 2016.
25.	Tea Trillingsgaard and Dion Sommer, 'Associations between older maternal age, use of sanctions, and children's socio-emotional development through 7, 11, and 15 years', *European Journal of Developmental Psychology*, November 2016.
26.	*Ali Wong: Baby Cobra*, Netflix, 2016.
27.	J. Walter Thompson Women's Index, 2015/16.
28.	J. Walter Thompson Women's Index, 2015/16.

29. 'The South Korean tutoring boom', *The Tutor Website*, 9 September 2014, https://www.thetutorwebsite.co.uk/articles/108,the-south-korean-tutoring-boom.html.

30. J. Walter Thompson Women's Index 2015/16

31. Tess Gerritsen, 'Confessions of a Failed Tiger Mom', 25 January 2011, http://www.tessgerritsen.com/confessions-of-a-failed-tiger-mom.

32. 'Losing her stripes', *Economist*, 22 September 2012.

33. 'World population prospects 2017', UN DESA/Population Division, 2017, https://esa.un.org/unpd/wpp/Download/Standard/Population.

34. *Baby Products Market Analysis*, Grandview Research, 2014, http://www.grandviewresearch.com/industry-analysis/baby-products-market/methodology.

35. J. Walter Thompson Women's Index, 2015/16.

36. Pope Francis, St Peter's Square address, 2015.

37. 'Heffernan targets "barren" Gillard', *Bulletin*, 1 May 2007.

38. Mark Latham, *The Latham Diaries*, Melbourne University Press, 2005.

39. Ann Rosenfield, 'No kidding – children, bequests, and charity', *Hilborn: Charity eNews*, 4 September 2017, https://www.charityinfo.ca/articles/No-kidding-children-bequests-and-charity.

40. J. Walter Thompson Women's Index, 2015/16.

41. Maureen Brookbanks, *Daily Mail*, 14 January 2016.

42. J. Walter Thompson Women's Index, 2016.

43. 'Women Want More (in Financial Services)', *BCG Perspectives*, 2009, https://www.bcg.com/documents/file31680.pdf.

44. 'The flight from marriage', *Economist*, 20 August 2011, https://www.economist.com/node/21526329.

45. J. Walter Thompson Women's Index, 2015/16.

46. Didi Kirsten Tatlow, 'Chinese law could make divorced women homeless', *China Legal*, 7 September 2011, http://www.chinalegal.org/chinese-law-could-make-divorced-women-homeless.

47. Christina Larson, 'China's "Leftover Ladies" are anything but', *Bloomberg*, 23 August 2012, https://www.bloomberg.com/news/articles/2012-08-23/chinas-leftover-ladies-are-anything-but.

48. 'Driving growth: the female economy in India and China', *BCG Perspectives*, 2012, https://www.bcg.com/documents/file119925.pdf.

49. Radha Chadha, 'The Asian "luxe-explosion"', *The Atlas Society*, 7 June 2010, https://atlassociety.org/commentary/commentary-blog/5437-the-asia-luxe-explosion.

50. Yang Jian, 'Audi reaches out to China's younger car buyers', 18 February 2016, *AdAge*, http://adage.com/article/global-news/audi-reaches-china-s-younger-car-buyers/302742.

51. 'Women and Consumerism', *BCG*, 2009.

52. 'Wealth Management Investment Study', Barclays, 2009.

Chapter 6: Women and Sex

1. Dr Lara Tavoschi, Joana Gomes Dias and Anastasia Pharris, 'New HIV diagnoses among adults aged 50 years or older in 31 European countries, 2004–15: an analysis of surveillance data', *Lancet*, vol. 4, no. 11, November 2017.

2. 'Parents call on schools to teach subjects related to porn', FPA, 11 September 2017, https://www.fpa.org.uk/news/parents-call-schools-teach-subjects-related-porn.

3. Sarah Buckley, 'China's high-speed sexual revolution', *BBC News*, 27 February 2016, http://www.bbc.co.uk/news/magazine-35525566.
4. Kathleen A. Ethier, Laura Kann and Timothy McManus, 'Sexual Intercourse Among High School Students – 29 States and United States Overall, 2005–2015', *Disclosures*, vol. 66, nos 51–2, 2018.
5. Public Workshop on Female Sexual Dysfunction, Food and Drug Administration, 27–8 October 2014.
6. Manjula Lusti-Narasimhan and John R. Beard, 'Sexual health in older women', *Bulletin of the World Health Organization*, vol. 91, no. 9, September 2013.
7. Laurie Penny, 'We don't need female Viagra, we need feminism', *New Statesman*, 1 September 2015.
8. Holly Thomas, Rachel Hess and Rebecca Thurston, 'Correlates of sexual activity and satisfaction in midlife and older women', *Annals of Family Medicine*, vol. 13, no. 4, July/August 2015.
9. K. Stoddard, *Saints and Shrews: Women and Aging in American Popular Film*, Greenwood Press, 1983.
10. Dr Susan Liddy, '"Missing persons": representations of mature female sexuality In British and Irish film 1998–2011', *Postgraduate Journal of Women, Ageing and Media*, no. 1, June 2014.
11. Jan Antfolk, Benny Salo, Katarina Alanko *et al.*, 'Women's and men's sexual preferences and activities with respect to the partner's age: evidence for female choice', *Evolution and Human Behaviour*, vol. 36, no. 1, January 2015.
12. Milaine Alarie and Jason T. Carmichael, 'The "Cougar" Phenomenon: An Examination of the Factors That Influence Age-Hypogamous Sexual Relationships Among Middle-Aged Women', *Journal of Marriage and Family*, vol. 77, no. 5, October 2015.
13. Dale Markowitz, 'Undressed: what's the deal with the age gap in relationships?', *Okcupid*, 1 June 2017, https://theblog.okcupid.com/undressed-whats-the-deal-with-the-age-gap-in-relationships-3143a2ca5178
14. '"Age shaming" men who only want younger women is justified', *Cafe Mom*, 15 February 2014. http://thestir.cafemom.com/love/168379/ageshaming_men_who_only_want.
15. Petronella Wyatt, 'Love in the time of austerity', *Daily Telegraph*, 20 July 2012.
16. Yoko Harada, 'Beauty secrets of the "Bimajyo" – beauty witch in Japanese', *Okoii's Beauty Blog*, 19 February 2011, https://okoii.wordpress.com/2011/02/19/beauty-se-crets-of-the-%E2%80%9Cbimajyo%E2%80%9D-beauty-witch-in-japanese.
17. Justin J. Lehmiller and Christopher R. Agnew, 'Commitment in age-gap heterosexual romantic relationships: a test of evolutionary and socio-cultural predictions', *Psychology of Women Quarterly*, vol. 32, no. 1, March 2008.
18. Ellen Fein and Shelley Schneider, *The Rules: Time-tested Secrets for Capturing the Heart of Mr Right*, Warner, 1995.
19. Tinder, expandedramblings.com.
20. 'Match.com State of the Date Report', US Data, 2016.
21. Ibid.
22. Candy, 'On marriage', *Journal of an elegant and modern day mistress* (courtesan), 30 August 2005, armcandy.blogspot.co.uk.
23. Jonathan Heaf, 'The future on online dating?', *GQ*, 29 March 2012, http://www.gq-magazine.co.uk/article/seeking-arrangement-sugar-babies-daddies.
24. Tracy McVeigh, 'Belle du Jour, aka Brooke Magnanti, stands up to her feminist critics', *Observer*, 10 April 2011, https://www.theguardian.com/books/2011/apr/10/brooke-magnanti-belle-de-jour.

25. Rachel Tan, 'When I grow up I want to be a WAG', *The Boar*, 27 February 2010, https://theboar.org/2010/02/when-i-grow-i-want-be-wag.
26. John Millward, 'Down the rabbit-hole', *John Millward – Data Journalist*, 8 September 2014, http://jonmillward.com/blog/studies/down-the-rabbit-hole-analysis-1-million-sex-toy-sales.
27. J. Walter Thompson Women's Index, 2015/16.
28. *Global Sex Toys Market 2017–2023*, Technavio, April 2017, https://www.technavio.com/report/global-female-sex-toys-market-2017-2021?utm_source=T2&utm_medium=B-W&utm_campaign=Media.
29. '96% women feel unsafe after dark in Delhi', *Times of India*, 8 March 2013, https://timesofindia.indiatimes.com/city/delhi/96-women-feel-unsafe-after-sunset-in-Delhi-Survey/articleshow/18856470.cms.
30. J. Walter Thompson Women's Index, 2015/16.
31. Jean M. Twenge, Ryne A. Sherman and Brooke E. Wells, 'Changes in American adults' reported same-sex sexual experiences and attitudes, 1973–2014', *Archives of Sexual Behaviour*, vol. 45, no. 7, October 2016.
32. Saga UK Investment Services, 2016/'The Elastic Generation', J. Walter Thompson, 2015.
33. Raphael Silberzahn and Jochen Menges, 'Reading the face of a leader: women with low facial masculinity are perceived as competitive', *Academy of Management Discoveries*, vol. 2. no. 3, 2017.

Chapter 7: Religion Rewritten

1. Gary Macy, 'The meaning of ordination and how women were gradually excluded', *National Catholic Reporter*, 16 January 2013.
2. Frederick Solt, Philip Habel and J. Tobin Grant, 'Economic inequality, relative power and religiosity', *Social Science Quarterly*, vol. 92, no. 2, April 2011.
3. 'Country comparison: distribution of family income – GINI Index', *The World Factbook*, Central Intelligence Agency, 2017, https://www.cia.gov/library/publications/the-world-factbook/rankorder/2172rank.html.
4. Tobin Grant, 'Religion and inequality go hand-in-hand', *Christianity Today*, 16 September 2011, http://www.christianitytoday.com/news/2011/september/religioninequality.html.
5. Michelle Boorstein, 'Can atheist Sam Harris become a spiritual figure?', *Washington Post*, 12 September 2014.
6. 'Theories explaining gender differences in religion', *The Gender Gap in Religion around the World*, Pew Research Center, 2016, http://www.pewforum.org/2016/03/22/theories-explaining-gender-differences-in-religion.
7. 'Theories explaining gender differences in religion', *The Gender Gap in Religion around the World*, Pew Research Center, 2016, http://www.pewforum.org/2016/03/22/theories-explaining-gender-differences-in-religion.
8. Giselle Vincett, 'Why are women attracted to goddess feminism?', *Wiccanweb*, 9 March 2013, http://wp.wiccanweb.ca/2013/03/09/why-are-women-attracted-to-goddess-feminism.
9. J. Walter Thompson Women's Index, 2015/16.
10. Timothy Shriver, 'Women and the new spirituality', *On Faith*, undated, https://www.onfaith.co/onfaith/2008/10/30/the-spirit-within-women-and-th/8602.
11. Ibid.

12. Neopaganism.com.
13. Allen Salkin, 'Seeing yourself in their light', *New York Times*, 18 September 2009.
14. Ibid.
15. Mary Douglas, *Purity and Danger*, Routledge & Kegan Paul, 1966.
16. Barbara O'Brien, 'Buddhism and sexism', *ThoughtCo.*, 10 July 2017, https://www.thoughtco.com/buddhism-and-sexism-449757.
17. Emma Tomalin, 'The Thai Bhikkhuni movement and women's empowerment', *Gender and Development*, vol. 14, no. 3, November 2006.
18. M. A. Mueke, 'Mother sold food, daughter sells her body', *Social Science and Medicine*, vol. 35, no. 7, 1992.
19. C. H. Jacquet, *Women Ministers in 1977: A Report*, National Council of Churches, 1978.
20. Barbara G. Wheeler and Anthony T. Ruger, 'Sobering figures point to overall enrolment decline', *InTrust*, Spring 2013, http://www.intrust.org/portals/39/docs/it413wheeler.pdf.
21. Vicki Wiltse, 'Midlife Women's Journey to Seminary', *Academia*, undated, http://www.academia.edu/11644034/Midlife_Womens_Journeys_to_Seminary.
22. Cooperative Congressional Election Study, 2016, https://cces.gov.harvard.edu/pages/welcome-cooperative-congressional-election-study.
23. Beverly J. Anderson, 'Women Clergy, how their presence is changing the Church', *Christian Century*, 7–14 February 1979.
24. Emma Tomalin, 'The Thai Bhikkhuni movement and women's empowerment', *Gender and Development*, vol. 14, no. 3, November 2006.
25. Dr Barbara Brown Zikmund, 'Women Clergy, how their presence is changing the Church', *Christian Century*, 7–14 February 1979.
26. L. J. Peach, 'Human rights, religion and slavery', *Annual of the Society of Christian Ethics*, no. 25, 2000.
27. Utpal M. Dholakia, 'Brands are behaving like organized religions', *Harvard Business Review*, 18 February 2016, https://hbr.org/2016/02/brands-are-behaving-like-organized-religions.
28. Grand View Research, 'Halal cosmetics market worth $52.02 billion by 2025/CAGR: 12.3%: Grand View Research, Inc.', *Market Insider*, 22 March 2017, http://markets.businessinsider.com/news/stocks/halal-cosmetics-market-worth-52-02-billion-by-2025-cagr-12-3-grand-view-research-inc-1001856869.
29. Faegheh Shirazi, 'How the hijab has grown into a fashion industry', *The Conversation*, 8 May 2017, http://theconversation.com/how-the-hijab-has-grown-into-a-fashion-industry-74740.
30. 'Nearly 47 per cent of global population now online – UN report', *UN News*, 15 September 2016, https://news.un.org/en/story/2016/09/539112-nearly-47-cent-global-population-now-online-un-report.
31. ITU ICT Facts and Figures, 2017, ITU, 2017, https://www.itu.int/en/ITU-D/Statistics/Pages/facts/default.aspx.
32. J. Walter Thompson Women's Index, 2015/16.

Chapter 8: The Cultural Icons

1. J. Walter Thompson Women's Index, 2015/16.
2. Catherine Filene, *Careers for Women*, Houghton Mifflin, 1920.
3. *Photoplay*, 1924; *Moving Picture World*, 1927.
4. Ashley Strobridge, 'Women's leadership roles in filmmaking', *Academia*, April 2011, http://www.academia.edu/4821503/Womens_Leadership_Roles_in_Filmmaking.

5. Joan Simon (ed.), *Alice Guy Blaché: Cinema Pioneer*, Yale University Press, 2009.
6. 'A brief history of Gaumont', *Variety*, 14 May 2014, http://variety.com/2014/film/news/intl-film-award-a-brief-history-of-gaumont-1201181084.
7. Giuliana Musico, 'American women screenwriters of the 1920s', in Christine Gledhill and Julia Knight (eds), *Doing Women's Film History*, University of Illinois Press, 2015.
8. Rosemary Hanes with Brian Taves, 'Moving Image Section – Motion Picture, Broadcasting and Recorded Sound Division', in Sheridan Harvey *et al.* (eds), *American Memory*, Library of Congress, 2001, https://wfpp.cdrs.columbia.edu/pioneer/ccp-lois-weber.
9. 'Episode 1: Frances Marion', *Women of Hollywoodland*, 2017. http://www.hollywoodland-series.com/episode-1-frances-marion.
10. Musico, 'American women screenwriters of the 1920s'.
11. Hanes with Taves, 'Moving Image Section'.
12. Richard Brody, 'Ida Lupino's prescient "Outrage"', *New Yorker*, 16 June 2014.
13. Kevin Thomas, 'UCLA series studies Dorothy Arzner films', *Los Angeles Times*, 23 January 2003, http://articles.latimes.com/2003/jan/23/news/wk-screen23.
14. Richard Falcon, 'Obituary: Leni Riefenstahl', *Guardian*, 9 September 2003.
15. Anthony Slide, *The Silent Feminists: America's First Women Directors*, Scarecrow Press, 1996.
16. Strobridge, 'Women's leadership roles in filmmaking'.
17. Steve Goodson, 'Handout 14: women and work', University of West Georgia History Course, 2014, https://www.westga.edu/~hgoodson/Women%20and%20Work.htm.
18. Linda Seger, *When Women Called the Shots*, Henry Holt & Company, 1996.
19. Musico, 'American women screenwriters of the 1920s'.
20. Rory Carroll, 'Female filmmakers still locked out of big Hollywood productions, study finds', *Guardian*, 6 May 2014.
21. Susan Wloszczyna, 'Dear Hollywood, hiring women directors could rescue the superhero movie. Love, half the human race', *Balder & Dash*, 8 July 2013, https://www.rogerebert.com/balder-and-dash/who-says-a-woman-cant-direct-a-superhero-film-hollywood-so-far.
22. Rory Carroll, 'Female filmmakers still locked out of big Hollywood productions, study finds', *Guardian*, 6 May 2014.
23. Kevin O'Keefe, 'Here's exactly how much movies about women make at the box office versus movies about men', *Mic*, 23 October 2013, https://mic.com/articles/127095/here-s-exactly-how-much-movies-about-women-make-at-the-box-office-versus-movies-about-men#.BgzTIhnKJ.
24. Rachel Montpelier, 'MPAA Report 2016', *Women and Hollywood*, 24 March 2017, https://blog.womenandhollywood.com/mpaa-report-2016-52-of-movie-audiences-are-women-other-takeaways-12320da989b4.
25. Julie Hinds, 'TV female superheroes are leaping over the glass ceiling', *Detroit Free Press*, 31 October 2015.
26. *What Women Want*, The 3% Movement, March 2016, https://www.3percentmovement.com/sites/default/files/resources/WhatWomenWant%20-%20Final.pdf.
27. Rachel Kranz, *African-American Business Leaders and Entrepreneurs*, Infobase, 2004.
28. 'Superachiever Barbara Proctor', *Selling Power*, 2 February 2010.
29. 'Advertising, she does', *Time*, 11 August 1967.
30. Jen Doll, 'Reviewing the "Mad Men" world by someone who was there', *Atlantic*, 9 April 2012.
31. 'J. Walter Thompson Advertising Handbook for Women', 1963.
32. B. L. Smith, T. D. Smith, L. Taylor and M. Hobby, 'Relationship between intelligence and vocabulary', *Perceptual and Motor Skills*, vol. 100, no. 1, February 2005, https://www.ncbi.nlm.nih.gov/pubmed/15773700.

33. Press Association, 'University gender gap at record high as 30,000 more women accepted', *Guardian*, 28 August 2017, https://www.theguardian.com/education/2017/aug/28/university-gender-gap-at-record-high-as-30000-more-women-accepted.

34. Ali Hanan, 'Creativity's female future', *Campaign*, 30 March 2017, https://www.campaignlive.co.uk/article/creativitys-female-future/1428824.

35. Ian Begg and Victoria Armour, 'Repetition and the ring of truth: biasing comments', *Canadian Journal of Behavioural Science*, vol. 23, no. 2, 1991, http://psycnet.apa.org/record/1992-00382-001.

36. Charles Q. Choi, 'How "Jaws" changed forever our view of great white sharks', *Live Science*, 20 June 2010, http://www.livescience.com/8309-jaws-changed-view-great-white-sharks.html.

37. J. Walter Thompson Women's Index, 2016.

38. 'How is open government related to violence against women in Brazil?', Open Government Partnership, 7 March 2017, https://www.opengovpartnership.org/stories/how-open-government-related-violence-against-women-brazil.

39. Kira Cochrane, 'Women in art: why are all the "great" artists men?', *Guardian*, 24 May 2013.

40. 'The 100 most expensive artists at auction', *Artsy*, 2016, https://www.artsy.net/article/artsy-editorial-the-100-most-expensive-artists.

41. J. Walter Thompson Women's Index, 2015/16.

42. 'The Guerrilla Girls', *The Art Story*, undated, http://www.theartstory.org/artist-guerrilla-girls.htm.

43. Kitty Knowles, 'Artfinder exposes shameless art world sexism – join the protest', *The Memo*, 9 February 2017, https://www.thememo.com/2017/02/09/artfinder-artworld-sexism-campaign-artfinder-gender-equality-report.

44. Andrew Johnson, 'There's never been a great woman artist', *Independent*, 5 July 2008.

45. Virginia Hughes, 'Were the first artists mostly women?', *National Geographic*, 9 October 2013.

46. Bonnie Rosenberg, 'Cindy Sherman: artist overview and analysis', *The Art Story*, 2018, http://www.theartstory.org/artist-sherman-cindy.htm.

47. 'Aesthetics, athletics and the Olympics', Cambridge University Press, 5 August 2016, http://www.cambridge.org/about-us/news/aest.

48. Sen Jia, Thomas Lansdall-Welfare, Saatviga Sudhahar, Cynthia Carner and Nello Cristianini, 'Women are seen more than heard in online newspapers', *PLOS One*, 3 February 2016.

49. Home page, Women's Media Center, https://www.womensmediacenter.com.

50. *Who Makes the News?*, Global Media Monitoring Project, 2015, http://www.presscouncil.org.au/uploads/52321/ufiles/Who_makes_the_news_-_Global_Media_Monitoring_Project_2015.pdf.

51. Ida Tarbell, *The History of the Standard Oil Company*, McClure, Phillips & Co, 1904.

52. Dr Stacy L. Smith, Marc Choueiti and Dr Katherine Pieper, *Gender Bias without Borders: An investigation of female characters in popular films across 11 countries*, Geena Davis Institute on Gender in Media, 2014, https://seejane.org/wp-content/uploads/gender-bias-without-borders-full-report.pdf

53. Phumzile Mlambo-Ngcuka, 'Media has key role to play in gender equality agenda – chief executive', *UN Women*, 22 September 2014, http://www.unwomen.org/en/news/stories/2014/9/ed-remarks-gender-in-media.

54. Helen Fraser, 'Britain's exam boards must stop writing famous women out of the school curriculum. Now', *Daily Telegraph*, 4 September 2015, http://www.telegraph.co.uk/

women/womens-life/11841976/Britain-schools-Exam-boards-must-stop-writing-women-out-of-curriculum.html.

55. For Books' Sake, '#BalanceTheBooks: commit to gender equality and better diversity in terms of class, race and sexuality in set texts for GCSE English Literature', 2014, https://www.change.org/p/balancethebooks-commit-to-gender-equality-and-better-diversity-in-gcses-set-texts.

56. J. Walter Thompson Women's Index, 2015/16.

57. Martha M. Lauzen, 'It's a Man's (Celluloid) World: Portrayals of Female Characters in the 100 Top Films of 2017', *Women in Television & Film*, 2018, https://womenintvfilm.sdsu.edu/research.

58. Anna Leszkiewicz, 'Ryan Adams's 1989 and the mansplaining of Taylor Swift', *New Statesman*, 24 September 2015.

59. Justin Tindall and Chaka Sobhani, 'Private view: this is getting boring', *Campaign*, 16 October 2017, https://www.campaignlive.co.uk/article/private-view-getting-boring-with-justin-tindall-chaka-sobhani/1447303.

60. J. Walter Thompson Women's Index, 2015/16.

61. J. Walter Thompson Women's Index, 2016.

62. 'People Insights: how gender-positive ads pay off', *Facebook IQ*, 3 August 2017, https://www.facebook.com/iq/articles/how-gender-positive-ads-pay-off.

Conclusions: A Time for Women

1. J. Walter Thompson Women's Index, 2015/16.

2. 'Divorce, Russian Style', *Russia Beyond*, 16 October 2013.

3. J. Walter Thompson Women's Index, 2016.

4. J. Walter Thompson Women's Index, 2016.

5. J. Walter Thompson Cannes Advertising Study in partnership with Google and the Geena Davis Institute on Gender in Media, 2017.

6. 'UNICEF says education for women and girls a lifeline to development', UNICEF, 4 May 2011, https://www.unicef.org/media/media_58417.html.

7. Betsey Stevenson, 'Beyond the classroom: using Title IX to measure the return to high school sports', University of Pennsylvania Scholarly Commons Working Paper Series, 31 January 2010,

8. https://repository.upenn.edu/cgi/viewcontent.cgi?article=1017&context=psc_working_papers

9. Marcus Noland and Tyler Moran, 'Women in the C-Suite are more profitable', *Harvard Business Review*, 8 February 2016, https://hbr.org/2016/02/study-firms-with-more-women-in-the-c-suite-are-more-profitable.

10. 'Women CEOs of the S&P 500', *Catalyst*, 13 March 2018, http://www.catalyst.org/knowledge/women-ceos-sp-500.

11. Jonathan Woetzel *et al.*, *The Power of Parity: How Advancing Women's Equality Can Add $12 Trillion to Global Growth*, McKinsey Global Institute, 2015, https://www.mckinsey.com/global-themes/employment-and-growth/how-advancing-womens-equality-can-add-12-trillion-to-global-growth.

ACKNOWLEDGEMENTS

I thank my husband James for his encouragement and unwavering belief that I could in fact write a book, convincing me it wasn't a mad flight of fancy and supporting me while I wrote in earnest … despite being heavily pregnant.

I'm hugely grateful to Sarah Such, my literary agent, for her enthusiasm, wisdom and candour. Without her energy, conviction and patience this would not have been possible: she's made me a much better writer and I'm very thankful.

I'm very appreciative of Carey Smith, Samantha Crisp, Howard Watson and the team at Penguin Random House for their enthusiasm and support. Working with them has been such a huge privilege.

At J. Walter Thompson I thank Noel Bussey, an ardent feminist and supporter of Female Tribes from its inception, Ngen Yap and Lucy Barton for their unfailing support, vision and passion for the project, Phil Lancaster – my boss – for his wisdom and encouragement, and Chips Hardy for his sanguine advice: always appreciated. I would also like to thank our CEO Tamara Ingram for being such an inspiration, James Whitehead and Louise Whitaker for being such advocates for the consultancy, and Jaspar Shelbourne who has championed Female Tribes creatively.

Special mention should also go to Mark Truss and Diana Orrico, from our New York Sonar Team, for making the Women's Index a reality, and for all their hard work, enterprise and wisdom, and for going above and beyond to make the study what it is today.

Finally, I'd like to thank Geena Davis and Madeline Di Nonno of the Geena Davis Institute on Gender in Media. We are so honoured to work with them and share their vision and passion for changing the way the world works for women through popular culture.

INDEX

activism: Altruists and xiii; art world and 217–18; be your own activist 239–40; 'erotic activism' 162; hedonism and 165–6; history/legacy of female 72; peacekeeping and 80; 'physical activism' 103; religion and 175, 179; rise of female 7–9, 110; Teen Activist 244

Adams, Ryan 17, 222

Adidas Pure Boost X 109

advertising xi, xii, xiii, 11, 28, 111, 138–9, 169, 170, 216, 223, 233, 238, 244; female pioneers in 202–5; female talent in 193–4, 195, 201, 202–12, 213; femvertising 23; life script and 21–3; moving image, impact of 212–13, 224–5; persuasion and 211–12; role models and 235–6; studies of women in 207–11; women side-lined in 205–7

Afghanistan 76, 77, 104

Africa: female leadership and 65–70, 241–2

African Alpha 65, 69, 70, 241–2

African-Americans 2, 19, 91, 97, 122, 123, 204

African Political Class 65, 242

Agility Research and Strategy 51

Alba, Jessica 33

Albright, Madeleine 226

All About Eve (film) 150–1

Alpha Female xii, xiii, 81, 227, 228, 231; African Alpha 65, 69, 70, 241–2; African Political Class 65, 242; ambition and 28; Asian Alpha 43–52, 241, 242; confidence and 38–9; defined 31–2, 241–2; GI Jane and 75–7, 242; Hedonists and 164, 165; Latina Matriarch and 69–75, 242; motherhood and 30–1, 139; Mumbai Millennial and 39, 242; Not Mum/Child Free and 35, 36, 242 *see also* Child Free; rise of 31–3; role models 3, 24–5; sports and 100, 103, 105; universality of characteristics 29–30

Altman, Ros 53

Altruists xiii, 243–4 *see also under individual tribe name*

Always: 'Like a Girl' campaign 105, 112–13

Amazon (online retailer) 45, 201

ambition, attitudes towards xi, xii, xiii, 18, 28–9, 30, 31, 32, 33, 44, 45, 47, 48, 49, 51, 55, 66, 69, 73, 90, 113, 128, 212, 225, 228, 241, 242

Amelio, Thomas 180

American Red Cross 96

Amex 26

Andersen, Jens Jakob 102

Antheil, George 90

Apfel, Iris 169

Apple Health app 109

Arazie, Ilana 180

armed forces 75–7, 231, 242

Armstrong, Lance 101

Artfinder 217–18

art world 213–18

Arzner, Dorothy 197–8

Asia: Beauty Witches (*Bimajyo*) in 153, 154–5; brand owners recognise female spending power in 51; childbirth/motherhood in 50, 117, 120–2, 128–34, 136–7; education in 131–2 *see also* Tiger Mother; femininity in 145–6; Golden Misses in 136–8, 141–2; marriage in 4–5, 47–8, 120–2, 136–7; Modern Courtesan in 158; Nurturers/Spouse Focused in 186; religion in 176–7; rural communities in 48–9; sexual empowerment in 145–7; sexual fulfilment in 147, 148; technology, attitudes towards 92; Tiger Mother in *see* Tiger Mother

Asian Alpha 43–52, 241, 242

atheism 173, 175–6, 188

Atomic Blonde (film) 2

Audi 142

Australia xi, 10; armed forces in 76; childbirth in 134; femininity, attitudes towards within 246; school curriculum 221; sexuality, attitudes towards within 5, 159, 168; success, attitudes towards within 245

Baby Boomers 21, 52, 69, 146–8, 169, 170, 194

baby brain 35–6, 239

Bachelet, Michelle 75

Balshaw, Maria 218

Banda, Joyce 67

Banta, Amritt 51

Bar Ilan University, Israel 36

Barclays Women in Leadership Total Return Index 25

Bartlett, William 96–7

Bartoli, Marion 16

'Battle of the Sexes' (tennis match) (1973) 15–16

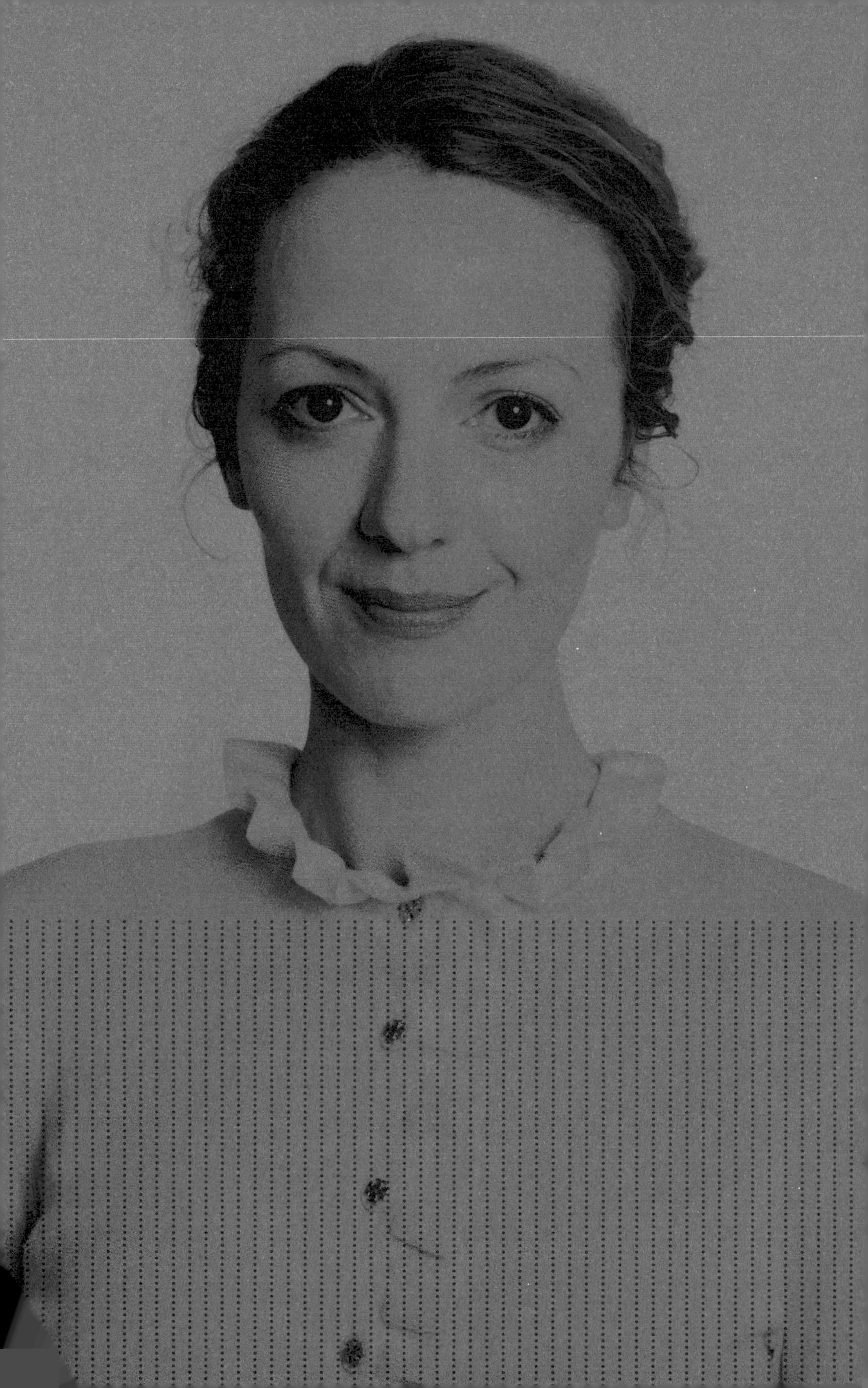